W9-AOB-685

A Dictionary *of* Common Wildflowers *of* Texas *&* the Southern Great Plains

A Dictionary *of* Common Wildflowers *of* Texas *&* the Southern Great Plains

Written & Compiled by
Joel E. Holloway, M.D.

✳

Edited by Amanda Neill

T C U P r e s s • F o r t W o r t h

Also by Joel E. Holloway, M.D.

A Dictionary of Birds of the United States

Library of Congress Cataloging-in-Publication Data

Holloway, Joel Ellis.
  A dictionary of common wildflowers of Texas and the Southern Great Plains / written and compiled by Joel E. Holloway ; edited by Amanda Neill.
       p. cm.
  ISBN 0-87565-309-X (trade paper)
  1. Wild flowers--Texas--Nomenclature--Dictionaries. 2. Wild flowers--Great Plains--Nomenclature--Dictionaries. 3. Wild flowers--Texas--Nomenclature (Popular)--Dictionaries. 4. Wild flowers--Great Plains--Nomenclature (Popular)--Dictionaries. I. Neill, Amanda. II. Title.
  QK188.H65 2005
  582.13'09764--dc22
                          2005015304

Images provided by the Botanical Research Institute of Texas
Cover & Book Design/Margie Adkins West

Printed in Canada.

~ Dedication ~

This work is dedicated to William R. Johnson, D.D.S.,
for his inspiration and example.

∼ Introduction ∼

This dictionary is intended to function chiefly as a companion resource to the field guides of common flowers of Texas and the southern Great Plains. These guides provide pictures for identification and information about the plants, as well as their scientific binomial names and their common names. Both the scientific name and common name can be referenced in this dictionary. The scientific binomial name, the genus and specific epithet, is translated from its Latinized form and the common name is explained. The original language for the scientific name may be Latin, Greek, some other European, Asian, or American Indian language, or even a person's name. If, as is fairly common, the original language was Greek, the base word is first written in Greek, without accents and breathing marks, for ease of printing, then transliterated and translated into English. The common names for flowers in the covered area are usually derived from English or Mexican Spanish, or an American Indian language.

The Principle of Priority is a phrase that will be found following some of the scientific name translations when a mistake, usually in spelling, is present. The Principle of Priority states that the original name assigned, once published in a recognized source, will remain the official name, even if it contains mistakes.

Some of the scientific names of plants (and animals) do not translate with ease or clarity. The main reason for this was the lack of peer review of the assigned names in the past. An individual would discover a plant or have one brought to him or her (as an authority) and assign it a Latinized name. If the name was not explained in the original publication, and the authority got it wrong, it becomes quite a problem to ferret out the intended meaning. This is why some of the scientific names will be translated as "most probably" or "intended to mean."

There can be many common names for the same plant, depending on the local language or folklore. In this dictionary, the one most commonly used was the basis for its selection.

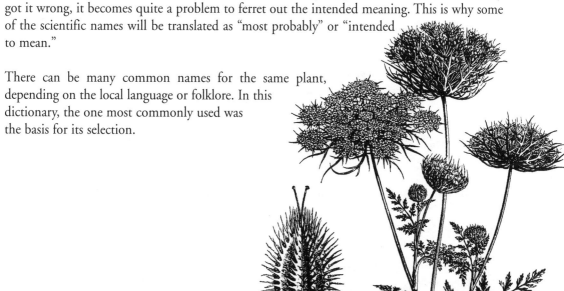

Daucus carota Queen Anne's Lace

Abronia ameliae **Amelia's Sand Verbena**

SCIENTIFIC NAME: *Abronia*, from Greek, αβρος, *abros*, graceful, delicate, pretty. Reference is to the involucre, the whorl of bracts below the inflorescence + *ameliae*, for Amelia Lundell (1908-1998) by her husband, Cyrus Longworth Lundell (1907-1993), founder and director of the Texas Research Foundation at Renner, Texas.

COMMON NAME: Amelia's, same as species name. Sand, for the habitat. Verbena, Latin name for plants used in ceremony or sacred rites.

Abronia angustifolia
Narrowleaf Sand Verbena

SCIENTIFIC NAME: *Abronia* + *angustifolia*, Latin for narrow-leaved.

COMMON NAME: Narrowleaf, descriptive. Sand Verbena, see *Abronia ameliae*.

Abronia fragrans **Pink Abronia**

SCIENTIFIC NAME: *Abronia* + *fragrans*, Latin for fragrant, sweet-smelling.

COMMON NAME: Pink, for the flower color. Abronia, same as genus name.

Abutilon fruticosum **Indian Mallow**

SCIENTIFIC NAME: *Abutilon*, from *aubutilun*, the Arabic name for this plant + *fruticosum*, Latin for pertaining to or resembling a shrub.
COMMON NAME: Indian, for the range

in India. Mallow, from the name of the family of these plants, *Malvaceae*, Latin name for this plant group.

Abutilon theophrasti **Velvetleaf**

SCIENTIFIC NAME: *Abutilon* + *theophrasti*, from Greek, Τηεοπηραστυς, *Theophrastus* divine speaker, a Greek philosopher who was a student of Aristotle. Aristotle appointed him as his successor as head of the Peripatetic school.

COMMON NAME: Velvetleaf, descriptive of the appearance and feel of the leaves.

Acacia angustissima **Prairie Acacia**

SCIENTIFIC NAME: *Acacia*, from the Greek name for the acacia tree, ακακια, *akakia*, in turn from Greek, ακις, *akis*, a pointed object. Reference is to the thorns on some members of this genus, although this species is thornless + *angustissima*, Latin for the most narrow. Reference is to the narrow leaves.

COMMON NAME: Prairie, for the habitat. Acacia, same as genus name.

Acacia berlandieri **Huajillo**

SCIENTIFIC NAME: *Acacia* + *berlandieri*, for Jean Louis Berlandier (1805-1851), a French botantist who collected plants in Texas and Mexico.

COMMON NAME: Huajillo, the Mexican Spanish name for this plant.

Acacia farnesiana   Huisache

SCIENTIFIC NAME: *Acacia + farnesiana,* Latin for pertaining to Farnese, for Cardinal Odoardo Farnese (1573-1626), who grew these plants in the gardens of his palace in Rome.

COMMON NAME: Huisache, a Mexican Spanish word, derived from the Nahuatl, *huixachin,* a thorny tree or bush.

Acacia greggii   Catclaw

SCIENTIFIC NAME: *Acacia + greggii,* for Josiah Gregg (1806-1850), an American plant collector.

COMMON NAME: Catclaw, for the thorns.

Acacia rigidula   Blackbush Acacia

SCIENTIFIC NAME: *Acacia + rigidula,* Latin for stiff, for the rigid stems.

COMMON NAME: Blackbush, for the black stems. Acacia, same as genus name.

Acacia roemeriana   Roemer's Acacia

SCIENTIFIC NAME: *Acacia + roemeriana,* Latin for pertaining to Roemer, for Ferdinand Roemer (1818-1891), a German geologist and explorer.

COMMON NAME: Roemer's Acacia, same as scientific name.

Achillea lanulosa   Woolly Yarrow

SCIENTIFIC NAME: *Achillea,* for the Greek hero Achilles (Αχιλλευς). In Greek myth Achilles learned the medicinal uses of this plant from Chirōn (Χιρων), the centaur + *lanulosa,* Latin for pertaining to or resembling wool. Reference is to the fuzzy appearance of the stems.

COMMON NAME: Woolly, same as species name. Yarrow, origin unknown, most probably from *gearwe,* an Anglo-Saxon word for this plant.

Achillea millefolium   Milfoil

SCIENTIFIC NAME: *Achillea + millefolium,* Latin for a thousand leaves.

COMMON NAME: Milfoil, same as species name.

Acleisanthes longiflora   Angel Trumpets

SCIENTIFIC NAME: *Acleisanthes,* an unclosed flower, from Greek, ακλειστος, *akleistos,* not closed or fastened and ανθος, *anthos,* blossom, flower. This is a night-blooming flower and the blooms are open when most other flowers are closed + *longiflora,* Latin for a long flower. The flowers are long trumpet-shaped tubes.

COMMON NAME: Angel Trumpets, for the trumpet-shaped flowers that open at night.

Acleisanthes obtusa   Vine Four O'Clock

SCIENTIFIC NAME: *Acleisanthes + obtusa,*

Latin for lacking in brilliance, dull. Reference is to the pale flowers.

COMMON NAME: Vine, this plant is a trailing or climbing vine. Four-O'Clock, so called because the flowers open in the afternoon.

Adonis annua Pheasant's Eye

SCIENTIFIC NAME: *Adonis,* the Greek name for this flower, from Αδωνις, *Adōnis* of Greek mythology. Adonis was the epitome of male beauty and was loved by both Aphroditē (Αφροδιτη) and Persephonē (Περσεφονη). Zeus (Ζευς) decreed that each of them could have Adonis for one-third of the year and Adonis could choose with whom he would spend the other third. He chose Aphrodite. When Adonis died he was turned into a beautiful flower with no scent. *Adonis + annua,* Latin for of the year, annual.

COMMON NAME: Pheasant's Eye, the red petals surrounding the black center of this flower was thought to resemble the red facial skin surrounding the black eye of the ring-necked pheasant.

Aesculus arguta White Buckeye

SCIENTIFIC NAME: *Aesculus,* Latin for a variety of oak tree + *arguta,* Latin for sharply toothed or notched, for the leaf edges.

COMMON NAME: White, for the flower color. Buckeye, from the appearance of the seed, thought to look like the eye of a buck in size and color, originally named for *Aesculus hippocastanum.*

Aesculus pavia Red Buckeye

SCIENTIFIC NAME: *Aesculus + pavia,* for Peter Paaw (d. 1617) of Leyden. The Principle of Priority allows the misspelling to stand.

COMMON NAME: Red, for the color of the flowers. Buckeye, see *Aesculus glabra.*

Agalinis auriculata Earleaf Gerardia

SCIENTIFIC NAME: *Agalinis,* a New Latin formation meaning "wonder flax," from Doric Greek, αγα, *aga,* wonder, "very" and Latin, *linum,* flax. So named because this plant superficially resembles flax + *auriculata,* Latin for eared, for the leaf shape.

COMMON NAME: Earleaf, for the ear-shaped leaves. Gerardia, for John Gerard (1545-1612), an English herbalist.

Agalinis densiflora Fineleaf Gerardia

SCIENTIFIC NAME: *Agalinis + densiflora,* Latin for densely flowered.

COMMON NAME: Fineleaf, for the slender leaves. Gerardia, see *Agalinis auriculata.*

Agalinis edwardsiana Plateau Gerardia

SCIENTIFIC NAME: *Agalinis + edwardsiana,* Latin for pertaining to Edwards, for the habitat on the Edwards Plateau of Texas, for Haden (or Hayden) Edwards (1771-1849), an early settler in the area.

COMMON NAME: Plateau, for the range on the Edwards Plateau. Gerardia, see *Agalinis auriculata*.

Agalinis fasciculata   Beach Gerardia

SCIENTIFIC NAME: *Agalinis + fasciculata,* Latin for clustered, grouped in bundles.

COMMON NAME: Beach, for the habitat. Gerardia, see *Agalinis auriculata*.

Agalinis gattingeri   Gattinger's Gerardia

SCIENTIFIC NAME: *Agalinis + gattingeri,* for Augustin Gattinger (1825-1903), an American botanist.

COMMON NAME: Gattinger's, same as species name. Gerardia, see *Agalinis auriculata*.

Agalinis heterophylla   Prairie Agalinis

SCIENTIFIC NAME: *Agalinis + heterophylla,* different leaves, from Greek, ετερος, *(h)eteros,* different and φυλλον, *phullon,* leaf, for having different kinds of leaves on the same plant.

COMMON NAME: Prairie, for the habitat. Agalinis, same as genus name.

Agalinis homalantha   Flatflower Gerardia

SCIENTIFIC NAME: *Agalinis + homalantha,* flat flower, from Greek,

ομαλος, *(h)omalos,* flat and ανθος, *anthos,* flower, for the flower shape.

COMMON NAME: Flatflower, descriptive. Gerardia, see *Agalinis auriculata*.

Agalinis purpurea   Purple Gerardia

SCIENTIFIC NAME: *Agalinis + purpurea,* Latin for purple. Reference is to the color of the flowers.

COMMON NAME: Purple, for the flower color. Gerardia, see *Agalinis auriculata*.

Agalinis tenuifolia   Slender Gerardia

SCIENTIFIC NAME: *Agalinis + tenuifolia,* Latin for thin leaves.

COMMON NAME: Slender, for the thin leaves. Gerardia, see *Agalinis auriculata*.

Agave lechuguilla   Lechuguilla

SCIENTIFIC NAME: *Agave,* from Greek, αγαυος, *agauos,* of things, noble, brilliant, glorious + *lechuguilla,* little lettuce, the Spanish diminutive of *lechuga,* lettuce.

COMMON NAME: Lechuguilla, same as species name.

Agave americana   Century Plant

SCIENTIFIC NAME: *Agave + americana,* Latin for pertaining to America.

COMMON NAME: Century Plant, century

plants got their name because it seemed to take them a century to bloom. Actually, they bloom on average of twelve to fifteen years.

Ageratina wrightii   Wright's Snakeroot

SCIENTIFIC NAME: *Ageratina,* a Latin diminutive for the genus *Ageratum,* for the appearance + *wrightii,* for Charles Wright (1811-1885), a Texas plant collector.

COMMON NAME: Wright's, same as species name. Snakeroot, the American Indians used this plant to treat snakebites.

Agrimonia microcarpa
Smallfruit Agrimony

SCIENTIFIC NAME: *Agrimonia,* a mistransliteration of Greek, αργεμωνη, *argemōnē,* a certain plant (Pliny), also αργεμον, *argemon,* a white speck in the eye, for which this plant was used as a treatment + *microcarpa,* small fruit, from Greek, μικρος, *micros,* small and καρπος, *karpos,* fruit.

COMMON NAME: Smallfruit, descriptive. Agrimony, same as genus name.

Agrimonia parviflora
Manyflower Agrimony

SCIENTIFIC NAME: *Agrimonia* + *parviflora,* Latin for small-flowered.

COMMON NAME: Manyflower, for the crowded flowers. Agrimony, same as genus name.

Agrimonia rostellata   Woodland Agrimony

SCIENTIFIC NAME: *Argimonia* + *rostellata,* Latin for a small beak, for the beaked fruit.

COMMON NAME: Woodland, for the habitat. Agrimony, same as genus name.

Agrostemma githago   Common Corn Cockle

SCIENTIFIC NAME: *Agrostemma,* field garland, from Greek, αγρος, *agros,* field and στεμμα, *stemma,* garland + *githago,* an old name for this genus, Latin for a plant that takes root.

COMMON NAME: Common, common in its range. Corn, in Old English this refered to grain crops. This flower grew in the grain fields. Cockle, form Old English, *coccul,* their name for this plant and others considered weeds in the grain fields.

Ajuga reptans   Carpet Ajuga

SCIENTIFIC NAME: *Ajuga,* no yoke, from Greek, α, *a,* without, none and Latin, *iugum,* a yoke. Reference is to the apparently missing upper corolla lip + *reptans,* Latin for creeping or crawling, for the growth pattern.

COMMON NAME: Carpet, for the growth pattern. Ajuga, same as genus name.

Aletris aurea   Colic Root

SCIENTIFIC NAME: *Aletris,* from Greek, αλετρις, *aletris,* a female slave who grinds corn or a noble maiden who prepares offering cakes. The root of this plant is ground and used as a medicine for colic + *aurea,* Latin for gold, for the color of the flowers.

COMMON NAME: Colic Root, see genus name.

Alisma subcordatum Water Plantain

SCIENTIFIC NAME: *Alisma,* from Greek, αλισμα, *alisma,* their name for this type of plant + *subcordatum,* Latin for somewhat heart-shaped, for the leaves.

COMMON NAME: Water, for the habitat. Plantain, from Latin, *plantago,* in turn from *planta,* the sole of the foot. Reference is to the shape of the leaves in some of this genus.

Allionia choisyi
Smooth Trailing Four O'Clock

SCIENTIFIC NAME: *Allionia,* for Carlo Ludovico Allioni (1728-1804), an Italian botanist + *choisyi,* for Jacques Denis Choisy (1799-1859), a Swiss botanist.

COMMON NAME: Smooth, for the smooth stems. Trailing, for the growth pattern. Four O'Clock, although this genus belongs to the afternoon-blooming four o'clock family, it opens in the morning and closes in the evening.

Allionia incarnata Trailing Four O'Clock

SCIENTIFIC NAME: *Allionia + incarnata,* Latin for flesh colored, pink.

Reference is to the color of the flowers.

COMMON NAME: Trailing Four O'Clock, see *Allionia choisyi.*

Allium ampeloprasum Wild Leek

SCIENTIFIC NAME: *Allium,* a form of Latin, *alium,* garlic + *ampeloprasum,* vineyard leek, from Greek, αμπελος, *ampelos,* vine, vineyard and πρασον, *prason,* leek. This leek commonly grows in vineyards.

COMMON NAME: Wild, for the habitat. Leek, from Old English, *leac,* their name for this plant.

Allium canadense Wild Onion

SCIENTIFIC NAME: *Allium + canadense,* Latin for belonging to Canada. Reference is to the area of the type specimen.

COMMON NAME: Wild, occurs naturally in the wild. Onion, from Latin, *unio, unionis,* a large single pearl.

Allium cepa Onion

SCIENTIFIC NAME: *Allium + cepa,* Latin for onion.

COMMON NAME: Onion, see *Allium canadense.*

Allium drummondii
Drummond's Wild Onion

SCIENTIFIC NAME: *Allium +*

drummondii, for Thomas Drummond (c. 1790-1831) a British plant collector.

COMMON NAME: Drummond's, same as species name. Wild Onion, see *Allium canadense.*

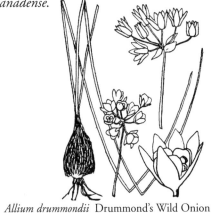

Allium drummondii Drummond's Wild Onion

Allium perdulce **Plains Wild Onion**

SCIENTIFIC NAME: *Allium +perdulce,* Latin for very sweet.

COMMON NAME: Plains, for the habitat. Wild Onion, see *Allium canadense.*

Allium runyonii **Runyon's Onion**

SCIENTIFIC NAME: *Allium + runyonii,* for H. Everett Runyon (1881-1968), an American botanist.

COMMON NAME: Runyon's, same as species name. Onion, see *Allium canadense.*

Allium stellatum **Prairie Onion**

SCIENTIFIC NAME: *Allium + stellatum,* Latin for starlike, for the flower shape.

COMMON NAME: Prairie, for the habitat. Onion, see *Allium canadense.*

Alophia drummondii **Purple Pleatleaf**

SCIENTIFIC NAME: *Alophia,* a form of the Greek, αλορος, *allophos,* without a crest + *drummondii,* for Thomas Drummond (c. 1790-1831) a British plant collector.

COMMON NAME: Purple, for the flower color. Pleat leaf, descriptive.

Aloysia gratissima **Whitebrush**

SCIENTIFIC NAME: *Aloysia,* for Maria Louisa (1751-1819), princess of Parma, she was the wife of Charles IV (1748-1819), king of Spain + *gratissima,* Latin for most pleasing, for its appearance when in bloom.

COMMON NAME: Whitebrush, when in bloom the white flowers cover the plant entirely.

Alternanthera caracasana **Mat Chaff Flower**

SCIENTIFIC NAME: *Alternanthera,* Latin for alternate anther, in this genus the stamens are alternately barren and fertile + *caracasana,* Latin for pertaining to Caracas, Venezuela, for the area of the type specimen.

COMMON NAME: Mat, for the low growth pattern. Chaff Flower, for the appearance on the ground.

Alternanthera philoxeroides
Alligator Weed

SCIENTIFIC NAME: *Alternanthera* + *philoxeroides,* to look like a *Philoxerus,* from the genus *Philoxerus* and Greek, ειοδος, *eiodos,* resembling. Reference is to the leaves.

COMMON NAME: Alligator Weed, this plant grows in waterways in the southeastern United States, in the same areas that alligators occur.

Amblyolepis setigera **Huisache Daisy**

SCIENTIFIC NAME: *Amblyolepis,* blunt scale, from Greek, αμβλυς, *amblus,* blunt, dulled, with the point or edge taken off and λεπος, *lepos,* rind, husk, scale + *setigera,* Latin for bristle-bearing.

COMMON NAME: Huisache, Spanish, from Nahuatl, *huixachin,* a thorny tree or bush. Daisy, from Anglo-Saxon, *daeges-eage,* day's eye, a daisy, for the eyelike appearance and the opening of the rays in the morning.

Amelanchier arborea **Common Shadbush**

SCIENTIFIC NAME: *Amelanchier,* the Old French common name for this plant + *arborea,* Latin for of or belonging to trees, for the appearance.

COMMON NAME: Common, abundant in its range. Shadbush, in New England, this bush blooms at the same time the shad appear in the rivers.

Ammannia auriculata **Earleaf Toothcup**

SCIENTIFIC NAME: *Ammannia,* for Paul Ammann (1634-1691) a German physician and botanist. He was a professor at Leipzig + *auriculata,* Latin for shaped like an ear. Reference is to the shape of the leaves.

COMMON NAME: Earleaf, for the shape of the leaves. Toothcup, for the shape of the fruit.

Ammannia coccinea **Purple Toothcup**

SCIENTIFIC NAME: *Ammannia* + *coccinea,* from Greek, κοκκινος, *kokkinos,* scarlet, for the color of the flower.

COMMON NAME: Purple, for the flower color. Toothcup, for the shape of the fruit.

Ammannia robusta **Lavender Toothcup**

SCIENTIFIC NAME: *Ammannia* + *robusta,* Latin for robust.

COMMON NAME: Lavender, for the flower color. Toothcup, for the shape of the fruit.

Amorpha canescens **Lead Plant**

SCIENTIFIC NAME: *Amorpha,* from Greek, αμορφος, *amorphos,* misshapen, without form. Reference is to the flower having only one petal + *canescens,* Latin for to be somewhat like a thing covered in white, gray with age. Reference is to the short white or grayish hairs on the leaves.

COMMON NAME: Lead Plant, from the belief that the presence of this plant indicated lead deposits in the area.

Amorpha fruticosa **False Indigo**

SCIENTIFIC NAME: *Amorpha + fruticosa*, Latin for pertaining to or resembling a shrub.

COMMON NAME: False, because it looks like true indigo. Indigo, from Spanish, *indico*, in turn from Latin, *indicum*, a blue pigment from India.

Amorpha paniculata **Panicled Amorpha**

SCIENTIFIC NAME: *Amorpha + paniculata*, Latin for having flowers in panicles.

COMMON NAME: Panicled Amorpha, same as scientific name.

Ampelopsis arborea **Pepper Vine**

SCIENTIFIC NAME: *Ampelopsis*, to look like a vine, from Greek, αμπελος, *ampelos*, any climbing plant with tendrils, a grapevine and οψις, *opsis* appearance + *arborea*, Latin for of or belonging to trees. Reference is to this plant climbing trees.

COMMON NAME: Pepper, for the pungent fruit. Vine, from Latin, *vinca*, a vineyard or vine, for the growth pattern.

Ampelopsis cordata **Heartleaf Ampelopsis**

SCIENTIFIC NAME: *Ampelopsis + cordata*, Latin for heart-shaped, for the heart-shaped leaves.

COMMON NAME: Heartleaf Ampelopsis, same as scientific name.

Amphiachyris dracunculoides **Broomweed**

SCIENTIFIC NAME: *Amphiachyris*, on both sides chaff, from Greek, αμφι, *amphi*, on both sides and αχυρον, *akhuron*, chaff, bran, for the appearance of the achenes + *dracunculoides,* to resemble dracunculus, for its resemblance to *Artemisia dracunculus* (tarragon) and the Greek, ειδος, *eidos,* to resemble.

COMMON NAME: Broomweed, For the appearance.

Amphicarpaea bracteata **Hog Peanut**

SCIENTIFIC NAME: *Amphicarpaea*, two kinds of fruit, from Greek, αμφι, *amphi*, on both sides, around, two kinds and καρπος, *karpos,* fruit. This plant has two types of flowers and two types of fruit. One fruit is underground on the lower part of the plant and is edible, the other occurs on the upper part of the plant and is not + *bracteata*, Latin for having bracts.

COMMON NAME: Hog Peanut, hogs will eat the underground fruit, *see* genus name.

Amsonia ciliata **Blue Star**

SCIENTIFIC NAME: *Amsonia,* for Charles Amson, an eighteenth century American physician and botanist + *ciliata,* Latin for fringed with soft hairs, from Latin, *cilium,* eyelid, then to eyelash.

COMMON NAME: Blue Star, for the color and shape of the five-petaled flowers.

Amsonia longiflora **Trumpet Slimpod**

SCIENTIFIC NAME: *Amsonia* + *longiflora,* Latin for long flower, for the trumpet-shaped flowers.

COMMON NAME: Trumpet, for the flower shape. Slimpod, for the thin seedpod.

Amsonia tabernaemontana
Willow Slimpod

SCIENTIFIC NAME: *Amsonia* + *tabernaemontana,* for Jacob Theodore von Berzabern (?-1590), a German botanist. He Latinized his name to Tabernaemontanus.

COMMON NAME: Willow, the leaves are shaped like those of the willow. Slimpod, for the thin seedpod.

Anagallis arvensis **Scarlet Pimpernel**

SCIENTIFIC NAME: *Anagallis,* again glorified, from Greek, ανα, *ana,* again and αγαλλο, *agallo,* glorify, exalt. Dioscorides

(Διοσκοριδες) (fl. first century A.D.), gave this name to this plant + *arvensis,* Latin for belonging to plowed fields.

COMMON NAME: Scarlet, for the flower color. Pimpernel, from Medieval Latin, *pipinella,* their name for this flower.

Anagallis minima **False Pimpernel**

SCIENTIFIC NAME: *Anagallis* + *minima,* Latin for the smallest.

COMMON NAME: False Pimpernel, the flower resembles the Scarlet Pimpernel.

Androsace occidentalis
Western Rock Jasmine

SCIENTIFIC NAME: *Androsace,* male buckle, from Greek, ανδρος, *andros,* man, male and σακος, *sakos,* buckle, shield, for the shape of the anthers + *occidentalis,* Latin for western, for the range in the United States.

COMMON NAME: Western, for the range in the United States. Rock, for the habitat in rocky areas. Jasmine, for the appearance of the flowers.

Androstephium caeruleum
Blue Funnel Lily

SCIENTIFIC NAME: *Androstephium,* stamen crowned, from Greek, ανδρος, *andros,* of man, stamen and στεφος, *stephos,* crown. Reference is to the stamens forming a central crown + *caeruleum,* dark blue, for the flower color.

COMMON NAME: Blue, for the flower color. Funnel, for the flower shape. Lily, from Latin, *lilium*, the name for this type of flower.

Anemone berlandieri **Tenpetal Anemone**

SCIENTIFIC NAME: *Anemone,* from Greek, ανεμωνη, *Anemōnē,* the windflower. Literal translation is "daughter of the wind." As early as 1551 in the *Turner Herbal,* it was believed that the flowers required the spring wind in order to open + *berlandieri,* for Jean Louis Berlandier (1805-1851), a French botanist who worked in Texas.

COMMON NAME: Tenpetal, actually the anemone has no petals but ten or more petal-like sepals form the apparent blossom. Anemone, same as genus name.

Anemone caroliniana **Carolina Anemone**

SCIENTIFIC NAME: *Anemone* + *carolinana,* Latin for pertaining to Carolina, the area of the type specimen.

COMMON NAME: Same as scientific name.

Anemone decapetala **Southern Anemone**

SCIENTIFIC NAME: *Anemone* + *decapetala,* Latin for having ten petals. Actually the Anemone has no petals, rather ten or more petal-like sepals on the blossom.

COMMON NAME: Southern, for the range in the United States. Anemone, same as genus name.

Anemopsis californica **Yerba Mansa**

SCIENTIFIC NAME: *Anemopsis,* to look like an anemone, from the genus *Anemone* and Greek, οψις, *opsis,* appearance + *californica,* Latin for of California, for the area of the type specimen.

COMMON NAME: Yerba Mansa, Spanish for gentle or tame herb.

Anisacanthus quadrifidus
Hummingbird Bush

SCIENTIFIC NAME: *Anisacanthus,* unequal thorn, from Greek, ανισα, *anisa,* unequal and ακανθος, *akanthos,* thorn + *quadrifidus,* Latin for cut into four.

COMMON NAME: Hummingbird Bush, the flowers attract hummingbirds.

Antennaria neglecta **Field Pussytoes**

SCIENTIFIC NAME: *Antennaria,* from New Latin, *antenna,* a feeler, horn of an insect. Reference is to the pappus, which was thought to resemble the antennae of the butterfly + *neglecta,* Latin for neglected.

COMMON NAME: Field, for the habitat. Pussytoes (cats' toes), for the appearance of the blossom.

Antennaria parlinii
Largeleaf Pussytoes

SCIENTIFIC NAME: *Antennaria* + *parlinii,* for John Crawford Parlin (1863-1948), an American who discovered this species.

COMMON NAME: Largeleaf, descriptive. Pussytoes, see *Antennaria neglecta.*

Anthemis cupula   **Stinkweed**

SCIENTIFIC NAME: *Anthemis,* from Greek, ανθεμις, *anthemis,* the chamomile + *cupula,* Latin for little cup.

COMMON NAME: Stinkweed, for the unpleasant scent.

Anthericum torreyi   **Crag Lily**

SCIENTIFIC NAME: *Anthericum,* from Greek, ανθερικος, *antherikos,* the flowering stem of asphodel + *torreyi,* for John Torrey (1796-1873), an American botanist, he was co-author, with Asa Gray (1810-1888), of *The Flora of North America* (1838-1843).

COMMON NAME: Crag, for the habitat in rocky canyons. Lily, from Latin, *lilium,* the name for this type of plant.

Aphanostephus pilosus   **Hairy Lazy Daisy**

SCIENTIFIC NAME: *Aphanostephus,* unseen crown, from Greek, αφανης, *aphanēs,* unseen and στεφανος, *stephanos,* circle, crown, wreath. Reference is to the

flowers staying closed until midday + *pilosus,* Latin for downy, having long soft hairs. Reference is to the downy stems and leaves.

COMMON NAME: Hairy, same as species name. Lazy, because the flowers do not open until midday. Daisy, from Anglo-Saxon, *daeges-eage,* day's eye, a daisy, for the eyelike appearance and the opening of the rays in the morning in most species.

Aphanostephus ramosissimus
Plains Lazy Daisy

SCIENTIFIC NAME: *Aphanostephus* + *ramosissimus,* Latin for much branched.

COMMON NAME: Plains, for the habitat. Lazy Daisy, see *Aphanostephus pilosus.*

Aphanostephus riddellii
Riddell's Lazy Daisy

SCIENTIFIC NAME: *Aphanostephus* + *riddellii,* for John Leonard Riddell (1807-1865), an American botanist.

COMMON NAME: Riddell's, same as species name. Lazy Daisy, *see Aphanostephus pilosus.*

Aphanostephus skirrhobasis
Arkansas Lazy Daisy

SCIENTIFIC NAME: *Aphanostephus* + *skirrhobasis,* hard base, from Greek, σκερρος, *skerros,* a form of σκιρος, *skiros,* hard and βασις, *basis,* base. The bases of

Aphanostephus skirrhobasis Arkansas Lazy Daisy

both the ray and disk flowers harden with age.

COMMON NAME: Arkansas, for the area of the type specimen. Lazy Daisy, see *Aphanostephus pilosus.*

Apios americana **Groundnut**

SCIENTIFIC NAME: *Apios,* from Greek, απιος, *apios,* a pear. Reference is to the tuberlike thickenings of the rhizomes + *americana,* of America, for the range.

COMMON NAME: Groundnut, for the tuber-like thickenings of the rhizomes.

Apocynum androsaemifolium **Spreading Dogbane**

SCIENTIFIC NAME: *Apocynum,* from Greek, αποκυνον, *apokunon,* dog's-bane, a poison cake made from this plant was used to kill dogs + *androsaemifolium,* Latin for to have leaves like *Androsaemum,* a plant genus related to St. John's Wort. From the genus *Androsaemum* and Latin, *folium,* leaves.

COMMON NAME: Spreading, for the sprawling growth pattern. Dogbane, historically used as a dog poison.

Apocynum cannabinum **Indian Hemp**

SCIENTIFIC NAME: *Apocynum + cannabinum,* Latin for to be like the genus *Cannabis.* Reference is to this plant being used to make cordage and ropes.

COMMON NAME: Indian Hemp, for the use by North American Indians to make cordage and rope.

Aquilegia canadensis **Common Columbine**

SCIENTIFIC NAME: *Aquilegia,* from Latin, *aquila,* an eagle, for the flower spurs thought to resemble the claws of an eagle + *canadensis,* Latin for belonging to Canada, for the area of the type specimen.

COMMON NAME: Common, abundant in its range. Columbine, from Latin, *columba,* doves. The flower looks like a dule of doves drinking when viewed from above.

Arbutus xalapensis **Texas Madrone**

SCIENTIFIC NAME: *Arbutus,* Latin for the wild strawberry tree + *xalapensis,* Latin for belonging to Xalapa, Mexico, the area of the type specimen.

COMMON NAME: Texas, for the range. Madrone. From Spanish, *madrono,* the madrono tree, silk tassel.

Arenaria benthamii **Hilly Sandwort**

SCIENTIFIC NAME: *Arenaria,* from Latin, *arena,* sand, for the habitat of many in this genus + *benthamii,* for George Bentham (1800-1884), an English taxonomist.

COMMON NAME: Hilly, for the habitat. Sandwort, sand, for the habitat and wort from Old English, *wort,* a plant used for food or medicine.

Arenaria serpyllifolia
Thymeleaf Sandwort

SCIENTIFIC NAME: *Arenaria* + *serpyllifolia,* Latin for having leaves like *Thymus serpyllum,* a species of thyme.

COMMON NAME: Thymeleaf, descriptive. Sandwort, see *Arenaria benthamii.*

Argemone albiflora **White Prickly Poppy**

SCIENTIFIC NAME: *Argemone,* from Greek, αργεμονε, *argemone,* the windrose, *Papaver argemone,* which this plant resembles + *albiflora,* Latin for white flower.

COMMON NAME: White, for the flower color. Prickly, for the spiny leaves and stem. Poppy, from Latin, *papauum,* their name for this type of plant.

Argemone aurantiaca **Prickly Poppy**

SCIENTIFIC NAME: *Argemone* + *aurantiaca,* Latin for orange-colored, for the flower color.

COMMON NAME: Prickly Poppy, see *Argemone albiflora.*

Argemone chisosensis **Pink Prickly Poppy**

SCIENTIFIC NAME: *Argemone* + *chisosensis,* Latin for belonging to Chisos, for the range in the Chisos Mountains of Texas.

COMMON NAME: Pink, for the flower color. Prickly Poppy, see *Argemone albiflora.*

Argemone intermedia
Bluestem Prickly Poppy

SCIENTIFIC NAME: *Argemone* + *intermedia,* Latin to indicate an intermediate position in color or form.

COMMON NAME: Bluestem, for the bluish cast of the stem. Prickly Poppy, see *Argemone albiflora.*

Argemone mexicana **Mexican Poppy**

SCIENTIFIC NAME: *Argemone* + *mexicana,* Latin for pertaining to Mexico. This flower was actually brought to Mexico from the West Indies.

COMMON NAME: Mexican, same as species name. Poppy, see *Argemone albiflora.*

Argemone polyanthemos
Crested Prickly Poppy

SCIENTIFIC NAME: *Argemone +
polyanthemos,* from Greek, πολυανθεμος,
poluanthemos, rich in flowers, many flowers.

COMMON NAME: Crested, for the
prominent sphere of yellow stamens at the
center of the bloom. Prickly Poppy, see
Argemone albiflora.

Argemone rosea   **Rose Prickly Poppy**

SCIENTIFIC NAME: *Argemone + rosea,*
Latin for rose, the flower color ranges
from pink to dark rose.

COMMON NAME: Rose, for the flower
color. Prickly Poppy, see *Argemone albiflora.*

Argemone sanguinea   **Rose Prickly Poppy**

SCIENTIFIC NAME: *Argemone + sanguinea,* Latin for bloody, colored like
blood. Reference is to the flower color.

COMMON NAME: Rose, for the color
of the flowers. Prickly Poppy, see
Argemone albiflora.

Argemone squarrosa
Hedgehog Prickly Poppy

SCIENTIFIC NAME: *Argemone +
squarrosa,* Latin for having parts that
spread or recurve at the ends.

COMMON NAME: Hedgehog, for the
spines. Prickly Poppy, see *Argemone albiflora.*

Arisaema dracontium   **Green Dragon**

SCIENTIFIC NAME: *Arisaema,* arum
blood, from Latin, *arum,* and Greek αιμα,
haema, blood. Reference is to the close
relationship to the genus *Arum* or to the
spots resembling blood on some of these
plants + *dracontium,* the ancient Greek
name for *Arum dracunculus,* which this
plant resembles. This comes from Greek,
δρακοντιον, *drakontion,* little dragon. The
elongated spadix of this plant was thought
to look like a dragon's tongue.

COMMON NAME: Green, for the
green spadix and spathe. Dragon, see
species name.

Arisaema quinatum
Fiveleaf Jack-in-the-Pulpit

SCIENTIFIC NAME: *Arisaema + quina-
tum,* Latin for in fives, for the five leaflets
forming the leaf.

COMMON NAME: Fiveleaf, same as
species name. Jack-in-the-Pulpit, for the
thick spadix and the canopied spathe,
which reminds one of a small priest in an
old style canopied pulpit.

Arisaema triphyllum   **Jack-in-the-Pulpit**

SCIENTIFIC NAME: *Arisaema + triphyllum,* three-leaved, from Greek, τρι, *tri,*
three and φυλλον, *phullon,* leaf, for the
three leaflets that make up the leaf.

COMMON NAME: Jack-in-the-Pulpit,
see *Arisaema quinatum.*

Arnoglossum plantagineum
Prairie Plantain

SCIENTIFIC NAME: *Arnoglossum,* lamb tongue, from Greek, αρνος, *arnos,* a lamb, and γλωσσα, *glōssa,* tongue, for the leaves + *plantaginea,* Latin for resembling a plantain.

COMMON NAME: Prairie, for the habitat. Plantain, for its resemblance to plantain (plantago).

Asclepias amplexicaulis
Bluntleaf Milkweed

SCIENTIFIC NAME: *Asclepias,* from Greek, ασκληπιας, *asklēpias,* the swallow-wort, *Vincetoxicum officinale. Vincetoxicum* is Latin for "to conquer or overcome poison"; it was used as a treatment for snakebite. This Greek common name, in turn, came from Ασκληπιος, *Asklēpios,* the Greek hero and god of healing + *amplexicaulis,* Latin for stem clasping, the bases of the leaves encircle the stem.

COMMON NAME: Bluntleaf, for the ovate leaves. Milkweed, for the milky sap.

Asclepias arenaria   **Sand Milkweed**

SCIENTIFIC NAME: *Asclepias* + *arenaria,* from Latin, *harenaria,* a sandpit. Reference is to the habitat.

COMMON NAME: Sand, for the habitat. Milkweed, for the milky sap.

Asclepias asperula   **Antelope Horn**

SCIENTIFIC NAME: *Asclepias* + *asperula,* Latin for rough to the touch.

COMMON NAME: Antelope Horn, for the shape of the fruting pods.

Asclepias engelmanniana
Engelmann's Milkweed

SCIENTIFIC NAME: *Asclepias* + *engelmanniana,* Latin for pertaining to Engelmann, for George Engelmann (1809-1884), a German American physician and botanist.

COMMON NAME: Engelmann's, same as species name. Milkweed, for the milky sap.

Asclepias incarnata   **Swamp Milkweed**

SCIENTIFIC NAME: *Asclepias* + *incarnata,* Latin for flesh-colored. Reference is to the pink flowers.

COMMON NAME: Swamp, for the habitat. Milkweed, for the milky sap.

Asclepias latifolia   **Broadleaf Milkweed**

SCIENTIFIC NAME: *Asclepias* + *latifolia,* Latin for having broad leaves.

COMMON NAME: Broadleaf, for the elliptical leaves that are wider than those of most milkweeds. Milkweed, for the milky sap.

Asclepias linearis **Slim Milkweed**

SCIENTIFIC NAME: *Asclepias + linearis,* Latin for narrow, with sides almost parallel, for the thin leaves.

COMMON NAME: Slim, for the narrow leaves. Milkweed, for the milky sap.

Asclepias oenotheroides
Sidecluster Milkweed

SCIENTIFIC NAME: *Asclepias + oenotheroides,* to look like *Oenothera,* from the genus *Oenothera* and Greek, ειδος, *eidos,* resembling.

COMMON NAME: Sidecluster, for the flower arrangement. Milkweed, for the milky sap.

Asclepias perennis **Shore Milkweed**

SCIENTIFIC NAME: *Asclepias + perennis,* Latin for perennial.

COMMON NAME: Shore, for the habitat along streams and swampy areas. Milkweed, for the milky sap.

Asclepias quadrifolia
Fourleaf Milkweed

SCIENTIFIC NAME: *Asclepias + quadrifolia,* Latin for having four leaves. Reference is to the leaf pattern of the middle leaves, which form a whorl of four.

COMMON NAME: Fourleaf, same as species name. Milkweed, for the milky sap.

Asclepias speciosa **Showy Milkweed**

SCIENTIFIC NAME: *Asclepias + speciosa,* Latin for showy, attractive in appearance. Reference is to the rose-pink inflorescences.

COMMON NAME: Showy, same as species name. Milkweed, for the milky sap.

Asclepias stenophylla
Narrowleaf Milkweed

SCIENTIFIC NAME: *Asclepias + stenophylla,* narrow-leaved, from Greek, στενος, *stenos,* narrow and φυλλον, *phullon,* leaf.

COMMON NAME: Narrowleaf, descriptive. Milkweed, for the milky sap.

Asclepias subverticillata
Poison Milkweed

SCIENTIFIC NAME: *Asclepias + subverticillata,* Latin for a whorl below. Reference is to the whorled pattern of leafy shoots that form at the bases of the leaves.

COMMON NAME: Poison, toxic to livestock. Milkweed, for the milky sap.

Asclepias sullivantii   **Sullivant Milkweed**

SCIENTIFIC NAME: *Asclepias +
sullivantii,* for William Starling Sullivant
(1803-1873), an American botanist.

COMMON NAME: Sullivant, same as
species name. Milkweed, for the milky sap.

Asclepias syriaca   **Common Milkweed**

SCIENTIFIC NAME: *Asclepias + syriaca,*
of Syria, Syrian, for the range of the type
specimen.

COMMON NAME: Common,
common in its range in the United States.
Milkweed, for the milky sap.

Asclepias texana   **Texas Milkweed**

SCIENTIFIC NAME: *Asclepias + texana,*
Latin for pertaining to Texas, for the range.

COMMON NAME: Texas, for the
range. Milkweed, for the milky sap.

Asclepias tuberosa   **Butterfly Milkweed**

SCIENTIFIC NAME: *Asclepias +
tuberosa,* Latin for having tubers.
Reference is to the tuberous roots used as
a laxative and for treating pleurisy by
American Indians.

COMMON NAME: Butterfly, the flow-
ers are attractive to a variety of butterflies.
Milkweed, this plant is in the milkweed
family but lacks the milky sap of the other
members.

Asclepias variegata
Whiteflower Milkweed

SCIENTIFIC NAME: *Asclepias +
variegata,* Latin for variegated, to have
different colors. Reference is to the white
flowers with purple gynostegia.

COMMON NAME: Whiteflower,
descriptive. Milkweed, for the milky sap.

Asclepias verticillata   **Whorled Milkweed**

SCIENTIFIC NAME: *Asclepias +
verticillata,* Latin for whorled. Reference is
to the pattern of leaf arrangement.

COMMON NAME: Whorled, same as
species name. Milkweed, for the milky sap.

Asclepias viridiflora   **Green Milkweed**

SCIENTIFIC NAME: *Asclepias +
viridiflora,* Latin for having green flowers.

COMMON NAME: Green, same as
species name. Milkweed, for the milky sap.

Asclepias tuberosa
Butterfly Milkweed

Asclepias viridis **Green Antelope Horn**

SCIENTIFIC NAME: *Asclepias + viridis,* Latin for to be green, for the green flowers.

COMMON NAME: Green, same as species name. Antelope Horn, for the shape of the seed pods.

Astragalus canadensis **Canada Milk Vetch**

SCIENTIFIC NAME: *Astragalus,* from Greek, αστραγαλος, *astragalos,* their name for this plant, it means "star milk," for the flower shape and the belief that it increased milk production in goats that ate it + *canadensis,* Latin for belonging to Canada, for the area of the type specimen.

COMMON NAME: Canada, same as species name. Milk Vetch, milk, for the belief that it increased the milk production of goats, Vetch, from the Latin name for this plant, *vicia.*

Astragalus crassicarpus **Ground Plum**

SCIENTIFIC NAME: Astragalus + *crassicarpus,* having thick fruit, from Latin, *crassus,* thick and Greek, καρπος, karpos, fruit.

COMMON NAME: Ground Plum, for the thick fruits.

Astragalus distortus **Bentpod Milk Vetch**

SCIENTIFIC NAME: *Astragalus + distortus,* Latin for distorted, twisted, for the twisted fruit.

COMMON NAME: Bentpod, same as species name. Milk Vetch, see *Astragalus canadensis.*

Astragalus giganteus **Giant Milk Vetch**

SCIENTIFIC NAME: *Astragalus + giganteus,* Latin for relating to giants, for the relative size.

COMMON NAME: Giant, same as species name. Milk Vetch, see *Astragalus canadensis.*

Astragalus leptocarpus
Slimpod Milk Vetch

SCIENTIFIC NAME: *Astragalus + leptocarpus,* having thin fruit, from Greek, λεπτος, *leptos,* thin and καρπος, *karpos,* fruit.

COMMON NAME: Slimpod, the fruiting pod is relatively thin. Milk Vetch, see *Astragalus canadensis.*

Astragalus lindheimeri
Lindheimer's Milk Vetch

SCIENTIFIC NAME: *Astragalus + lindheimeri,* for Ferdinand Jacob Lindheimer (1809-1879), a German political exile who collected plants in Texas.

COMMON NAME: Lindheimer's, same as species name. Milk Vetch, see *Astragalus canadensis.*

Astragalus lotiflorus **Lotus Milk Vetch**

SCIENTIFIC NAME: *Astragalus +
lotiflorus,* Latin for having flowers like the
genus *Lotus.*

COMMON NAME: Lotus, same as
species name. Milk Vetch, see *Astragalus
Canadensis.*

Astragalus missouriensis
Missouri Milk Vetch

SCIENTIFIC NAME: *Astragalus +
missouriensis,* Latin for belonging to
Missouri, for the area of the type specimen.

COMMON NAME: Missouri, same as
species name. Milk Vetch, see *Astragalus
canadensis.*

Astragalus mollissimus **Woolly Locoweed**

SCIENTIFIC NAME: *Astragalus +
mollissimus,* the Latin superlative of *mollis,*
soft. Therefore, very soft, softest.
Reference is to the soft, downy leaves.

COMMON NAME: Wooly, for the silky
hairs of the leaves. Locoweed, this plant
contains lococine, which is poisonous to
livestock. The dyskinetic spasmotic mus-
cular actions induced by this toxin makes
the affected animal appear "loco," the
common word in Spanish for crazy.

Astragalus nuttallianus **Turkey Pea**

SCIENTIFIC NAME: *Astragalus +
nuttallianus,* Latin for pertaining to

Nuttall, for Thomas Nuttall (1786-1859),
an English botanist, explorer, printer,
ornithologist, and plant collector. He was
a fellow of the Linnaean Society.

COMMON NAME: Turkey Pea, for the
seeds, which are eaten by turkeys and
other birds.

Astragalus plattensis
Platte River Milk Vetch

SCIENTIFIC NAME: *Astragalus +
plattensis,* Latin for belonging to the
Platte, for the Platte River, for the area
of the type specimen.

COMMON NAME: Platte River, same
as species name. Milk Vetch, see *Astragalus
canadensis.*

Astragalus racemosus **Creamy Milk Vetch**

SCIENTIFIC NAME: *Astragalus + racemosus,* Latin for to grow in racemes.
Reference is to the flowers opening along
a central stalk from the bottom up.

COMMON NAME: Creamy, for the
flower color. Milk Vetch, *see Astragalus
canadensis.*

Astragalus reflexus **Texas Milk Vetch**

SCIENTIFIC NAME: *Astragalus +
reflexus,* Latin for bent back sharply.

COMMON NAME: Texas, for the
range. Milk Vetch, *see Astragalus
canadensis.*

Astragalus wrightii **Wright's Milk Vetch**

SCIENTIFIC NAME: *Astragalus +
wrightii,* for Charles Wright (1811-1885),
a Texas plant collector.

COMMON NAME: Wright's, same as
species name. Milk Vetch, *see Astragalus
canadensis.*

Astranthium integrifolium
Western Daisy

SCIENTIFIC NAME: *Astranthium,* star
flower, from Greek, αστρον, *astron,* star
and ανθος, *anthros,* flower, for the flower
shape + *integrifolium,* Latin for having
entire leaves.

COMMON NAME: Western, for the
range in the United States. Daisy, from
Anglo-Saxon, *daeges-eage,* day's eye, a
daisy, for the eyelike appearance and the
opening of the rays in the morning.

Aureolaria grandiflora **Downy Oakleech**

SCIENTIFIC NAME: *Aureolaria,* from
Latin, *aureo,* golden, for the flower color +
grandiflora, Latin for large flowers.

COMMON NAME: Downy, for the soft
hairs on the stems. Oakleech, this plant is
hemiparasitic on oaks.

Bahia absinthifolia **Yerba Raton**

SCIENTIFIC NAME: *Bahia,* for Juan
Francisco de Bahi y Fonseca (1775-1841),
a Spanish physician and botanist +

absinthifolia, Latin for having leaves like
absinthe, *Artemisia absinthium.*

COMMON NAME: Yerba Raton,
Spanish for mouse herb or mouse grass.

Baileya multiradiata **Desert Marigold**

SCIENTIFIC NAME: *Baileya,* for Jacob
Whitman Bailey (1811-1857), an
American botanist + *multiradiata,* Latin
for many spokes, for the multiple rows of
ray petals.

COMMON NAME: Desert, for the
habitat. Marigold, Mary's gold, from the
proper name Mary, with reference to the
Virgin Mary and gold for the color of the
flowers.

Baptisia australis **Blue False Indigo**

SCIENTIFIC NAME: *Baptisia,* from
Greek, βαπτω, *baptō,* to dip, to dye.
Reference is to this plant genus being used
as a dye + *australis,* Latin for of the south
wind, southern.

COMMON NAME: Blue, for the flower
color. False, not true indigo, although it
looks like it. Indigo, a blue dye from
India, from Greek, ινδικος, *indikos,*
Indian. Obtained from *Indigofera tinctoria.*

Baptisia bicolor **Two-Color Wild Indigo**

SCIENTIFIC NAME: *Baptisia + bicolor,*
Latin for having two colors, the flowers
have two shades of blue-violet.

COMMON NAME: Two-color, same as species name. Wild, for the habitat. Indigo, see *Baptisia australis.*

Baptisia bushii Bush's Wild Indigo

SCIENTIFIC NAME: *Baptisia + bushii,* for Benjamin Franklin Bush (1858-1937), an American plant collector.

COMMON NAME: Bush's, same as species name. Wild, for the habitat. Indigo, see *Baptisia australis.*

Baptisia bracteata
Longbract Wild Indigo

SCIENTIFIC NAME: *Baptisia + bracteata,* Latin for having bracts. Reference is to the long bracts.

COMMON NAME: Longbract, descriptive. Wild, for the habitat. Indigo, see *Baptisia australis.*

Baptisia lactea Wild White Indigo

SCIENTIFIC NAME: *Baptisia + lactea,* Latin for milky, of milk. Reference is to the white flowers.

COMMON NAME: Wild, for the habitat. White, for the flower color. Indigo, see *Baptisia australis.*

Baptisia leucantha White Indigo

SCIENTIFIC NAME: *Baptisia + leucantha,* white flowered, from Greek, λευκος, *leukos,* white and ανθη, *anthē,* bloom, flower.

COMMON NAME: White, for the flower color. Indigo, see *Baptisia australis.*

Baptisia leucophaea Plains Wild Indigo

SCIENTIFIC NAME: *Baptisia + leucophaea,* white-brown, from Greek, λευκος, *leukos,* white and φαεο, *phaeo,* brown. Reference is to the dark yellow flowers.

COMMON NAME: Plains, for the habitat. Wild, for the habitat. Indigo, see *Baptisia australis.*

Baptisia nuttalliana Nuttall's Baptisia

SCIENTIFIC NAME: *Baptisia + nuttalliana,* Latin for pertaining to Nuttall, for Thomas Nuttall (1786-1859), an English botanist, explorer, printer, ornithologist, and plant collector. He was a fellow of the Linnaean Society.

COMMON NAME: Nuttall's, same as species name. Baptisia, see *Baptisia australis.*

Baptisia sphaerocarpa Green Wild Indigo

SCIENTIFIC NAME: *Baptisia + sphaerocarpa,* ball or globe fruited, from Greek, σφαιρα, *sphaira,* a ball or globe and καρπος, *karpos,* fruit.

COMMON NAME: Green, for the blue-green leaves. Wild, for the habitat. Indigo, see *Baptisia australis.*

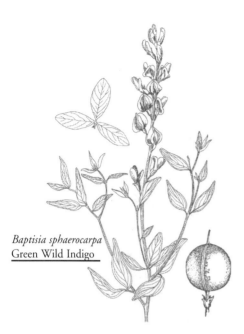

Baptisia sphaerocarpa
Green Wild Indigo

Baptisia variicolor
Varicolor Wild Indigo

SCIENTIFIC NAME: *Baptisia* + *variicolor,* Latin for having various colors, the flower color ranges from red, yellow, orange to blue-violet.

COMMON NAME: Varicolor, same as species name. Wild, for the habitat. Indigo, see *Baptisia australis.*

Bastardia viscosa **Bastardia**

SCIENTIFIC NAME: *Bastardia,* for Toussaint Bastard (1784-1846), a French physician and botanist + *viscosa,* Latin for sticky. Reference is to the sticky hairs which cover the plant.

COMMON NAME: Bastardia, same as genus name.

Berberis trifoliolata **Wild Currant**

SCIENTIFIC NAME: *Berberis,* the Latinized form of the Arabian word, *barbaris,* their name for the fruit, is the commonly accepted definition. *Barbaris* was actually the Latin name employed by Arabian botanists to name this plant, it is not known what the base word or language was. *The Oxford English Dictionary, 2nd Edition,* 1989, states that no such Arabic or Persian word exists and lists the derivation as unknown + *trifoliolata,* Latin for having three leaves, the leaves are made up of three leaflets.

COMMON NAME: Wild, for the habitat. Currant, for the edible fruit, currant comes from Anglo-French, *raisins de Corauntz* (raisins of Cornith).

Berlandiera betonicifolia **Texas Greeneyes**

SCIENTIFIC NAME: *Berlandiera,* for Jean Louis Berlandier (1805-1851), a French physician and botanist, who collected plants in Texas and Mexico + *betonicifolia,* Latin for having leaves like the genus *Betonica.*

COMMON NAME: Texas, for the range. Greeneyes, for the green central disk.

Berlandiera lyrata **Greeneyes**

SCIENTIFIC NAME: *Berlandiera* + *lyrata,* Latin for shaped like a lyre, for the leaves.

COMMON NAME: Greeneyes, for the green central disk.

Berlandiera pumila **Soft Greeneyes**

SCIENTIFIC NAME: *Berlandiera, + pumila,* Latin for a dwarf or midget. This flower resembles a small sunflower.

COMMON NAME: Soft, for the velvety leaves. Greeneyes, for the green central disk.

Bidens aristosa **Western Tickseed**

SCIENTIFIC NAME: *Bidens,* Latin for "two-toothed." Reference is to the two bristles on the achenes + *aristosa,* Latin for having a beard or bristle. Again the reference is to the bristles on the achenes.

COMMON NAME: Western, for the range in the United States. Tickseed, for the appearance and the adherence of the achenes.

Bidens bipinnata **Spanish Needles**

SCIENTIFIC NAME: *Bidens + bipinnata,* Latin for "two-feathered" or "two-winged." Reference is to the bristles on the achenes.

COMMON NAME: Spanish Needles, for the barbs on the achenes.

Bidens cernua **Nodding Beggar Ticks**

SCIENTIFIC NAME: *Bidens + cernua,* Latin for drooping or nodding. Reference is to the flowers.

COMMON NAME: Nodding, for the appearance of the flowers. Beggar Ticks,

for the appearance and adherence of the achenes.

Bidens frondosa **Beggar Ticks**

SCIENTIFIC NAME: *Bidens + frondosa,* Latin for being full of leaves, having well-developed leaves.

COMMON NAME: Beggar Ticks, see *Bidens cernua.*

Bidens laevis **Smooth Bidens**

SCIENTIFIC NAME: *Bidens + laevis,* Latin for smooth. Reference is to the smooth stems.

COMMON NAME: Smooth Bidens, same as scientific name.

Bifora americana **Prairie Bishop's Weed**

SCIENTIFIC NAME: *Bifora,* Latin for having two doors or openings. Reference is to the mericarp + *americana,* Latin for pertaining to America.

COMMON NAME: Prairie, for the habitat. Bishop's Weed, common name first applied in Scotland because it was almost impossible to get rid of, as it would be to remove a bishop from the church.

Bigelowia nuttallii **Rayless Goldenrod**

SCIENTIFIC NAME: *Bigelowia,* for Jacob Bigelow (1787-1879), an American physician and plant collector + *nuttallii,* for Thomas Nuttall (1786-1858), an English botanist, explorer, printer, ornithologist, and plant collector. He was a fellow of the Linnaean Society.

COMMON NAME: Rayless, for the rayless flowers. Goldenrod, for the appearance of the yellow inflorescence.

Bignonia capreolata **Cross Vine**

SCIENTIFIC NAME: *Bignonia,* for Abbe Jean Paul Bignon (1662-1743), librarian to King Louis XIV + *capreolata,* Latin for provided with tendrils.

COMMON NAME: Cross, a cross section of the stem reveals a cross. Vine, for the growth habit.

Boerhavia linearifolia **Narrowleaf Spiderling**

SCIENTIFIC NAME: *Boerhavia,* for Herman Boeraave (1668-1739), a Dutch physician and botanist. The Principle of Priority allows the misspelling to stand. + *linearifolia,* Latin for having linear leaves.

COMMON NAME: Narrowleaf, descriptive of the linear leaves. Spiderling, for the spiderly appearance of the slender branches.

Boerhavia purpurascens **Purple Spiderling**

SCIENTIFIC NAME: *Boerhavia* + *purpurascens,* Latin for somewhat purple, for the color of the flowers.

COMMON NAME: Purple, for the flower color. Spiderling, for the spiderly appearance of the slender branches.

Boltonia asteroides **White Boltonia**

SCIENTIFIC NAME: *Boltonia,* for James Bolton (1758-1799), an English botanist + *asteroides,* to look like a star, from Greek, αστερ, *aster* and ειδος, *eidos,* resembling, for the flower shape.

COMMON NAME: White, for the flower color. Boltonia, same as genus name.

Boltonia diffusa **Smallhead Boltonia**

SCIENTIFIC NAME: *Boltonia* + *diffusa,* Latin for diffuse, spreading, for the growth pattern.

COMMON NAME: Smallhead, for the small flower heads. Boltonia, same as genus name.

Borrichia frutescens **Sea Oxeye**

SCIENTIFIC NAME: *Borrichia,* for Olaf Borrick, a Danish botanist + *frutescens,* Latin for shrublike.

COMMON NAME: Sea, for the habitat along the coast. Oxeye, for the appearance of the heads, which have a large central disk.

Brassica juncea **India Mustard**

SCIENTIFIC NAME: *Brassica,* Latin for cabbage + *juncea,* from Latin, *iunceus,* resembling rushes.

COMMON NAME: India, for the original range. Mustard, from Spanish, *mostaza,* mustard. The name comes from the condiment, prepared by grinding the seeds of the plant with must (new wine), not from the plant.

Brickellia cylindracea
Gravelbar Brickellbush

SCIENTIFIC NAME: *Brickellia,* for John Brickell (1749-1809), an American plant collector + *cylindracea,* Latin for cylindrical.

COMMON NAME: Gravelbar, for the habitat. Brickellbush, same as genus name.

Brickellia eupatorioides **Brickellbush**

SCIENTIFIC NAME: *Brickellia* + *eupatorioides,* to look like *Eupatorium,* from the genus *Eupatorium* and Greek, ειοδος, *eiodos,* resembling.

COMMON NAME: Brickellbush, same as genus name.

Buchnera americana
American Blueheart

SCIENTIFIC NAME: *Buchnera,* for Johann Gottfried Buchner (1695-1749), a

German botanist + *americana,* Latin for pertaining to America.

COMMON NAME: American, for the range. Blueheart, for the usually blue flower.

Caesalpinia gilliesii **Bird-of-Paradise**

SCIENTIFIC NAME: *Caesalpinia,* for Andrea Cesalpino (1519-1603), an Italian physician and botanist + *gilliesii,* for John Gillies (1792-1834), a Scottish physician and botanist.

COMMON NAME: Bird-of-Paradise, for the appearance of the flower.

Calamintha arkansana
Arkansas Calamint

SCIENTIFIC NAME: *Calamintha,* beautiful mint, from Greek, καλος, *kalos,* beautiful and μινθη, *minthē,* mint + *arkansana,* Latin for pertaining to Arkansas, for the area of the type specimen.

COMMON NAME: Arkansas Calamint, same as scientific name.

Calibrachoa parviflora **Wild Petunia**

SCIENTIFC NAME: *Calibrachoa,* for Antonio de Cal y Bracho, a nineteenth century Mexican botanist + *parviflora,* Latin for small flower.

COMMON NAME: Wild, for the habitat. Petunia, for the appearance of the flower, some in this genus are often classified in the *Petunia* genus.

Callicarpa americana   French Mulberry

SCIENTIFIC NAME: *Callicarpa,* from Greek, καλος, *kalos,* beautiful and καρπος, *karpos,* fruit + *americana,* Latin for pertaining to America.

COMMON NAME: French Mulberry, for the appearance of the fruit.

Callirhoe alcaeoides
Plains Poppy Mallow

SCIENTIFIC NAME: *Callirhoe,* from Greek, καλλιρροη, *kallirroē,* one of the Oceanids of Greek mythology. Her name means "beautiful flowing" + *alcaeoides,* to look like a mallow, from *Alcea,* the genus of mallow and Greek, ειδος, *eidos,* resembling.

COMMON NAME: Plains, for the habitat. Poppy Mallow, for the appearance of the blossom.

Callirhoe involucrata   Wine Cup

SCIENTIFIC NAME: *Callirhoe + involucrata,* Latin for having an involucre, a ring of bracts beneath the flower.

COMMON NAME: Wine Cup, for the color and shape of the blossom.

Calliroe leiocarpa   Tall Wine Cup

SCIENTIFIC NAME: *Calliroe + leiocarpa,* smooth fruit, from Greek, λειος, *leios,* smooth and καρπος, *karpos,* fruit.

COMMON NAME: Tall, for the relative height. Wine Cup, for the color and shape of the blossom.

Callirhoe pedata   Finger Poppy Mallow

SCIENTIFIC NAME: *Callirhoe + pedata,* Latin for footed, for the lobes at the foot of the leaf.

COMMON NAME: Finger, for the shape of the leaf lobes. Poppy Mallow, for the appearance of the blossom.

Callirhoe pedata
Finger Poppy Mallow

Calochortus kennedyi
Desert Mariposa Lily

SCIENTIFIC NAME: *Calochortus,*
beautiful grass, from Greek, καλος, *kalos,*
beautiful and χορτος, *khortos,* grass, any
fodder. Reference is to the grasslike leaves
+ *kennedyi,* for John Kennedy (1775-1842),
a Scottish nurseryman.

COMMON NAME: Desert, for the
habitat. Mariposa, Spanish for butterfly.
Lily, from Latin, *lilium,* their name for
this type of flower.

Calopogon barbatus **Bearded Grass Pink**

SCIENTIFIC NAME: *Calopogon,* beautiful beard, from Greek, καλος, *kalos,*
beautiful and πωγων, *pōgōn,* beard, for
the bearded lip petal + *barbatus,* Latin for
having barbs.

COMMON NAME: Bearded, same as
genus name. Grass Pink, for the grasslike
leaves and the pink flowers.

Calopogon oklahomensis
Oklahoma Grass Pink

SCIENTIFIC NAME: *Calopogon +
oklahomensis,* Latin for belonging to
Oklahoma, for the area of the type
specimen.

COMMON NAME: Oklahoma, same as
species name. Grass Pink, see *Calopogon
barbatus.*

Calopogon tuberosus **Grass Pink**

SCIENTIFIC NAME: *Calopogon +
tuberosus,* Latin for having tubers.

COMMON NAME: Grass Pink, see
Calopogon barbatus.

Calylophus berlandieri
Squarebud Day Primrose

SCIENTIFIC NAME: *Calylophus,* calyx
crest, from Greek, καλυξ, *kalux,* calyx
and λοφος, *lophos,* a crest or ridge.
Reference is to the raised mid-nerve of the
sepals covering the bud + *berlandieri,* for
Jean Louis Berlandier (1805-1851), a
French botanist who made extensive plant
collections in Texas.

COMMON NAME: Squarebud,
descriptive. Day Primrose, in contrast
with the evening primrose, the flowers
stay open during the day. Primrose, from
Middle English, prime rose, first rose.
Refers to the *Primula* genus, one of the
first flowers to bloom in the spring. The
American flowers that reminded early
botanists of the English Primrose aquired
the name, even though they were
not related.

Calylophus hartwegii
Hartweg's Evening Primrose

SCIENTIFIC NAME: *Calylophus +
hartwegii,* for Karl Theodore Hartweg
(1812-1871), a German botanist who
collected in North and South America.

COMMON NAME: Hartweg's, same as

species name. Evening, the flowers open in the evening. Primrose, see *Calylophus berlandieri.*

Calylophus lavandulifolius
Lavenderleaf Evening Primrose

SCIENTIFIC NAME: *Calylophus + lavandulifolius,* Latin for lavender-leaved.

COMMON NAME: Lavenderleaf, descriptive. Evening Primrose, see *Calylophus hartwegii.*

Calylophus serrulatus
Plains Yellow Evening Primrose

SCIENTIFIC NAME: *Calylophus + serrulatus,* Latin for somewhat serrate. Reference is to the notched leaves.

COMMON NAME: Plains, for the habitat. Yellow, for the flower color. Evening Primrose, see *Calylophus hartwegii.*

Calyptocarpus vialis   Hierba Del Caballo

SCIENTIFIC NAME: *Calyptocarpus,* covered fruit, from Greek, καλυπτο, *kalupto* a caplike covering, and καρπος, *karpos,* fruit, for the cortex of the achene + *vialis,* Latin for of or belonging to the highways, for the common habitat along roadsides.

COMMON NAME: Hierba Del Caballo, Spanish for herb of the horse.

Calystegia macounii   Hedge Bindweed

SCIENTIFIC NAME: *Calystegia,* calyx roof, from Greek, καλυξ, *kalux,* calyx and στεγη, *stegē,* roof, covering, tent. Reference is to the large bracteoles + *maucounii,* for John Macoun (fl. 1895), who collected the type specimen.

COMMON NAME: Hedge, for the habitat. Bindweed, for the trailing stems.

Calystegia sepium
Trailing Hedge Bindweed

SCIENTIFIC NAME: *Calystegia + sepium,* Latin for relating to hedges or fences. Reference is to the habitat.

COMMON NAME: Trailing, for the growth pattern. Hedge, for the habitat. Bindweed, for the trailing stems.

Camassia scilloides   Wild Hyacinth

SCIENTIFIC NAME: *Camassia,* from the Chinook Indian *camass* or *lakamas,* their name for this plant + *scilloides,* resembling *Scilla,* from the genus *Scilla,* the old genus for hyacinth and Greek, ειδος, *eidos,* resembling.

COMMON NAME: Wild, for the habitat. Hyacinth, from Greek, υακινθος, *uakinthos,* a flower and a gem. The word was originally used for the name of a youth beloved by Apollo.

Campsis radicans **Trumpet Creeper**

SCIENTIFIC NAME: *Campsis,* from Greek, καμπσις, *kampsis,* bending, having a bend. Reference is to the stamens + *radicans,* Latin for producing adventitious roots along the stem. This vine will put down roots along its course.

COMMON NAME: Trumpet, for the shape of the flowers. Creeper, for the growth pattern.

Cardamine bulbosa **Spring Cress**

SCIENTIFIC NAME: *Cardamine,* from Greek, καρδαμινη, *kardaminē,* a watercress + *bulbosa,* Latin for bulbous, for the tuber.

COMMON NAME: Spring, grows in springs and streams. Cress, from Old High German, *chresan,* to creep.

Cardamine hirsuta **Hairy Bittercress**

SCIENTIFIC NAME: *Cardamine* + *hirsuta,* Latin for hairy, for the hairs on the leaves.

COMMON NAME: Hairy, same as species name. Bitter, for the taste. Cress, see *Cardamine bulbosa.*

Cardamine parviflora **Sand Bittercress**

SCIENTIFIC NAME: *Cardamine* + *parviflora,* Latin for small flowers.

COMMON NAME: Sand, for the habitat. Bittercress, see *Cardamine hirsuta.*

Cardamine pensylvanica **Bittercress**

SCIENTIFIC NAME: *Cardamine* + *pensylvanica,* Latin for of Pennsylvania, for the area of the type specimen. The Principle of Priority allows the misspelling to stand.

COMMON NAME: Bittercress, *see Cardamine hirsuta.*

Carduus nutans **Nodding Thistle**

SCIENTIFIC NAME: *Carduus,* Latin for thistle + *nutans,* Latin for nodding. Reference is to the movement of the flower head.

COMMON NAME: Nodding, same as species name. Thistle, from Old Teutonic, *pistil-o,* their name for this plant.

Carduus tenuiflorus
Slender Bristle Thistle

SCIENTIFIC NAME: *Carduus* + *tenuiflorus,* Latin for slender flowers.

COMMON NAME: Slender, for the flowers. Bristle, for the spines. Thistle, see *Carduus nutans.*

Carphephorous pseudoliatris **False Liatris**

SCIENTIFIC NAME: *Carphephorous,* to bear a dry body, from Greek, καρφος, *karphos,* any dry body, a dry stalk and φορος, *phoros,* bearing + *pseudoliatris,* false liatris, from Greek, ψευδης, *pseudēs,* false and the genus *Liatris,* for the appearance.

COMMON NAME: False Liatris, same as species name.

Carthamus lanatus   Saffron Thistle

SCIENTIFIC NAME: *Carthamus,* from Arabic, *quarthami,* to paint. Reference is to the dye extracted from *Carthamus tinctorius* + *lanatus,* Latin for woolly, for the white hairs on the stems.

COMMON NAME: Saffron, for the flower. Thistle, see *Carduus nutans.*

Carthamus tinctorius   Safflower

SCIENTIFIC NAME: *Carthamus* + *tinctorius,* Latin for pertaining to dyes, a dye can be extracted from this species.

COMMON NAME: Safflower, a contraction of Saffron Flower, for the appearance.

Castilleja coccinea   Indian Paintbrush

SCIENTIFIC NAME: *Castilleja,* for Domingo Castillejo (fl. 1781), a Spanish botanist + *coccinea,* Latin for scarlet. Reference is to the color of the flowers.

COMMON NAME: Indian Paintbrush, from the appearance of the inflorescence and calyx that resemble a brush dipped in paint. The American Indians did obtain dye from this plant.

Castilleja indivisa   Texas Paintbrush

SCIENTIFIC NAME: *Castilleja* + *indivisa,* Latin for not split or cloven, indivisible, for the entire leaves.

COMMON NAME: Texas, for the range. Paintbrush, see *Castilleja coccinea.*

Castilleja integra   Scarlet Paintbrush

SCIENTIFIC NAME: *Castilleja* + *integra,* Latin for entire, undivided, for the leaves.

COMMON NAME: Scarlet, for the flower color. Paintbrush, see *Castilleja coccinea.*

Castilleja purpurea   Lemon Paintbrush

SCIENTIFIC NAME: *Castilleja* + *purpurea,* Latin for purple. Reference is to the color of the flowers of one variety of this species.

COMMON NAME: Lemon, for the yellow color of the flowers of one variety. Paintbrush, see *Castilleja coccinea.*

Castilleja sessiliflora   Downy Paintbrush

SCIENTIFIC NAME: *Castilleja* + *sessiliflora,* Latin for having flowers without stalks.

COMMON NAME: Downy, for the soft hairy appearance. Paintbrush, see *Castilleja coccinea.*

Catalpa bignonioides Southern Catalpa

SCIENTIFIC NAME: *Catalpa,* for the Catawba Indians of South Carolina, the area of the type specimen + *bignonioides,* to look like a *Bignonia,* from the genus *Bignonia* and Greek, ειδος, *eidos,* resembling, for the flowers.

COMMON NAME: Southern, for the range in the United States. Catalpa, same as genus name.

Catalpa speciosa Catalpa

SCIENTIFIC NAME: *Catalpa* + *speciosa,* Latin for showy, attractive, for the flowers that cover the tree in the spring.

COMMON NAME: Catalpa, same as genus name.

Ceanothus americanus New Jersey Tea

SCIENTIFIC NAME: *Ceanothus,* from Greek, κεανοθος, *keanothos,* the corn-thistle, used by Theophrastus (θεοφραστυς) + *americanus,* Latin for pertaining to America.

COMMON NAME: New Jersey Tea, the leaves were used to make tea.

Ceanothus herbaceus Redroot

SCIENTIFIC NAME: *Coeanothus* + *herbaceus,* Latin for like a herb, not woody.

COMMON NAME: Redroot, descriptive.

Ceanothus ovatus Smaller Redroot

SCIENTIFIC NAME: *Ceanothus* + *ovatus,* Latin for oval. Reference is to the shape of the leaves.

COMMON NAME: Smaller, shorter than the others in this genus. Redroot, descriptive.

Centaurea americana Basket Flower

SCIENTIFIC NAME: *Centaurea,* from Greek, κενταυρος, *kentaura,* a Centaur, of or for Centaurs. Used as a medicinal by the American Indians, the Centaurs of Greek mythology were involved in healing + *americana,* Latin for pertaining to America.

COMMON NAME: Basketflower, for the shape of the involucre.

Centaurea cyanus Bachelor's Button

SCIENTIFIC NAME: *Centaurea* + *cyanus,* from Greek, κυανος, *kuanos,* dark blue, for the flower color.

COMMON NAME: Bachelor's Button, for the shape of the flower.

Centaurea melitenis   Tocalote

SCIENTIFIC NAME: *Centaurea + melitenis,* Latin for belonging to Malta, its ancient name was Melita. Reference is to the range of the type specimen.

COMMON NAME: Tocalote, a variety of *chicalote,* the Nahuatl (Mexico) Indian word for the prickly poppy, which this plant resembles.

Centaurea solstitialis   Yellow Star Thistle

SCIENTIFIC NAME: *Centaurea + solstitialis,* Latin for the summer solstice. Reference is to this flower blooming in midsummer.

COMMON NAME: Yellow, for the flower color. Star, for the flower shape. Thistle, see *Carduus nutans.*

Centaurium beyrichii   Rock Centaury

SCIENTIFIC NAME: *Centaurium,* from Greek, κενταυρα, *kentaura,* a Centaur, of or for the Centaurs. Used by the American Indians as a medicinal, the Centaurs of Greek mythology were involved in healing + *beyrichii,* for Heinrich Kral Beyrich (1796-1834), a Prussian botanist.

COMMON NAME: Rock, for the habitat. Centaury, same as genus name.

Centaurium calycosum   Centaury

SCIENTIFIC NAME: *Centaurium + calycosum,* pertaining to a calyx, form Greek, καλυξ, *kalux,* cup, calyx, for the large calyx.

COMMON NAME: Centaury, same as genus name.

**Centaurium floribundum
June Centaury**

SCIENTIFIC NAME: *Centaurium + floribundum,* Latin for abundant flowers.

COMMON NAME: June, for the time of flowering. Centaury, same as genus name.

Centaurium pulchellum   Centaury

SCIENTIFIC NAME: *Centaurium + pulchellum,* Latin for little pretty.

COMMON NAME: Centaury, same as genus name.

Centaurium texense   Texas Centaury

SCIENTIFIC NAME: *Centaurium + texense,* Latin for belonging to Texas, for the range.

COMMON NAME: Texas Centaury, same as scientific name.

Centrosema virginianum **Spurred Pea**

SCIENTIFIC NAME: *Centrosema,* from Greek, κεντρον, *kentron,* any sharp point, a spur and στεμμα, *stemma,* a wreath or garland. Reference is to the small thorns on the stems + *virginianum,* Latin for pertaining to Virginia, for the area of the type specimen.

COMMON NAME: Spurred, same as genus name. Pea, for the fruit.

Cephalanthus occidentalis **Button Bush**

SCIENTIFIC NAME: *Cephalanthus,* head flower, from Greek, κεφαλη, *kephalē,* head and ανθος, *anthos,* flower, for the shape + *occidentalis,* Latin for of or pertaining to the west.

COMMON NAME: Button Bush, for the shape of the inflorescences.

Cerastium brachypetalum
Gray Chickweed

SCIENTIFIC NAME: *Cerastium,* from Greek, κεραστης, *kerastēs,* horned. Reference is to the shape of the seed capsules + *brachypetalum,* Latin for short petals.

COMMON NAME: Gray, for the hairs covering the stems, which give the plant a gray-green appearance. Chickweed, birds are attracted to the seeds as a food source.

Cerastium brachypodum
Shortstalk Chickweed

SCIENTIFIC NAME: *Cerastium* + *brachypodum,* Latin for short-stalked.

COMMON NAME: Shortstalk, descriptive. Chickweed, see *Cerastium brachypetalum.*

Cerastium fontanum
Common Mouse Ear

SCIENTIFIC NAME: *Cerastium* + *fontanum,* Latin for pertaining to springs or fountains, growing in moving water.

COMMON NAME: Common, abundant in its range. Mouse Ear, for the shape of the leaves, which are opposite on the stem.

Cerastium glomeratum **Chickweed**

SCIENTIFIC NAME: *Cerastium* + *glomeratum,* Latin for clustered, for the grouped flowers.

COMMON NAME: Chickweed, see *Cerastium brachypetalum.*

Cerastium nutans **Nodding Chickweed**

SCIENTIFIC NAME: *Cerastium* + *nutans,* Latin for nodding, for the flowers, on slender stems, that nod in the breeze.

COMMON NAME: Nodding, same as species name. Chickweed, see *Cerastium brachypetalum.*

Cerastium pumilum
Dwarf Mouse-Ear Chickweed

SCIENTIFIC NAME: *Cerastium +
pumilum,* Latin for dwarf, for the relative
size.

COMMON NAME: Dwarf, for the
relative size. Mouse-Ear Chickweed, see
Cerastium fontanum.

Cercis canadensis   **Red Bud**

SCIENTIFIC NAME: *Cercis,* from
Greek, κερκις, *kerkis,* their name for this
tree + *canadensis,* Latin for belonging to
Canada, for the area of the type specimen.

COMMON NAME: Red Bud, this tree
is covered with pink or red buds and then
pink flowers in the spring before it
produces leaves.

Chaerophyllum tainturieri   **Chervil**

SCIENTIFIC NAME: *Chaerophyllum,*
pleasing leaf, from Greek, χαιρω, *chairō,*
rejoice at, take pleasure in and φυλλον,
phullon, leaf. Reference is to the fragrance
+ *tainturieri,* for L. F. Tainturier des
Essarts, a plant collector who sent plants
from Louisiana to England.

COMMON NAME: Chervil, a potherb
used for its aromatic qualities.

Chaerophyllum texanum
Spreading Chervil

SCIENTIFIC NAME: *Chaerophyllum +*

texanum, Latin for pertaining to Texas.

COMMON NAME: Spreading, for the
growth pattern. Chervil, a pot-herb used
for its aromatic qualities.

Chaetopappa asterodes
Common Least Daisy

SCIENTIFIC NAME: *Chaetopappa,*
bristling pappus, from Greek, χαιτη,
khaitē, a horse's mane, flowing hair,
bristles and παππος, *pappos,* down on the
achenes of certain plants + *asterodes,*
starlike, from Greek, αστεροειδης, *aster-
oeidēs,* starlike. Reference is to the shape of
the flowers.

COMMON NAME: Common, abun-
dant in its range. Least, for the small size.
Daisy, from Anglo-Saxon, *daeges-eage,*
day's eye, a daisy, for the eyelike appearance and the opening of the rays in the
morning.

Chaetopappa ericoides   **Baby White Aster**

SCIENTIFIC NAME: *Chaetopappa +
ericoides,* to look like *Erica,* from the
genus *Erica* and Greek, ειδος, *eidos,*
resembling.

COMMON NAME: Baby, for the small
size. White, for the petal color. Aster, from
the Greek, αστερ, *astēr,* a star, for the
flower shape.

Chamaecrista fasciculata
Showy Partridge Pea

Chamaecrista fasciculata
Showy Partridge Pea

SCIENTIFIC NAME: *Chamaecrista*, a crest on the ground, from Greek, χαμαι, *khamai*, on the ground and Latin, *crista*, a crest + *fasciculate*, Latin for clustered.

COMMON NAME: Showy, for the large flowers. Partridge Pea, this plant produces legumes, which are eaten by partridges and other game birds.

Chamaecrista nictitans **Sensitive Pea**

SCIENTIFIC NAME: *Chamaecrista + nictitans*, Latin for winking or blinking. Reference is to the flower movement in the breeze.

COMMON NAME: Sensitive, the leaves curl up when stroked. Pea, for the pod it produces.

Chamaesaracha coniodes **Chamaesaracha**

SCIENTIFIC NAME: *Chamaesaracha*, from Greek, χαμαι, *khamai*, on the

ground, low, dwarf and the genus *Saracha*, therefore, a plant that looks like a small *Saracha + coniodes*, to appear dusty, from Greek, κονιος, *konios*, dusty and ειδος, *eidos*, resembling. Reference is to dust on the sticky leaves.

COMMON NAME: Chamaesaracha, same as genus name.

Chamaesaracha coronopus
Green False Nightshade

SCIENTIFIC NAME: *Chamaesaracha + coronopus*, crow-foot, from Greek, κορονη, *korone*, crow, and πους, *pous*, foot.

COMMON NAME: Green False Nightshade, so called because it resembles silvery nightshade, but the leaves are greener.

Chamaesaracha edwardsiana
Plateau False Nightshade

SCIENTIFIC NAME: *Chamaesaracha + edwardsiana*, Latin for pertaining to Edwards, for the range on the Edwards Plateau of Texas, named for Haden (or Hayden) Edwards (1771-1849), an early settler in the area.

COMMON NAME: Plateau, for the range on the Edwards Plateau of Texas. False Nightshade, for the appearance, which resembles the silver nightshade.

Chamaesaracha sordida
Hairy False Nightshade

SCIENTIFIC NAME: *Chamaesaracha* + *sordida,* Latin for dirty, the plants of this genus are sticky and usually covered with dust.

COMMON NAME: Hairy, for the dense pubescent hairs that cover the stems and leaves. False Nightshade, *see Chamaesaracha edwardsiana.*

Chamaesaracha villosa
Woolly False Nightshade

SCIENTIFIC NAME: *Chamaesaracha* + *villosa,* Latin for shaggy or hairy. Reference is to the glandular hairs that cover the plant.
COMMON NAME: Woolly, same as species name. False Nightshade, see *Chamaesaracha edwardsiana.*

Chilopsis linearis   Desert Willow

SCIENTIFIC NAME: *Chilopsis,* to resemble a lip, from Greek, χειλος, *kheilos,* lip and οψις, *opsis,* appearance. Reference is to the shape of the calyx + *linearis,* Latin for narrow, with sides nearly parallel. Reference is to the leaves.

COMMON NAME: Desert, for the habitat. Willow, the leaves resemble those of the willow.

Chionanthus virginicus   Fringe Tree

SCIENTIFIC NAME: *Chionanthus,* snow flower, from Greek, χιον, *khion,* snow and ανθος, *anthos,* flower. Reference is to the abundant white flowers + *virginicus,* Latin for of Virginia, the area of the type specimen.

COMMON NAME: Fringe Tree, for the flowers whose strap-shaped petals hang like a fringe.

Chloracantha spinosa
Mexican Devil Wood

SCIENTIFIC NAME: *Choloracantha,* green thorns from Greek, χλορος, *khloros,* green and ακανθα, *akantha,* thorn + *spinosa,* Latin for full of spines. Reference is to the spines at the base of the stems.

COMMON NAME: Mexican, for the range of the type specimen. Devil Wood, for the spines on the stems.

Chorispora tenella   Blue Mustard

SCIENTIFIC NAME: *Chorispora,* separate seeds, from Greek, χωρις, *khōris,* separate, apart and spora, *spora,* seed. Reference is to the septate fruits + *tenella,* Latin for physically soft or tender.

COMMON NAME: Blue for the color of the flowers. Mustard, from Spanish, *mostaza,* mustard, in turn from Old French, moutarde. Originally from Latin, mustum ardens. The name came from the condiment, prepared by grinding the seeds of the plant with must (new wine), not from the plant itself.

Chrysactinia mexicana Damianita

SCIENTIFIC NAME: *Chrysactinia,* gold ray, from Greek, χρυσος, *khrusos,* gold and ακτις, *aktin,* a ray, for the flowers + *mexicana,* Latin for pertaining to Mexico.

COMMON NAME: Damianita, the Mexican Spanish vernacular name for this plant.

Chrysopsis pilosa Golden Aster

SCIENTIFIC NAME: *Chrysopsis,* to resemble gold, from Greek, χρυσος, *khrusos,* gold and οψις, *opsis,* appearance, for the flower color + *pilosa,* Latin for hairy. Reference is to the hairy stems.

COMMON NAME: Golden, for the gold disk and rays. Aster, from Greek, αστηρ, *astēr,* a star, for the flower shape.

Chrysopsis texana Mauchia

SCIENTIFIC NAME: *Chrysopsis + texana,* Latin for pertaining to Texas, for the range.

COMMON NAME: Mauchia, the Mexican Spanish vernacular name for this plant.

Cichorium intybus Chicory

SCIENTIFIC NAME: *Cichorium,* from Arabic, *chikourych,* a salad vegetable + *intybus,* from Greek, ιντυβος, *intubos,* the endive or chicory plant.

COMMON NAME: Chicory, from another Greek word for chicory, κιχορα, *kikhora.*

Cicuta maculata
Common Water Hemlock

SCIENTIFIC NAME: *Cicuta,* the Latin name for hemlock + *maculata,* Latin for variegated, spotted or striped. Reference is to the purple spots on the stems.

COMMON NAME: Common, common in its range. Water, for the occurrence near water. Hemlock, from *hymlic,* the Old English name for this plant.

Cirsium altissimum Tall Thistle

SCIENTIFIC NAME: *Cirsium,* from Greek, κιρσιον, *kirsion,* a type of thistle + *altissimum,* Latin for the tallest. This is the tallest plant in the genus.

COMMON NAME: Tall, may reach ten feet in height. Thistle, from Old Teutonic, *pistil-o,* their name for this type of plant.

Cirsium engelmannii Blackland Thistle

SCIENTIFIC NAME: *Cirsium + engelmannii,* for George Engelmann (1809-1884) a German physician and botanist.

COMMON NAME: Blackland, for the Blackland area of Texas. Thistle, see *Cirsium altissimum.*

Cirsium horridulum   Yellow Thistle

SCIENTIFIC NAME: *Cirsium + hor-ridulum,* Latin for very thorny.

COMMON NAME: Yellow, for the yellow color phase of the flowers; the flower color ranges from yellow to violet. Thistle, see *Cirsium altissimum.*

Cirsium horridulum
Yellow Thistle

Cirsium ochrocentrum
Yellow Spine Thistle

SCIENTIFIC NAME: *Cirsium + ochrocentrum,* Latin for having a reddish-yellow center.

COMMON NAME: Yellow Spine, for the color of the flowers. Thistle, see *Cirsium altissimum.*

Cirsium texanum   Texas Thistle

SCIENTIFIC NAME: *Cirsium + texanum,* Latin for pertaining to Texas.

COMMON NAME: Texas, for the range. Thistle, see *Cirsium altissimum.*

Cirsium undulatum   Wavyleaf Thistle

SCIENTIFIC NAME: *Cirsium + undulatum,* Latin for wavy. Reference is to the leaves.

COMMON NAME: Wavyleaf, descriptive. Thistle, see *Cirsium altissimum.*

Cirsium vulgare   Bull Thistle

SCIENTIFIC NAME: *Cirsium + vulgare,* Latin for common.

COMMON NAME: Bull, for the spines on the leaves. Thistle, see *Cirsium altissimum.*

Claytonia virginica   Spring Beauty

SCIENTIFIC NAME: *Claytonia,* for John Clayton (1686-1773), a British physician and botanist who moved to Virginia in 1705 + *virginica,* for Virginia, for the area of the type specimen.

COMMON NAME: Spring Beauty, this is one of the earliest flowers to appear in the spring.

Claytonia virginica
Spring Beauty

Clematis crispa Curl Flower

SCIENTIFIC NAME: *Clematis,* from Greek, κλεματις, *klematis,* their name for this type of plant, meaning small vine + *crispa,* Latin for curly or curled, for the curled flower petals.

COMMON NAME: Curl Flower, same as species name.

Clematis drummondii
Texas Virgin's Bower

SCIENTIFIC NAME: *Clematis + drummondii,* for Thomas Drummond (c. 1790-1831), a British naturalist and plant collector.

COMMON NAME: Texas, for the range. Virgin's Bower, for the white flowers and this climbing plant can form a bower as it grows over other plants.

Clematis pitcheri Pitcher's Clematis

SCIENTIFIC NAME: *Clematis + pitcheri,* for Zina Pitcher (1797-1872), an American physician and botanist.

COMMON NAME: Pitcher's Clematis, same as scientific name.

Clematis reticulata Netleaf Clematis

SCIENTIFIC NAME: *Clematis + reticulata,* Latin for having a netlike pattern, for the leaves.

COMMON NAME: Netleaf, for the leaf pattern. Clematis, same as genus name.

Clematis terniflora
Sweet Autumn Clematis

SCIENTIFIC NAME: *Clematis + terniflora,* Latin for having flowers in threes.

COMMON NAME: Sweet, for the fragrance. Autumn, for the time of blooming. Clematis, same as genus name.

Clematis texensis Scarlet Clematis

SCIENTIFIC NAME: *Clematis + texensis,* Latin for belonging to Texas.

COMMON NAME: Scarlet, for the flower color. Clematis, same as genus name.

Cleome hassleriana Spiderplant

SCIENTIFIC NAME: *Cleome,* Greek

name used by Theophrastus, (Θεοπηραστυς), reference is obscure, possibly from Greek, κλειω, *kleio,* to close, in reference to the flowers + *hassleriana,* Latin for pertaining to Hassler, for Emile Hassler (1861-1937), a Swiss physician and plant collector.

COMMON NAME: Spiderplant, for the pistils and stamens, which are much longer than the petals and give the flower a spidery appearance.

Cleome serrulata
Rocky Mountain Bee Plant

SCIENTIFIC NAME: *Cleome* + *serrulata,* Latin for somewhat serrate. Reference is to the leaf margins, which may be minutely toothed.

COMMON NAME: Rocky Mountain, for a common habitat. Bee Plant, the flowers attract numerous bees.

Cleomella angustifolia   Cleomella

SCIENTIFIC NAME: *Cleomella,* Latin for a little *Cleome, see Cleome hassleriana* + *angustifolia,* Latin for having narrow leaves.

COMMON NAME: Cleomella, same as genus name.

Clitoria mariana   Spoonflower

SCIENTIFIC NAME: *Clitoria,* from Latin, *clitoris,* for the keel, which restmbles a clitoris + *mariana,* Latin for

of Maryland, for the area of the type specimen.

COMMON NAME: Spoonflower, for the flower shape.

Cnidoscolus texanus   Bull Nettle

SCIENTIFIC NAME: *Cnidoscolus,* nettle thorn, from Greek, κνιδη, *knidē,* a nettle and σκλοψ, *sklops,* anything pointed, a thorn + *texanus,* Latin for pertaining to Texas.

COMMON NAME: Bull, for the large size, Nettle, from Old English, *netele,* in turn from Old High German, *nazza,* their name for this type of plant, for the stinging hairs on the leaves and stems.

Collinsia violacea   Violet Collinsia

SCIENTIFIC NAME: *Collinsia,* for Zaccheus Collins (1764-1831), a Philadelphia merchant and botanist + *violacea,* Latin for violet, for the flower color.

COMMON NAME: Violet Collinsia, same as scientific name.

Comandra umbellata   Bastard Toadflax

SCIENTIFIC NAME: *Comandra,* hairy stamen, from Greek, κομη, *kome,* the hair of the head and ανδρος, *andros,* male, man, stamen. Reference is to the bearded stamens + *umbellata,* Latin for having umbels. Reference is to the shape of the inflorescence.

COMMON NAME: Bastard Toadflax, when the flowers are not blooming this plant resembles toadflax.

Commelina communis
Common Dayflower

SCIENTIFIC NAME: *Commelina,* for the Dutch botanists Johan Commelin (1629-1692), his nephew Caspar Commelin (1667-1731)—both were well known botanists—and for Caspar's son also named Caspar, who was almost unknown. Reference is to the three-petaled flower with two conspicuous petals and one that is inconspicuous + *communis,* Latin for common or to grow in abundance. Reference is to these flowers growing in patches.

COMMON NAME: Common, common in its range. Dayflower, this flower opens in the morning and closes in the afternoon.

Commelina diffusaa
Spreading Dayflower

SCIENTIFIC NAME: *Commelina + diffusa,* Latin for diffuse, spreading, for the growth pattern.

COMMON NAME: Spreading, for the growth pattern. Dayflower, see *Commelina communis.*

Commelina erecta   Erect Dayflower

SCIENTIFIC NAME: *Commelina + erecta,* Latin for upright or erect.

COMMON NAME: Erect, for the erect stems. Dayflower, see *Commelina communis.*

Commelina virginica
Virginia Dayflower

SCIENTIFIC NAME: *Commelina + virginica,* Latin for of Virginia, for the area of the type specimen.

COMMON NAME: Virginia, for the area of the type specimen. Dayflower, see *Commelina communis.*

Conium maculatum   Poison Hemlock

SCIENTIFIC NAME: *Conium,* from Greek, κωνειον, *kōneion,* their name for hemlock + *maculatum,* Latin for variegated, spotted or striped. Reference is to the purple spots on the stems.

COMMON NAME: Poison, this plant contains alkaloids that can cause death in humans and animals. Hemlock, from Old English, *hymlic,* their name for this plant. This species is of European origin.

Consolida ajacis   Annual Larkspur

SCIENTIFIC NAME: *Consolida,* Latin for to consolidate, to become solid. Reference is to the use of this plant to heal wounds + *ajacis,* for Ajax (Αιας), the Greek hero, for the shield-shaped areas on the leaves.

COMMON NAME: Annual, for the timing of the growth. Larkspur, for the spur on the flower that resembles the spur of a lark.

Convolvulus arvensis   Field Bindweed

SCIENTIFIC NAME: *Convolvulus,* the Latin name for bindweed, from Latin, *convolvo,* to twist or roll up + *arvensis,* Latin for belonging to a plowed field.

COMMON NAME: Field, for the habitat. Bindweed, this vine wraps tightly around other plants.

Convolvulus equitans   Gray Bindweed

SCIENTIFIC NAME: *Convolvulus* + *equitans,* Latin for riding a horse, each flower petal seems to be riding on the adjacent petal.

COMMON NAME: Gray, for the gray-ish hairs on the leaves. Bindweed, see *Convolvulus arvensis.*

Cooperia drummondii
Evening-Star Rain Lily

SCIENTIFIC NAME: *Cooperia,* for Daniel Cooper (c. 1817-1842), an English botanist + *drummondii,* for Thomas Drummond (c. 1790-1831), a British plant collector.

COMMON NAME: Evening-Star, for the shape of the flower. Rain Lily, this plant blooms following a rain.

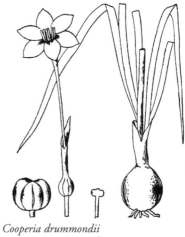

Cooperia drummondii
Evening-Star Rain Lily

Cooperia pedunculata   Rain Lily

SCIENTIFIC NAME: *Cooperia* + *pedunculata,* Latin for having many or well-developed flower stalks.

COMMON NAME: Rain Lily, see *Cooperia drummondii.*

Corallorhiza wisteriana
Early Southern Coral Root

SCIENTIFIC NAME: *Corallorhiza,* coral root, from Greek, κοραλλιον, *korallion,* coral, especially red coral and ριζα, *r(h)iza,* root. Reference is to the coral shaped root + *wisteriana,* Latin for pertaining to Wister, for Charles Jones Wister (1782-1865), he discovered the type specimen.

COMMON NAME: Early, blooms early in the spring. Southern, for the range in the United States. Coral Root, same as genus name.

Coreopsis grandiflora
Bigflower Coreopsis

SCIENTIFIC NAME: *Coreopsis,* to look like a bug, from Greek, κορις, *koris,* a bug and οψις, *opsis,* appearance, for the seeds + *grandiflora,* Latin for large flowers.

COMMON NAME: Bigflower, for the blossom size. Coreopsis, same as genus name.

Coreopsis lanceolata   **Tickseed**

SCIENTIFIC NAME: *Coreopsis* + *lanceolata,* Latin for spear-shaped, for the leaves.

COMMON NAME: Tickseed, for the appearance of the seeds.

Coreopsis palmata   **Finger Coreopsis**

SCIENTIFIC NAME: *Coreopsis* + *palmata,* Latin for having leaves like a palm.

COMMON NAME: Finger, for the leaf shape. Coreopsis, same as genus name.

Coreopsis tinctoria   **Plains Coreopsis**

SCIENTIFIC NAME: *Coreopsis* + *tinctoria,* Latin for pertaining to dyes. The White Mountain Apache and the Zuni used this plant to obtain a red dye.

COMMON NAME: Plains, for the habitat. Coreopsis, same as genus name.

Coreopsis wrightii   **Rock Coreopsis**

SCIENTIFIC NAME: *Coreopsis* + *wrightii,* for Charles Wright (1811-1885), a Texas plant collector.

COMMON NAME: Rock, for the common habitat. Coreopsis, same as genus name.

Cornus drummondii
Roughleaf Dogwood

SCIENTIFIC NAME: *Cornus,* Latin for the cornel or dogwood, from *cornu,* horn, for the hardness of the wood, + *drummondii,* for Thomas Drummond (c. 1790-1831), a British plant collector.

COMMON NAME: Roughleaf, descriptive. Dogwood, from Old English, *dagwood,* in turn from *dagge,* a dagger or pointed object. The branches of this wood were commonly sharpened and used as skewers to cook meat.

Cornus florida   **Flowering Dogwood**

SCIENTIFIC NAME: *Cornus* + *florida,* Latin for covered with or producing flowers, for the abundant flowers in the spring.

COMMON NAME: Flowering, the tree is covered with flowers in the spring before the leaves appear. Dogwood, see *Cornus drummondii.*

Coronilla varia **Crown Vetch**

SCIENTIFIC NAME: *Coronilla,* Latin for little crown. Reference is to the shape of the flowers + *varia,* Latin for variable.

COMMON NAME: Crown, for the shape of the flowers. Vetch, from the Latin name for this plant, *vicia.*

Corydalis aurea **Golden Fumewort**

SCIENTIFIC NAME: *Corydalis,* from Greek, κορυδος, *korudos,* a lark. The spur of the flower resembles a lark's spur + *aurea,* Latin for golden, for the flower color.

COMMON NAME: Golden, for the flower color. Fumewort, smoke plant. This plant is also called Golden Smoke for the appearance of the flowers at a distance.

Corydalis crystallina **Mealy Corydalis**

SCIENTIFIC NAME: *Corydalis* + *crystallina,* Latin for crystalline or transparent.

COMMON NAME: Mealy, for the appearance. Corydalis, same as genus name.

Corydalis curvisiliqua
Curvepod Corydalis

SCIENTIFIC NAME: *Corydalis* + *curvisiliqua,* Latin for a curved seed pod.

COMMON NAME: Curvepod,

descriptive. Corydalis, same as genus name.

Corydalis flavula **Pale Fumewort**

SCIENTIFIC NAME: *Corydalis* + *flavula,* Latin for yellow, for the flower color.

COMMON NAME: Pale, the yellow flower color is paler than the other fumeworts. Fumewort, see *Corydalis aurea.*

Corydalis micrantha **Scrambled Eggs**

SCIENTIFIC NAME: *Corydalis* + *micrantha,* Latin for small flowers.

COMMON NAME: Scrambled Eggs, for the color and appearance of the yellow grouped flowers.

Coryphantha echinus **Rhinoceros Cactus**

SCIENTIFIC NAME: *Coryphantha,* crown flower, from Greek, κορυφη, *koruphē,* top of the head, crown + ανθος, *anthos,* flower, the flowers are on the top of the stems + *echinus,* Latin for spiny.

COMMON NAME: Rhinoceros, for the spines. Cactus, from Greek, κακτος, *kaktos,* a prickly plant.

Coryphantha sulcata **Pineapple Cactus**

SCIENTIFIC NAME: *Coryphantha* + *sulcata,* Latin for furrowed.

COMMON NAME: Pineapple, for the

appearance. Cactus, see *Coryphantha echinus.*

Cosmos parviflorus Southwest Cosmos

SCIENTIFIC NAME: *Cosmos, from Greek,* κοσμειος, *kosmeios,* well adorned + *parviflorus,* Latin for having small flowers.

COMMON NAME: Southwest, for the range in the United States. Cosmos, same as genus name.

Crinum americanum Swamp Lily

SCIENTIFIC NAME: *Crinum,* from Greek, κρινων, *krinōn,* lily + *americanum,* Latin for pertaining to America.

COMMON NAME: Swamp, for the habitat. Lily, for the appearance of the flower.

Croptilon divaricatum
Slender Goldenweed

SCIENTIFIC NAME: *Croptilon,* according to the author of this genus, this means "col. feather," probably color or colored feather. The first part of the word is of uncertain derivation, the last part is from Greek, πτιλον, *ptilon,* feather + *divaricatum,* Latin for spreading, for the growth pattern.

COMMON NAME: Slender, for the thin stems. Goldenweed, for the yellow flowers.

Croptilon hookerianum
Hooker's Croptilon

SCIENTIFIC NAME: *Croptilon + hookerianum,* Latin for pertaining to Hooker, for William Jackson Hooker (1785-1865), an English botanist and a director of Kew Gardens in London.

COMMON NAME: Hooker's Croptilon, same as scientific name.

Croton alabamensis Texabama Croton

SCIENTIFIC NAME: *Croton,* from Greek, κροτων, *krotōn,* castorberry, sesame seed or a tick, for the appearance of the seeds + *alabamensis,* Latin for belonging to Alabama.

COMMON NAME: Texabama, for the range in Texas and Alabama. Croton, same as genus name.

Croton capitatus Woolly Croton

SCIENTIFIC NAME: *Croton + capitatus,* Latin for having or forming a head. Reference is to the compact inflorescences near the ends of the branches.

COMMON NAME: Woolly, for the woolly hairs covering the plant. Croton, same as genus name.

Croton fruticulosus Encinilla

SCIENTIFIC NAME: *Croton + fruticulosus,*

Latin for a shrubby dwarf.

COMMON NAME: Encinilla, the Mexican Spanish name for this plant.

Croton lindheimerianus
Three-Seed Croton

SCIENTIFIC NAME: *Croton + lindheimerianus,* Latin for pertaining to Lindheimer, for Ferdinand Jacob Lindheimer (1801-1879), a German botanist, who collected plants in Texas.

COMMON NAME: Three-Seed, descriptive, this plant produces three seeds per capsule. Croton, same as genus name.

Croton michauxii   Narrowleaf Rushfoil

SCIENTIFIC NAME: *Croton + michauxii,* for Andre Michaux (1746-1803), a French botanist.

COMMON NAME: Narrowleaf, descriptive. Rushfoil, for the appearance, the thin leaves (foils) resemble those of the Rush.

Croton monanthogynus
One-Seed Croton

SCIENTIFIC NAME: *Croton + monanthogynus,* one flower woman, from Greek, μονο, *mono,* one, ανθος, *anthos,* flower and γυνη, *gunē,* woman. Reference is to the production of one seed per fruit capsule.

COMMON NAME: One-seed, this plant produces one seed per capsule.

Croton, same as genus name.

Croton texensis   Texas Croton

SCIENTIFIC NAME: *Croton + texensis,* Latin for belonging to Texas.

COMMON NAME: Texas, for the range. Croton, same as genus name.

Cryptantha cinerea   Bownut Cryptantha

SCIENTIFIC NAME: *Cryptantha,* hidden flower, from Greek, κρυπτος, *kruptos,* hidden, secret and ανθος, *anthos,* flower. Reference is to the cleistogamous flowers, which self-fertilize before opening + *cinerea,* Latin for the color of ashes.

COMMON NAME: Bownut, for the shape of the seed. Cryptantha, same as genus name.

Cryptantha crassisepala
Thicksepal Cryptantha

SCIENTIFIC NAME: *Cryptantha + crassisepala,* thick sepals, from Latin, *crassus,* thick and *sepala,* a Latinized form of sepal.

COMMON NAME: Thicksepal, descriptive. Cryptantha, same as genus name.

Cryptantha minima   Little Cryptantha

SCIENTIFIC NAME: *Cryptantha + minima,* Latin for smallest, a superlative adjective to minor.

COMMON NAME: Little, this is the smallest Cryptantha. Cryptantha, same as genus name.

Cryptantha texana Texas Cryptantha

SCIENTIFIC NAME: *Cryptantha + texana,* Latin for pertaining to Texas.

COMMON NAME: Texas Cryptantha, same as scientific name.

Cucurbita foetidissima Buffalo Gourd

SCIENTIFIC NAME: *Cucurbita,* Latin for gourd + *foetidissima,* Latin for very foul smelling.

COMMON NAME: Buffalo, grows in the range of the Buffalo (American Bison). Gourd, from the French name for this plant, *gourde.*

Cucurbita foetidissima
Buffalo Gourd

Curcurbita texana Texas Gourd

SCIENTIFIC NAME: *Curcurbita + texana,* Latin for pertaining to Texas.

COMMON NAME: Texas, for the range. Gourd, see *Curcurbita foetidissima.*

**Cuscuta cephalanthi
Buttonbush Dodder**

SCIENTIFIC NAME: *Cuscuta,* Medieval Latin name for this plant + *cephalanthi,* for its resemblance to the genus *Cephalanthus.*

COMMON NAME: Buttonbush, same as species name. Dodder, from Middle English, *doder,* a bunch of thread, their name for this parasitic, stringlike plant.

Cuscuta compacta Compact Dodder

SCIENTIFIC NAME: *Cuscuta + compacta,* Latin for compact, for the growth pattern.

COMMON NAME: Compact, for the growth pattern. Dodder, see *Cuscuta cephalanthi.*

Cuscuta coryli Hazel Dodder

SCIENTIFIC NAME: *Cuscuta + coryli,* for the genus *Corylus* (hazel), on which this plant commonly grows.

COMMON NAME: Hazel, this plant commonly grows on hazel. Dodder, see *Cuscuta cephalanthi.*

Cuscuta cuspidata   Dodder

SCIENTIFIC NAME: *Cuscuta + cuspidata,* Latin for having a cusp. Reference is to the shape of the flowers.

COMMON NAME: Dodder, see *Cuscuta cephalanthi.*

Cuscuta exaltata   Tree Dodder

SCIENTIFIC NAME: *Cuscuta + exaltata,* Latin for very tall.

COMMON NAME: Tree, parasite on trees, especially oaks. Dodder, see *Cuscuta cephalanthi.*

Cuscuta glomerata   Cluster Dodder

SCIENTIFIC NAME: *Cuscuta + glomerata,* Latin for to form or gather into a ball. Reference is to the flower ball.

COMMON NAME: Cluster, for the clusters of flowers. Dodder, see *Cuscuta cephalanthi.*

Cuscuta gronovii   Gronovius' Dodder

SCIENTIFIC NAME: *Cuscuta + gronovii,* for Jan Fredrick Gronovius (1690-1762), who taught Carl Linnaeus (1707-1778).

COMMON NAME: Gronovius', same as species name. Dodder, see *Cuscuta cephalanthi.*

Cuscuta indecora   Dodder

SCIENTIFIC NAME: *Cuscuta + indecora,* Latin for not decorative, not ornamental, unadorned.

COMMON NAME: Dodder, see *Cuscuta cephalanthi.*

Cuscuta obtusiflora   Red Dodder

SCIENTIFIC NAME: *Cuscuta + obtusiflora,* Latin for obtuse (blunt) flower.

COMMON NAME: Red, for the flower color. Dodder, see *Cuscuta cephalanthi.*

Cuscuta pentagona   Five-Angled Dodder

SCIENTIFIC NAME: *Cuscuta + pentagona,* five-angled, from Greek, πεντα, *penta,* five and γωνον, *gōnon,* angle, for the calyx.

COMMON NAME: Five-angled, same as species name. Dodder, see *Cuscuta cephalanthi.*

Cymopterus acaulis   Stemless Corkwing

SCIENTIFIC NAME: *Cymopterus,* wave wing, from Greek, κυμα, *kuma,* a wave and πτερον, *pteron,* wing. Reference is to the winged seed pods + *acaulis,* Latin for stemless.

COMMON NAME: Stemless, descriptive. Corkwing, for the winged seed pods that look like a cork and have two wings.

Cymopterus macrorhizus
Bigroot Wavewing

SCIENTIFIC NAME: *Cymopterus +
macrorhizus,* big root, from Greek,
μακρος, *macros,* big, long and ριζα,
r(h)iza, root.

COMMON NAME: Bigroot, descriptive.
Wavewing, for the undulating wings on
the seed pods.

Cymopterus montanus
Mountain Corkwing

SCIENTIFIC NAME: *Cymopterus +
montanus,* Latin for pertaining to the
mountains.

COMMON NAME: Mountain, for the
range. Corkwing, see *Cymopterus acualis.*

Cynanchum barbigerum
Thicket Threadvine

SCIENTIFIC NAME: *Cynanchum,* dog
quinsy, (a sore throat), from Greek,
κυναγχη, *kunagkhē,* dog quinsy. Reference
is to the poisonous properties of this plant
+ *barbigerum,* Latin for bearded, for the
hairs on the corolla.

COMMON NAME: Thicket, for the
habitat. Threadvine, for the growth
pattern.

Cynanchum laeve   **Sand Vine**

SCIENTIFIC NAME: *Cynanachum +
laeve,* Latin for smooth, free of hairs.

COMMON NAME: Sand, for the
habitat. Vine, descriptive, from Latin,
vinea, a trailing or climbing plant.

Cypripedium calceolus
Yellow Lady's Slipper Orchid

SCIENTIFIC NAME: *Cypripedium,*
Aphrodite's Sandals, from Greek, Κυπρις,
Kupris, a name for Aphroditē (Αφροδιτη)
and πεδιλον, *pedilon,* sandals, any covering for the feet. Reference is to the slip-
per-shaped lip petal + *calceolus,* little shoe,
a diminutive of Latin, *calceus,* shoe.

COMMON NAME: Yellow, for the
flower color. Lady's Slipper, for the slip-
per-shaped lip petal. Orchid, from Greek,
ορχις, *orkhis,* testicle, for the shape of the
pseudobulbs.

Dalea aurea   **Golden Prairie Clover**

SCIENTIFIC NAME: *Dalea,* for Samuel
Dale (1659-1739), an English physician,
apothecary and botanist + *aurea,* Latin for
gold, for the flower color.

COMMON NAME: Golden, for the
petal color. Prairie Clover, for the habitat
and Anglo-Saxon, *clafre,* clover.

Dalea candida   **White Prairie Clover**

SCIENTIFIC NAME: *Dalea + candida,*
Latin for white, for the flower color.

COMMON NAME: White, for the
color of the petals. Prairie Clover, see
Dalea aurea.

Dalea formosa **Feather Dalea**

SCIENTIFIC NAME: *Dalea* + *formosa,* Latin for handsome, beautiful.

COMMON NAME: Feather, for the hairy sepals. Dalea, same as genus name.

Dalea greggii **Gregg's Dalea**

SCIENTIFIC NAME: *Dalea* + *greggii,* for Josiah Gregg (1806-1850), an American explorer and plant collector.

COMMON NAME: Gregg's Dalea, same as scientific name.

Dalea lanata **Silky Prairie Clover**

SCIENTIFIC NAME: *Dalea* + *lanata,* Latin for woolly. Reference is to the hairs on this plant.

COMMON NAME: Silky, for the flowers. Prairie Clover, see *Dalea aurea.*

Dalea lasiathera **Purple Dalea**

SCIENTIFIC NAME: *Dalea* + *lasiathera,* shaggy flower, from the Greek prefix, λασιος, *lasi,* shaggy and ανθηρος, *anthēro,* flower. Reference is to the inflorescence.

COMMON NAME: Purple, for the flower color. Dalea, same as genus name.

Dalea nana **Dwarf Dalea**

SCIENTIFIC NAME: *Dalea* + *nana,*

Latin for dwarf, for the small size.

COMMON NAME: Dwarf, for the small size. Dalea, same as genus name.

Dalea pogonathera **Bearded Awn**

SCIENTIFIC NAME: *Dalea* + *pogo-nathera,* bearded awn, from Greek, πωγων, *pōgōn,* beard and ανθερο, *anthēr,* awn. Reference is to the plumes on the calyx teeth.

COMMON NAME: Bearded Dalea, same as scientific name.

Dalea purpurea **Purple Prairie Clover**

SCIENTIFIC NAME: *Dalea* + *purpurea,* Latin for purple, for the flower color.

COMMON NAME: Purple, for the flower color. Prairie Clover, see *Dalea aurea.*

Dalea villosa **Silky Prairie Clover**

SCIENTIFIC NAME: *Dalea* + *villosa,* Latin for hairy. Reference is to the silky hairs on the flowers.

COMMON NAME: Silky, for the silky hairs on the flowers. Prairie Clover, see *Dalea aurea.*

Dasylirion leiophyllum **Desert Candle**

SCIENTIFIC NAME: *Dasylirion,* thick or hairy lily, from Greek, δασυς, *dasus,* thick, hairy and λειριον, *leirion,* lily, for the arrangement of the flowers + *leiophyllum*, smooth leaves, from Greek, λειος, *leios*, smooth and φυλλον, *phullon*, leaf.

COMMON NAME: Desert, for the habitat. Candle, for the appearance of the flower spike.

Datura inoxia Sacred Datura

SCIENTIFIC NAME: *Datura*, from the Sanskrit name for this plant, *dhatura* + *inoxia*, Latin for not injurious, harmless. Regardless of the assigned species name, this plant is poisonous.

COMMON NAME: Sacred, for its use in North American Indian rituals. The alkaloids in this plant produce hallucinations. Datura, same as genus name.

Datura quercifolia Oakleaf Datura

SCIENTIFIC NAME: *Datura* + *quercifolia*, Latin for oak-leaved.

COMMON NAME: Oakleaf, for the shape of the leaves. Datura, same as genus name.

Datura stramonium Jimsonweed

SCIENTIFIC NAME: *Datura*, + *stramonium*, from the French name for this plant, *stramonium*.

COMMON NAME: Jimsonweed, a corruption of Jamestown Weed, for Jamestown, Virginia, where it was first collected. Originally used as a potherb,

where its toxic properties were quickly discovered.

Datura wrightii Southern Thorn Apple

SCIENTIFIC NAME: *Datura* + *wrightii*, for Charles Wright (1811-1885), a Texas plant collector.

COMMON NAME: Southwestern, for the range in the United States. Thorn Apple, for the round, spiny seed capsule.

Daucus carota Queen Anne's Lace

SCIENTIFIC NAME: *Daucus*, from Greek, δαυκος, *daukos*, wild carrot + *carota*, Latin for carrot.

COMMON NAME: Queen Anne's Lace, for the lacelike appearance of the inflorescence.

Daucus carota
Queen Anne's Lace

Daucus pusillus Southwestern Carrot

SCIENTIFIC NAME: *Daucus + pusillus,* Latin for very small.

COMMON NAME: Southwestern, for the range in the United States. Carrot, from Latin, *carota,* a carrot.

Delphinium carolinianum Blue Larkspur

SCIENTIFIC NAME: *Delphinium* from Greek, δελφινιον, *delphinion* the Larkspur + *carolinianum,* Latin for pertaining to Carolina, for the area of the type specimen.

COMMON NAME: Blue, for the color of the flowers. Larkspur, the nectary of this flower is shaped like the spur on a lark's foot.

Delphinium carolinianum
Blue Larkspur

Delphinium tricorne Dwarf Larkspur

SCIENTIFIC NAME: *Delphinium + tricorne,* Latin for three horns.

COMMON NAME: Dwarf, for the size. Larkspur, see *Delphinium carolinianum.*

Descurainia incana Tansy Mustard

SCIENTIFIC NAME: *Descurainia,* for Francois Descourain (1658-1740), a French pharmacist and botanist. The Principle of Priority allows the misspelling to stand + *incana,* Latin for very gray, hoary.

COMMON NAME: Tansy, this plant resembles true tansy (*Tanacetum vulgare*). Mustard, from Spanish *mostaza,* mustard, in turn from Old French, *moustarde,* originally from Latin, *mustum ardens.* The name comes from the condiment, prepared by grinding the seeds of the plant with must (new wine), not from the plant.

Descurainia pinnata Tansy Mustard

SCIENTIFIC NAME: *Descurainia + pinnata,* Latin for to look like a feather. Reference is to the leaf arrangement.

COMMON NAME: Tansy Mustard, see *Descurainia incana.*

Descurainia sophia
Flixweed Tansy Mustard

SCIENTIFIC NAME: *Descurainia + sophia,* an old genus name.

COMMON NAME: Flixweed, a corruption of flaxweed, for the appearance. Tansy Mustard, see *Descurainia incana.*

Desmanthus illinoensis
Illinois Bundle Flower

SCIENTIFIC NAME: *Desmanthus,* bundled flower, from Greek, δεσμος, *desmos,* a bundle and ανθος, *anthos,* flower, for the clustered flowers +*illinoensis,* Latin for belonging to Illinois, for the area of the type specimen.

COMMON NAME: Illinois Bundle flower, same as scientific name.

Desmanthus leptolobus
Narrowpod Bundle Flower

SCIENTIFIC NAME: *Desmanthus* + *leptolobus,* narrow lobe, from Greek, λεπτος, *leptos,* thin, narrow and Latin, *lobos,* lobe. Reference is to the fruit pods.

COMMON NAME: Narrowpod Bundle Flower, same as scientific name.

Desmanthus velutinu Bundle Flower

SCIENTIFIC NAME: *Desmanthus* + *velutinus,* Latin for velvety.

COMMON NAME: Bundle Flower, same as genus name.

Desmanthus virgatus Bundle Flower

SCIENTIFIC NAME: *Desmanthus* + *virgatus,* Latin for twiggy.

COMMON NAME: Bundle Flower, same as genus name.

Desmodium canescens Hoary Tickclover

SCIENTIFIC NAME: *Desmodium,* from Greek, δεσμος, *desmos,* in this sense a chain, for the segments of the fruits resembling a chain + *canescens,* Latin for the very short hairs that give a white appearance.

COMMON NAME: Hoary, same as species name. Tickclover, the seedpods break apart easily and stick on people and animals; these pieces have the appearance of ticks.

Desmodium ciliare Littleleaf Tickclover

SCIENTIFIC NAME: *Desmodium* + *ciliare,* Latin for fringed.

COMMON NAME: Littleleaf, descriptive. Tickclover, see *Desmodium canescens.*

Desmodium glutinosum
Largeflower Tickclover

SCIENTIFIC NAME: *Desmodium* + *glutinosum,* Latin for glutinous, sticky. Reference is to the fruits.

COMMON NAME: Largeflower, has the largest flowers of this genus. Tickclover, see *Desmodium canescens.*

Desmodium illinoense
Illinois Tickclover

SCIENTIFIC NAME: *Desmodium + illinoense,* Latin for belonging to Illinois, for the area of the type specimen.

COMMON NAME: Illinois, same as species name. Tickclover, see *Desmodium canescens.*

Desmodium marilandicum
Maryland Tickclover

SCIENTIFIC NAME: *Desmodium + marilandicum,* Latin for of Maryland, for the area of the type specmen.

COMMON NAME: Maryland, for the area of the type specimen. Tickclover, see *Desmodium canescens.*

Desmodium nuttallii
Nuttall's Tickclover

SCIENTIFIC NAME: *Desmodium + nuttallii,* for Thomas Nuttall (1786-1856) an English botanist, explorer, printer, ornithologist, and plant collector. He was a fellow of the Linnaean Society.

COMMON NAME: Nuttall's, same as species name. Tickclover, see *Desmodium canescens.*

Desmodium obtusum   Rigid Tickclover

SCIENTIFIC NAME: *Desmodium + obtusum,* Latin for blunt, for the leaves.

COMMON NAME: Rigid, for the erect stems. Tickclover, see *Desmodium canescens.*

Desmodium paniculatum
Panicled Tickclover

SCIENTIFIC NAME: *Desmodium + paniculatum,* Latin for having flowers in panicles.

COMMON NAME: Panicled, same as species name. Tickclover, see *Desmodium canescens.*

Desmodium pauciflorum
Fewflower Tickclover

SCIENTIFIC NAME: *Desmodium + pauciflorum,* Latin for having few flowers.

COMMON NAME: Fewflower, descriptive. Tickclover, see *Desmodium canescens.*

Desmodium psilophyllum   Sticktights

SCIENTIFIC NAME: *Desmodium + psilophyllum,* smooth leaf, from Greek, ψιλος, *psilos,* smooth, bare and φυλλον, *phullon,* leaf.

COMMON NAME: Sticktights, for the seeds that stick to clothing and animals.

Desmodium sessilifolium
Sessileleaf Tickclover

SCIENTIFIC NAME: *Desmodium + sessilifolium,* Latin for having leaves without stalks.

COMMON NAME: Sessileleaf, same as species name. Tickclover, see *Desmodium canescens.*

Desmodium tweedyi **Tweedy's Tickclover**

SCIENTIFIC NAME: *Desmodium + tweedyi,* for Frand Tweedy (1854-1937), an American plant collector.

COMMON NAME: Tweedy's, same as species name. Tickclover, see *Desmodium canescens.*

Desmodium viridiflorum
Velvetleaf Tickclover

SCIENTIFIC NAME: *Desmodium + viridiflorum,* Latin for green flowers.

COMMON NAME: Velvetleaf, for the soft leaves. Tickclover, see *Desmodium canescens.*

Dimorphocarpa wislizeni **Spectacle Pod**

SCIENTIFIC NAME: *Dimorphocarpa,* two shape fruit, from Greek, δις, *dis,* two, μορφη, *morphe* a shape and καρπος, *karpos,* fruit. Reference is to the appearance of the seed pod + *wislizeni,* for Friedrich Adolph Wislizenus (1810-1889), a German physician and explorer.

COMMON NAME: Spectacle Pod, for the appearance of the seed pod, which resembles a pair of spectacles.

Dodecatheon meadia **Shooting Star**

SCIENTIFIC NAME: *Dodecatheon,* twelve gods, from Greek, δoδεκα, *dodeka,* twelve and θεος, *theos,* god. Pliny gave this name to the primrose (a related plant), because it was belived that it was protected by the twelve main Greek gods + *meadia,* for Richard Mead (1673-1754), an English physician.

COMMON NAME: Shooting Star, for the appearance of the flower.

Dracopis amplexicaulis
Claspingleaf Coneflower

SCIENTIFIC NAME: *Dracopis,* to look like a dragon or serpent, from Greek, δρακον, *drakon,* dragon, serpent and oψις, *opsis,* resembling. Reference is to the appendages on the style + *amplexicaulis,* Latin for to embrace the stem. Reference is to the base of the leaf, which is wrapped around the stem.

COMMON NAME: Claspingleaf, same as species name. Coneflower, for the cone-shaped disk.

Drosera breviflora **Sundew**

SCIENTIFIC NAME: *Drosera,* from Greek, δροσερος, *droseros,* dewy, for the clear glandular secretions that look like dew, these are sticky and trap insects for this insectivorous plant + *breviflora,* Latin for short flower.

COMMON NAME: Sundew, for the viscid, clear glandular secretions that glitter in the sun like dew.

Duchesnea indica   Yellow Strawberry

SCIENTIFIC NAME: *Duchesnea,* for Antoine Nicholas Duchesne (1747-1827), a French botanist + *indica,* Latin for of India, for the native range.

COMMON NAME: Yellow, for the flower color. Strawberry, from Anglo-Saxon, *streawberige* (strawberry), their name for this berry, origin of the derivation is obscure.

Dyschoriste linearis   Snake Herb

SCIENTIFIC NAME: *Dyschoriste,* difficult to separate, from Greek, δυς, *dus,* with difficulty, poorly and χοριστος, *khoristos,* separable. Reference is to the valves of the capsules + *linearis,* Latin for narrow, with sides nearly parallel, for the leaves.

COMMON NAME: Snake Herb, used for treatment of snakebite.

Dysodiopsis tagetoides   Fetid Marigold

SCIENTIFIC NAME: *Dysodiopsis,* bad smelling appearance, from Greek, δυσοσης, *dusosēs,* ill-smelling, stinking and οψις, *opsis,* for appearance resembling *Dyssodia thymophylla* + *tagetoides,* to look

like a *Tagetes,* from the genus *Tagetes* and Greek, ειδος, *eidos,* resembling.

COMMON NAME: Fetid, for the scent. Marigold, Mary's Gold, with reference to the Virgin Mary and the gold color of the flowers.

Dyssodia papposa   Fetid Marigold

SCIENTIFIC NAME: *Dyssodia,* from Greek, δυσοδια, *dusodia,* ill-smelling, stinking + *papposa,* from Greek, παππος, *pappos,* grandfather, down on seeds. Reference is to the hair on the achenes.

COMMON NAME: Fetid, for the strong odor. Marigold, see Dysodiopsis tagetoides.

Echinacea angustifolia
Narrowleaf Purple Coneflower

SCIENTIFIC NAME: *Echinacea,* similar to a hedgehog, from Greek, εχινος *ekhinos,* a hedgehog and the Latin suffix, *aceus,* similar to. Reference is to the spiny central disk + *angustifolia,* Latin for narrow leaves.

COMMON NAME: Narrow-leaf, for the lance-shaped leaves. Purple, for the color of the petals. Coneflower, for the shape of the central disk.

*Echinacea
angustifolia*
Narrowleaf
Purple
Coneflower

Echinacea atrorubens
Topeka Purple Coneflower

SCIENTIFIC NAME: *Echinacea +
atrorubens,* Latin for becoming dark red.
Reference is to the dark purple ray flower
petals.

COMMON NAME: Topeka, for the
area of the type specimen, Topeka, Kansas,
Purple Coneflower, see *Echinacea angustifolia. Echinacea,* same as genus name.

Echinacea pallida **Pale Coneflower**

SCIENTIFIC NAME: *Echinacea +
pallida,* Latin for pale, for the pale petals.

COMMON NAME: Pale, same as
species name. Coneflower, for the shape of
the central disk.

Echinacea purpurea **Purple Echinacea**

SCIENTIFIC NAME: *Echinacea +
purpurea,* Latin for purple, for the flower
color.

COMMON NAME: Purple Echinacea,
same as scientific name.

Echinacea sanguinea **Purple Coneflower**

SCIENTIFIC NAME: *Echinacea +
sanguinea,* Latin for of blood. Reference is
to the color of the petals.

COMMON NAME: Purple Coneflower,
see *Echinacea angustifolia.*

Echinocactus texensis **Horse Crippler**

SCIENTIFIC NAME: *Echinocactus,*
hedgehog cactus, from Greek, εχινος,
ekhinos, sea urchin and κακτος, *kaktos,* a
prickly plant + *texensis,* Latin for belonging to Texas.

COMMON NAME: Horse Crippler,
this cactus grows low to the ground and
has very strong spines, which can cause
severe injury to a horse if it steps on one.

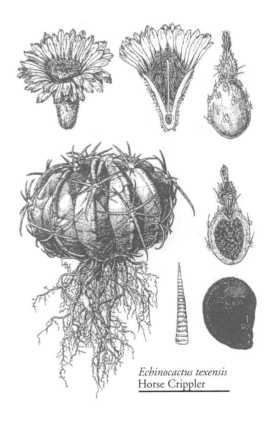

Echinocactus texensis
Horse Crippler

Echinocereus chisoensis   **Chisos Hedgehog**

SCIENTIFIC NAME: *Echinocereus,* from Greek, εχινος, *ekhinos,* hedgehog and *cereus,* Latin for a wax taper + *chisonensis,* Latin for belonging to Chisos, for the range in the Chisos Mountains of Texas.

COMMON NAME: Chisos Hedgehog, same as scientific name.

Echinocereus coccineu   **Claret-Cup Cactus**

SCIENTIFIC NAME: *Echinocereus + coccineus,* Latin for scarlet, for the flower color.

COMMON NAME: Claret-Cup, for the color and shape of the flower. Cactus, see *Echinocactus texensis.*

Echinocereus enneacanthus
Strawberry Cactus

SCIENTIFIC NAME: *Echinocereus + enneacanthus,* Latin for having nine spines.

COMMON NAME: Strawberry, the greenish fruits taste like strawberries. Cactus, see *Echinocactus texensis.*

Echinocereus pectinatus
Texas Rainbow Cactus

SCIENTIFIC NAME: *Echinocereus + pectinatus,* Latin for comblike, for the spines.

COMMON NAME: Texas, for the

range. Rainbow, the yellow flowers have streaks of magenta and green. Cactus, see *Echinocactus texensis.*

Echinocereus reichenbachii
Purple Candle

SCIENTIFIC NAME: *Echinocereus + reichenbachii,* for Heinrich Gottleib Ludwig Reichenbach (1793-1989) a German naturalist.

COMMON NAME: Purple Candle, the purple flower blooms at the top of this cactus, giving the illusion of a candle's flame.

Echinocereus russanthus
Rusty Hedgehog Cactus

SCIENTIFIC NAME: *Echinocereus + russanthus,* russet flower, from Latin, *russatus,* rust-colored and Greek, ανθος, *anthos,* flower.

COMMON NAME: Rusty, for the flower color. Hedgehog Cactus, see *Echinocactus texensis.*

Echinocereus triglochidiatus
Claret-Cup Cactus

SCIENTIFIC NAME: *Echinocereus + triglochidiatus,* Latin for having three glochids, the small spines, at the areoles.

COMMON NAME: Claret-cup, for the color and shape of the flower. Cactus, see *Echinocactus texensis.*

Echinocereus viridiflorus
Greenflower Hedgehog

SCIENTIFIC NAME: *Echinocereus* + *viridiflorus,* Latin for green-flowered.

COMMON NAME: Greenflower, descriptive. Hedgehog, for the spines.

Echinodorus berteroi   **Burrhead**

SCIENTIFIC NAME: *Echinodorus,* hedgehog bag, from Greek, εχινος, *ekhinos,* a hedgehog and δορος, *doros,* bag, wallet, bottle, for the grouped spiny achenes + *berteroi,* for C. G. L. Bertero (1789-1831), an Italian physician and plant collector.

COMMON NAME: Burrhead, for the rough, fruiting heads.

Echinodorus cordifolius
Creeping Burrhead

SCIENTIFIC NAME: *Echinodorus* + *cordifolius,* Latin for heart-shaped leaves.

COMMON NAME: Creeping, for the growth pattern. Burrhead, see *Echinodorus berteroi.*

Eichhornia crassipes   **Water Hyacinth**

SCIENTIFIC NAME: *Eichhornia,* for Johann Albrecht Friedrich Eichhorn (1779-1856), a Prussian education minister + *crassipes,* Latin for thick-footed, for the thick stem.

COMMON NAME: Water, for the habitat. Hyacinth, from Latin, *hyacinthus,* in turn from Greek, υακινθος, *uakinthos,* a precious gem of blue color, for the blue flower.

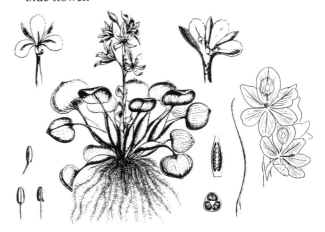

Eichhornia crassipes
Water Hyacinth

Engelmannia peristenia
Engelmann Daisy

SCIENTIFIC NAME: *Engelmannia,* for Geroge Engelmann (1809-1884), a German-born American physician and botanist + *peristenia,* extra bands, from Greek, περισσο, *perisso,* over and above and τενια, *tenia,* band, ribbon, for the featherlike leaves.

COMMON NAME: Engelmann, same as genus name. Daisy, from Anglo-Saxon, *daeges-eage,* day's eye, daisy, for the eyelike appearance and the opening of the rays in the morning.

Erigeron annuus   Annual Fleabane

SCIENTIFIC NAME: *Erigeron,* from Greek, ηριγερων, *ērigerōn,* early old man, their name for groundsel. Reference is to its early spring flowering and the hoary down + *annuus,* Latin for annual.

COMMON NAME: Annual, lives only one season. Fleabane, for the ability to kill or drive off fleas.

Erigeron bellidiastrum
Western Fleabane

SCIENTIFIC NAME: *Erigeron +* *bellidiastrum,* Latin for little wild daisy star, for the size and shape of the flowers.

COMMON NAME: Western, for the range in the United States. Fleabane, see *Erigeron annuus.*

Erigeron geiseri   **Basin Fleabane**

SCIENTIFIC NAME: *Erigeron + geiseri,* for Samuel Wood Geiser (1890-1983), professor at Southern Methodist University.

COMMON NAME: Basin, for the habitat. Fleabane, see *Erigeron annuus.*

Erigeron modestus   **Plains Fleabane**

SCIENTIFIC NAME: *Erigeron +* *modestus,* Latin for modest, gentle.

COMMON NAME: Plains, for the habitat. Fleabane, see *Erigeron annuus.*

Erigeron philadelphicus
Philadelphia Fleabane

SCIENTIFIC NAME: *Erigeron +* *philadelphicus,* for Philadelphia, Pennsylvania, the area of the type specimen.

COMMON NAME: Philadelphia, same as species name. Fleabane, see *Erigeron annuus.*

Erigeron strigosus   **Daisy Fleabane**

SCIENTIFIC NAME: *Erigeron +* *strigosus,* Latin for having stiff bristles.

COMMON NAME: Daisy, from Anglo-Saxon, *daeges-eage,* day's eye, a daisy, for the eyelike appearance and the opening of the rays in the morning. Fleabane, see *Erigeron annuus.*

Erigeron tenuis   **Slender Fleabane**

SCIENTIFIC NAME: *Erigeron + tenuis,* Latin for thin, slender, for the stems.

COMMON NAME: Slender, for the stems. Fleabane, see *Erigeron annuus.*

Eriogonum abertianum
Abert Wild Buckwheat

SCIENTIFIC NAME: *Eriogonum,* woolly knee, from Greek, εριον, *erion,* wool and γονυ, *gonu,* knee. Reference is to the downy nodes on the stems + *abertianum,* Latin for pertaining to Abert, for James William Abert (1820-1897), an American Army officer and explorer.

COMMON NAME: Abert, same as species name. Wild, for the habitat. Buckwheat, thought to be an original English word for this plant, originally beechwheat.

Eriogonum annuum Wild Buckwheat

SCIENTIFIC NAME: *Eriogonum* + *annuum,* Latin for annual.

COMMON NAME: Wild Buckwheat, see *Eriogonum abertianum.*

Eriogonum longifolium Longleaf Wild Buckwheat

SCIENTIFIC NAME: *Eriogonum* + *longifolium,* Latin for having long leaves, the leaves of this species are three to five times longer than those of the other species.

COMMON NAME: Longleaf, same as species name. Wild Buckwheat, see *Eriogonum annuum.*

Eriogonum multiflorum Heartsepal Wild Buckwheat

SCIENTIFIC NAME: *Eriogonum* + *multiflorum,* Latin for many flowers.

COMMON NAME: Heart Sepal, for the heart-shaped sepals. Wild Buckwheat, see *Eriogonum abertianum.*

Eriogonum wrightii Wild Buckwheat

SCIENTIFIC NAME: *Eriogonum* + *wrightii,* for Charles Wright (1713-1885), a Texas plant collector.

COMMON NAME: Wild Buckwheat, see *Eriogonum annuum.*

Erodium cicutarium Pin Clover

SCIENTIFIC NAME: *Erodium,* from Greek, ερωδιος, *erōdios,* a heron. Reference is to the shape of the fruit, which resembles the bill of a heron or stork + *cicutarium,* Latin for resembling the genus *Cicuta* (water hemlock).

COMMON NAME: Pin, for the pinlike seed pods. Clover, for the appearance of the leaves.

Erodium texanum Texas Stork's Bill

SCIENTIFIC NAME: *Erodium* + *texanum,* Latin for pertaining to Texas, for the range.

COMMON NAME: Texas, for the range. Stork's Bill, same as genus name.

Eryngium diffusum Bushy Eryngo

SCIENTIFIC NAME: *Eryngium,* from Greek, ερυγγιον, *eruggion,* their name for this type of plant, originally for *Eryngium campestre* + *diffusum,* Latin for spreading, for the growth pattern.

COMMON NAME: Bushy, for the overall appearance. Eryngo, same as genus name.

Eryngium heterophyllum
Mexican Thistle

SCIENTIFIC NAME: *Erygium + hetero-phyllum,* different leaves, from Greek, ετερος, *(h)etero,* different, other and φυλλον, *phullon,* leaf, for the two different kinds of leaves.

COMMON NAME: Mexican, for the range. Thistle, for the overall appearance, actually belongs to the carrot family.

Eryngium hookeri Hooker's Eryngo

SCIENTIFIC NAME: *Eryngium + hookeri,* for Willian Jackson Hooker (1785-1865), a director of Kew Gardens in London.

COMMON NAME: Hooker's Eryngo, same as scientific name.

Eryngium integrifolium
Simpleleaf Eryngo

SCIENTIFIC NAME: *Eryngium + integrifolium,* Latin for having entire leaves.

COMMON NAME: Simpleleaf, descriptive. Eryngo, same as genus name.

Eryngium leavenworthii
Leavenworth's Eryngo

SCIENTIFIC NAME: *Eryngium + leavenworthii,* for Melines Conklin Leavenworth (1796-1862), a United States Army surgeon and botanist.

COMMON NAME: Leavenworth's Eryngo, same as scientific name.

Eryngium prostratum Creeping Eryngo

SCIENTIFIC NAME: Eryngium + prostratum, Latin for prostrate, for the matlike growth pattern.

COMMON NAME: Creeping, for the growth pattern. Eryngo, same as genus name.

Eryngium yuccifolium Button Snakeroot

SCIENTIFIC NAME: *Eryngium + yucci-folium,* Latin for having leaves like a yucca.

COMMON NAME: Button, for the round shape of the flower spike. Snakeroot, this plant was used by Native American Indians as a snakebite remedy.

Erysimum asperum Plains Wallflower

SCIENTIFIC NAME: *Erysimum.* from Greek, ερυσιμον, *erusimon,* their name for hedge mustard; this plant is in the mustard family + *asperum,* Latin for rough, harsh.

COMMON NAME: Plains, for the habitat. Wallflower, for the growth on old walls, rocks, and quarries.

Erysimum capitatum   **Western Wallflower**

SCIENTIFIC NAME: *Erysimum* + *capitatum,* Latin for forming a head. Reference is to the showy terminal cluster of flowers.

COMMON NAME: Western, for the range in the United States. Wallflower, see *Erysimum asperum.*

Erysimum repandum   **Bushy Wallflower**

SCIENTIFIC NAME: *Erysimum* + *repandum,* Latin for wavy margins, for the leaves.

COMMON NAME: Bushy, for the appearance. Wallflower, see *Erysimum asperum.*

Erythrina herbacea   **Coral Bean**

SCIENTIFIC NAME: *Erythrina,* from Greek, ερυθρος, *eruthros,* red, for the flower and seed color of most species + *herbacea,* Latin for herbaceous, not woody.

COMMON NAME: Coral Bean, for the red beanlike seeds.

Erythronium albidum
White Dog-Tooth Violet

SCIENTIFIC NAME: *Erythronium,* from Greek, ερυθρονιον, *eruthronion,* a type of orchid, in turn from ερυθρος, *eruthros,* red, for the flower color of some of this species + *albidum,* Latin for white, for the flower color.

COMMON NAME: White, for the flower color. Dog-tooth, for the sharply recurved sepals of the flower, which remind one of the canine teeth of a dog. Violet, for the resemblance to the violet family.

Erythronium grandiflorum   **Glacier Lily**

SCIENTIFIC NAME: *Erythronium* + *grandiflorum,* Latin for large flower.

COMMON NAME: Glacier, this flower blooms just below the receding snow as it melts at high elevations. Lily, from Latin, *Lilium,* the name for this type of flower.

Erythronium mesochoreum
Dog-Tooth Violet

SCIENTIFIC NAME: *Erythronium* + *mesochoreum,* midland, from Greek, μεσοχωρος, *mesokhōros,* midland, for the range.

COMMON NAME: Dog-Tooth Violet, see *Erythronium albidum.*

Erythronium rostratum
Dog-Tooth Violet

SCIENTIFIC NAME: *Erythronium* + *rostratum,* Latin for beaked, for the flower.

COMMON NAME: Dog-Tooth Violet, see *Erythronium albidum.*

Eschscholzia californica
California Poppy

SCIENTIFIC NAME: *Eschscholzia,* for John Friedrich Gustav von Eschscholtz (1793-1831), an Estonian professor of medicine and anatomy, zoologist, biologist and explorer + *californica,* Latin for of California, for the area of the type specimen.

COMMON NAME: California, same as species name. Poppy, from Latin, *papaver,* a poppy.

Escobaria missouriensis
Plains Nipple Cactus

SCIENTIFIC NAME: *Escobaria,* for two Mexican brothers, Romulo and Numa Escobar (fl. early 1900s), plant collectors + *missouriensis,* Latin for of Missouri.

COMMON NAME: Plains, for the habitat. Nipple, for the overall shape. Cactus, from Greek, κακτος, *kaktos,* a prickly plant.

Escobaria vivipara   **Pincushion Cactus**

SCIENTIFIC NAME: *Escobaria* +

vivipara, Latin for bearing live young, this cactus produces asexual propagules.

COMMON NAME: Pincushion, for the appearance. Cactus, see *Escobaria missouriensis.*

Eucnide bartonioides   **Rock Nettle**

SCIENTIFIC NAME: *Eucnide,* good nettle, from Greek, ευ, *eu,* good, well and κνιδη, *knidē,* nettle + *bartonioides,* to look like a *Bartonia,* from the genus *Bartonia* and the Greek suffix, ειδος, *eidos,* to resemble.

COMMON NAME: Rock, for the habitat in dry, stony areas. Nettle, from Old English, *netele,* in turn from Old High German, *nazza,* their name for this type of plant.

Eupatorium altissimum
Tall Joe-Pie Weed

SCIENTIFIC NAME: *Eupatorium,* for Mithridates Eupator (132-63 B.C.), king of Pontus. This name was associated with the plant agrimony. The ancient Greek word for agrimony, ευπατεριον, *eupaterion,* was derived from this surname + *altissimum,* Latin for the tallest.

COMMON NAME: Tall, may grow to six feet in height. Joe-Pie, a name for an American Indian (possibly mythical) who used the *Eupatorium* genus for treatment of typhus. Weed, from Old English, *weod,* a herbaceous plant, growing wild, of no value for beauty or commerce.

Eupatorium capillifolium   **Dogfennel**

SCIENTIFIC NAME: *Eupatorium + capillifolium,* Latin for hairy leaves.

COMMON NAME: Dogfennel, for the unpleasant scent and the fennel-like leaves.

Eupatorium coelestinum   **Mistflower**

SCIENTIFIC NAME: *Eupatorium + coelestinum,* Latin for heavenly, sky blue. Reference is to the color of the flowers.

COMMON NAME: Mistflower, for the appearance of the multiple threadlike disk flowers.

Eupatorium greggii   **Gregg's Mistflower**

SCIENTIFIC NAME: *Eupatorium + greggii,* for Josiah Gregg (1806-1850), an American explorer and plant collector.

COMMON NAME: Gregg's, same as species name. Mistflower, see *Eupatorium coelestinum.*

Eupatorium havanense   **Shrubby Boneset**

SCIENTIFIC NAME: *Eupatorium + havanense,* Latin for pertaining to Havana, for the area of the type specimen.

COMMON NAME: Shrubby, for the appearance. Boneset, from its use, among many others, by the American Indians to aid in mending bones.

Eupatorium incarnatum
Pink Eupatorium

SCIENTIFIC NAME: *Eupatorium + incarnatum,* Latin for flesh-colored, for the pink flowers.

COMMON NAME: Pink, for the flower color. Eupatorium, same as genus name.

Eupatorium perfoliatum   **Boneset**

SCIENTIFIC NAME: *Eupatorium + perfoliatum,* Latin for a leaf that surrounds the stem.

COMMON NAME: Boneset, see *Eupatorium havanense.*

Eupatorium rugosum   **White Snakeroot**

SCIENTIFIC NAME: *Eupatorium + rugosum,* Latin for wrinkled.

COMMON NAME: White, for the bright white flowers. Snakeroot, used by the American Indians to treat snakebite.

Eupatorium serotinum
Late-Flowering Boneset

SCIENTIFIC NAME: *Eupatorium + serotinum,* Latin for late-flowering. This plant blooms in the fall.

COMMON NAME: Late-flowering, same as species name. Boneset, see *Eupatorium perfoliatum.*

Euphorbia antisyphilitica   Candelilla

SCIENTIFIC NAME: *Euphorbia,* the literal translation is good food, from Greek, ευ, *eu,* good and φορβη, *phorbē,* food, pasture, however, this plant was named after Euphorbus, physician to King Luba of Mauritania in the first century A.D. + *antisyphilitica,* Latin for against syphilis, for its use in treating venereal disease.

COMMON NAME: Candelilla, Spanish for little candle, for the thin stems topped by a cluster of white and pink flowers, which look like a candle flame. This plant also yields a wax used in making candles, soap, sealing wax and other products.

Euphorbia bicolor   Snow-on-the-Prairie

SCIENTIFIC NAME: *Euphorbia* + *bicolor,* Latin for having two colors, for the green and white bracts.

COMMON NAME: Snow-on-the-Prairie, from a distance a large number of these plants together looks like snow on the ground.

Euphorbia corollata   Flowering Spurge

SCIENTIFIC NAME: *Euphorbia* + *corollata,* Latin for corollalike. Reference is to the white petal-like appendages of the glands that surround the insignificant flowers. True petals are absent.

COMMON NAME: Flowering, same as species name. Spurge, a plant of the *Euphorbia* genus with milky sap.

Euphorbia cyathophora
Fire-on-the-Mountain

SCIENTIFIC NAME: *Euphorbia* + *cyathophora,* Latin for cup-bearing. Reference is to the cup-shaped involucral glands.

COMMON NAME: Fire-on-the-Mountain, for the yellow and red patches at the bases of the leaves and bracts, when viewed from a distance these appear as fire.

Euphorbia dentata   Toothed Spurge

SCIENTIFIC NAME: *Euphorbia* + *dentata,* Latin for provided with teeth. Reference is to the toothed margins of the leaves.

COMMON NAME: Toothed, same as species name. Spurge, see *Euphorbia corollata.*

Euphorbia hexagona   Green Spurge

SCIENTIFIC NAME: *Euphorbia* + *hexagona,* from Greek, εξαγωνος, *exagōnos,* six angles.

COMMON NAME: Green, for the overall color. Spurge, see *Euphorbia corollata.*

Euphorbia marginata
Snow-on-the-Mountain

SCIENTIFIC NAME: *Euphorbia* + *marginata,* Latin for relating to the border or margins. Reference is to the white borders of the showy bracts.

COMMON NAME: Snow-on-the-Mountain, patches of this plant look like snow in the distance.

Euphorbia marginata
Snow-on-the-Mountain

Euphorbia roemeriana
Roemer's Euphorbia

SCIENTIFIC NAME: *Euphorbia* + *roemeriana,* Latin for pertaining to Roemer, for Ferdinand Roemer (1818-1891), an American geologist.

COMMON NAME: Roemer's Euphorbia, same as scientific name.

Eustoma exaltatum   Bluebell Gentian

SCIENTIFIC NAME: *Eustoma,* good mouth, from Greek, ευ, *eu,* good and

στομα, *stoma,* mouth, used here in the sense of a large mouth. Reference is to the shape of the flowers + *exaltatum,* Latin for very tall.

COMMON NAME: Bluebell, for the color and shape of the flowers. Gentian, named for Gentius, king of Illyria.

Euthamia leptocephala
Slenderhead Euthamia

SCIENTIFIC NAME: *Euthamia,* well crowded, from Greek, ευ, *eu,* good, well and θαμεες, *thamees,* crowded. Reference is to the crowded flowers + *leptocephala,* thin headed, from Greek, λεπτος, *leptos,* thin, fine and κεφαλη, *kephalē,* head. Reference is to the slender inflorescences.

COMMON NAME: Slenderhead Euthamia, same as scientific name.

Evolvulus nuttallianus
Nuttall's Evolvulus

SCIENTIFIC NAME: *Evolvulus,* Latin for "do not twine," to untwist, this genus does not climb as others in this family do + *nuttallianus,* Latin for pertaining to Nuttall, for Thomas Nuttall (1786-1859), an English botanist, explorer, printer, ornithologist, and plant collector. He was a fellow of the Linnaean Society.

COMMON NAME: Nuttall's Evolvulus, same as scientific name.

Fallugia paradoxa **Apache Plume**

SCIENTIFIC NAME: Fallugia, for
Virgilio Fallugi (?-1707), an Italian botanist
+ *paradoxa,* Greek for paradoxical
(παραδοξα), contrary to what is expected.

COMMON NAME: Apache Plume, for
the range (Apache territory) and the
feathery plumes of the achenes.

Ferocactus hamatacanthus **Turk's Head**

SCIENTIFIC NAME: *Ferocactus,* Latin
for ferocious cactus, for the spines +
hamatacanthus, Latin for hooked thorn,
for the hooked spines.

COMMON NAME: Turk's Head, for
the overall shape, generally the shape of a
human head.

Ferocactus uncinatus **Catclaw Cactus**

SCIENTIFIC NAME: *Ferocactus* +
uncinatus, Latin for having hooks, for the
hooked spines.

COMMON NAME: Catclaw, for the
hooked spines. Cactus, from Greek,
κακτος, *kaktos,* a prickly plant.

Fouquieria splendens **Ocotillo**

SCIENTIFIC NAME: *Fouquieria,* for
Pierre Eloi Fouquier (1776-1850), a
French physician + *splendens,* Latin for
splendid, for the flowers.

COMON NAME: Ocotillo, a
diminutive of the Mexican Spanish,
ocote, a resinous Mexican pine, in turn
from, *ocotl,* the Nahautl Indian word for
the pine.

Froelichia arizonica
Arizona Snake Cotton

SCIENTIFIC NAME: *Froelichia,* for
Joseph Aloys Froelich (1766-1841) a
German botanist + *arizonica,* of Arizona,
for the range.

COMMON NAME: Arizona, same as
species name. Snake Cotton, Snake, for
the habitat in sandy and rocky soil (where
snakes are found) and Cotton, for the
white, woolly flowers that look like
cotton.

Froelichia floridana **Snake Cotton**

SCIENTIFIC NAME: *Froelichia* +
floridana, pertaining to Florida, for the
area of the type specimen.

COMMON NAME: Snake Cotton, see
Froelichia arizonica.

Froelichia gracilis **Slender Snake Cotton**

SCIENTIFIC NAME: *Froelichia* +
gracilis, Latin for slender, for the stems.

COMMON NAME: Slender, for the stems.
Snake Cotton, see *Froelichia arizonica.*

Gaillardia aestivalis **Prairie Gaillardia**

SCIENTIFIC NAME: *Gaillardia,* for Gaillard de Charentoneau (fl. late 1700s), a French magistrate and member of the Academie des Sciences, a patron of botany + *aestivalis,* Latin for summer, like the summer, or in this case summer-blooming.

COMMON NAME: Prairie, for the habitat. Gaillardia, same as genus name.

Gaillardia amblyodon **Red Gaillardia**

SCIENTIFIC NAME: *Gaillardia* + *amblyodon,* blunt toothed, from Greek, αμβλυς, *amblu,* blunt, dull and οδοντ, *odont,* tooth. Reference is to the blunt-toothed ends of the petals.

COMMON NAME: Red, for the color of the petals. Gaillardia, same as genus name.

Gaillardia multiceps
Gyp Indian Blanket

SCIENTIFIC NAME: *Gaillardia* + *multiceps,* Latin for having many heads. Reference is to the brown-red central disks that remain on the stems after the petals fall, they appear as multiple small heads.

COMMON NAME: Gyp, grows in areas where gypsum is found. Indian Blanket, for the colors and pattern of the flowers.

Gaillardia pulchella **Indian Blanket**

SCIENTIFIC NAME: *Gaillardia* + *pulchella,* meant to be Latin for little pretty. Actually a depreciatory or condescending diminutive of *pulcher,* Latin for pretty.

COMMON NAME: Indian Blanket, for the colors and pattern of the flowers.

Gaillardia suavis **Fragrant Gaillardia**

SCIENTIFIC NAME: *Gaillardia* + *suavis,* Latin for sweet, fragrant. Reference is to the heavy, pleasant scent.

COMMON NAME: Fragrant, for the scent. Gaillardia, same as genus name.

Gaura brachycarpa **Plains Gaura**

SCIENTIFIC NAME: *Gaura,* from Greek, γαυρος, *gauros,* splendid, for the flowers + *brachycarpa,* short fruit, from Greek , βραχυς, *brakhus,* short, and καρπος, *fruit.*

COMMON NAME: Plains, for the habitat. Gaura, same as genus name.

Gaura coccinea **Scarlet Gaura**

SCIENTIFIC NAME: *Gaura* + *coccinea,* Latin for scarlet, for the pink flowers.

COMMON NAME: Scarlet, for the pink flowers. Gaura, same as genus name.

Gaura drummondii Sweet Gaura

SCIENTIFIC NAME: *Gaura + drummondii,* for Thomas Drummond (1780-1835), a Scottish plant collector.

COMMON NAME: Sweet, for the scent. Gaura, same as genus name.

Gaura lindheimeri White Gaura

SCIENTIFIC NAME: *Gaura + lindheimeri,* for Ferdinand Jacob Lindheimer (1801-1879), a German plant collector who made a large collection of plants from Texas.

COMMON NAME: White, for the flower color. Gaura, same as genus name.

Gaura longiflora Largeflower Gaura

SCIENTIFIC NAME: *Gaura + longiflora,* Latin for having long flowers.

COMMON NAME: Largeflower, although the flowers on this species are no larger than some of the other *Gaura.* Gaura, same as genus name.

Gaura parviflora Velvety Gaura

SCIENTIFIC NAME: *Gaura + parviflora,* Latin for small-flowered. The flowers on this plant are less than one-eighth of an inch long.

COMMON NAME: Velvety, for the dense glandular hairs. Gaura, same as genus name.

Gaura sinuata Wavyleaf Gaura

SCIENTIFIC NAME: *Gaura + sinuata,* Latin for having wavy margins, for the leaves.

COMMON NAME: Wavyleaf, for the leaf margins. Gaura, same as genus name.

Gaura suffulta Wild Honeysuckle

SCIENTIFIC NAME: *Gaura + suffulta,* Latin for supported, for the growth pattern, supported by other plants.

COMMON NAME: Wild, for the habitat. Honeysuckle, for the "honey sucking" of bees, also called Bee Blossom.

Gaura villlosa Woolly Gaura

SCIENTIFIC NAME: *Gaura + villosa,* latin for having soft hair, for the hairs on the stems.

COMMON NAME: Woolly Gaura, same as scientific name.

Gelsemium sempervirens
Carolina Jessamine

SCIENTIFIC NAME: *Gelsemium,* from Italian, *gelsemino,* jessamine + *sempervirens,* Latin for always green, for the evergreen leaves.

COMMON NAME: Carolina, for the area of the type specimen. Jessamine, a form of jasmine, from Persian, *yasmin,* their name for this kind of flower.

Gentiana puberulenta **Prairie Gentain**

SCIENTIFIC NAME: *Gentiana,* Latin for gentian, from Gentius, a second century king of Illyria, said to have discovered the medicinal uses of this plant + *puberulenta,* Medieval Latin, a diminutive of *pubens,* downy, therefore, little downy. Reference is to the small hairs on this plant.

COMMON NAME: Prairie, for the habitat. Gentian, same as genus name.

Geranium carolinianum **Crane's Bill**

SCIENTIFIC NAME: *Geranium,* from Greek, γερανος, *geranos,* a crane, for the long beak on the fruit, thought to resemble the beak of a crane + *carolinianum,* Latin for pertaining to Carolina, for the area of the type specimen.

COMMON NAME: Crane's Bill, same as genus name.

Geranium dissectum **Crane's Bill**

SCIENTIFIC NAME: *Geranium* + *dissectum,* Latin for deeply cut, dissected, for the leaf margins.

COMMON NAME: Crane's Bill same as genus name.

Geranium texanum **Texas Geranium**

SCIENTIFIC NAME: *Geranium* + *texanum,* Latin for pertaining to Texas.

COMMON NAME: Texas, for the range. Geranium, same as genus name

Gilia incisa **Splitleaf Gilia**

SCIENTIFIC NAME: *Gilia,* for Felipe Gil (fl. eighteenth century), a Spanish botanist + *incisa,* Latin for cut, deeply lobed, for the leaves.

COMMON NAME: Splitleaf, for the deeply lobed leaves. Gilia, same as genus name.

Gilia rigidula **Blue Gilia**

SCIENTIFIC NAME: *Gilia* + *rigidula,* Latin for a little rigid, for the stems.

COMMON NAME: Blue, for the flower color. Gilia, same as genus name.

Grindelia adenodonta
Littlehead Gumweed

SCIENTIFIC NAME: *Grindelia,* for David Hieronymus Grindel (1777-1836), a German physician, apothecary, and botanist + *adenodonta,* Latin for gland tooth or sticky tooth, for the sticky resin.

COMMON NAME: Littlehead, has relatively small inflorescences. Gumweed, for the sticky resin.

Grindelia lanceolata   Gulf Gumweed

SCIENTIFIC NAME: *Grindelia +
lanceolata,* Latin for lance-shaped, for
the leaves.

COMMON NAME: Gulf, for the range.
Gumweed, for the sticky resin.

Grindelia nuda   Rayless Gumweed

SCIENTIFIC NAME: *Grindelia + nuda,*
Latin for nude, bare, for the absense of ray
flowers.

COMMON NAME: Rayless, descriptive.
Gumweed, for the sticky resin.

Grindelia papposa   Sawleaf Daisy

SCIENTIFIC NAME: *Grindelia +
papposa,* Latin for pappus, this plant has a
conspicuous pappus.

COMMON NAME: Sawleaf, for the
saw-toothed leaf edges. Daisy, for the
flowers resembling those of the daisy.

Grindelia papposa
Sawleaf Daisy

Grindelia squarrosa
Curlytop Gumweed

SCIENTIFIC NAME: *Grindelia +
squarrosa,* Latin for scaly. Reference is to
the bracts.

COMMON NAME: Curlytop, for the
recurved tips of the bracts. Gumweed, for
the sticky resin.

Gutierrezia amoena   **Broomweed**

SCIENTIFIC NAME: *Gutierrezia,* for
Pedro Gutierrez (fl. 1816), correspondent
for the Madrid botanical garden +
amoena, Latin for plesant, delightful.

COMMON NAME: Broomweed, was
used as a broom by American Indians and
early settlers.

Gutierrezia microcephala
Threadleaf Snakeweed

SCIENTIFIC NAME: *Gutierrezia +
microcephala,* small head, from Greek,
μικροκεφαλος, *mikrokephalos,* small head,
for the overall appearance of the
inflorescences.

COMMON NAME: Threadleaf, for the
thin leaves. Snakeweed, used in snakebite
remedies by the Navajo of the western
United States.

Gutierreza sarothrae   **Broom Snakeweed**

SCIENTIFIC NAME: *Gutierrezia, +
sarothrae,* a broom, from Greek,

σαροθρον, *sarothron,* a form of σαρον, *saron,* a broom.

COMMON NAME: Broom, used as a broom by some American Indians and early settlers. Snakeweed, see *Gutierrezia microcephala.*

Guterrezia texana   **Texas Broomweed**

SCIENTIFIC NAME: *Guterrezia + texana,* Latin for pertaining to Texas.

COMMON NAME: Texas, for the range. Broomweed, see *Gutierrezia amoena.*

Gymnosperma glutinosum   **Gumhead**

SCIENTIFIC NAME: *Gymnosperma,* naked seed, from Greek, γυμνος, *gumnos,* naked and σπερμα, *sperma,* seed + *glutinosum,* Latin for sticky, for the sticky leaves.

COMMON NAME: Gumhead, for the resinous exudate.

Habenaria nivea   **Snowy Orchid**

SCIENTIFIC NAME: *Habenaria,* from Latin, *habena,* that by which a thing is held, a strap, holder. Reference is to the spur on the lip petal + *nivea,* Latin for bright, shining, for the white flowers.

COMMON NAME: Snowy, for the white flowers. Orchid, from Greek, ορχις, *orkhis,* testicle, for the shape of the pseudobulbs of some members of the Orchid family.

Habenaria repens   **Creeping Orchid**

SCIENTIFIC NAME: *Habenaria + repens,* Latin for creeping, for the growth pattern.

COMMON NAME: Creeping, for the growth pattern. Orchid, see *Habenaria nivea.*

Habranthus texanus   **Copper Lily**

SCIENTIFIC NAME: *Habranthus,* pretty flower, from Greek, αβρος, *abros,* graceful, pretty and ονθος, *anthos,* flower, blossom + *texanus,* Latin for pertaining to Texas, for the range.

COMMON NAME: Copper, for the flower color. Lily, from Latin, *lilium,* lily.

Haplopappus ciliatus   **Wax Goldenweed**

SCIENTIFIC NAME: *Haplopappus,* single pappus, from Greek, απλος, *(h)aplos,* single and παππος, *pappos,* down on seeds. Reference is to the bristle on the tip of the achene + *ciliatus,* Latin for fringed with soft hairs. Reference is to the hairs on the edges of the leaves.

COMMON NAME: Wax, for the waxy yellow disk flowers. Goldenweed, for the flower color.

Haplopappus spinulosus
Cutleaf Ironweed

SCIENTIFIC NAME: *Haplopappus +
spinulosus,* Latin for somewhat spiny.
Reference is to the bristles on the leaves.

COMMON NAME: Cutleaf, for the
toothed, cut-out appearance of the leaves.
Ironweed, for the hard stem.

Hedyotis nigricans **Fineleaf Bluet**

SCIENTIFIC NAME: *Hedyotis ,* sweet
ear, from Greek, ηδυς, *ēdus,* sweet ,
pleasant to the taste or smell and ωτος,
ōtos, ear. Most probably a pet name +
nigricans, Latin for shading into black,
verging on black. Reference is to the leaves
turning black as they dry.

COMMON NAME: Fineleaf, for the
threadlike leaves. Bluet, see *Hedyotis
crassifolia.*

Helenium amarum **Bitter Sneezeweed**

SCIENTIFIC NAME: *Helenium,* from
Greek, ελενιον, *elenion,* the elechampane
(*Inula helenium*), which this plant resembles + *amarum,* Latin for bitter to taste,
pungent to smell. The bitter qualities of
this plant can be transfered to milk if cattle
eat it or to honey if bees collect from it.

COMMON NAME: Bitter, same as
species name. Sneezeweed, the odor of this
plant is reputed to cause sneezing.

Helenium autumnale **Sneezeweed**

SCIENTIFIC NAME: *Helenium +
autumnale,* Latin for of autumn.
Reference is to the fall blooming flowers.

COMMON NAME: Sneezeweed, see
Helenium amarum.

Helenium drummondii
Fringed Sneezeweed

SCIENTIFIC NAME: *Helenium +
drummondii,* for Thomas Drummond
(c. 1790-1831), a British plant collector.

COMMON NAME: Fringed, for the
fringed flower petals. Sneezeweed, see
Helenium amarum.

Helenium flexuosum
Purplehead Sneezeweed

SCIENTIFIC NAME: *Helenium + flexuosum,* Latin for full of bends and turns.
Reference is to the pattern of the stems.

COMMON NAME: Purplehead, for
the red-brown to purple disk flowers.
Sneezeweed, see *Helenium amarum.*

Helianthus angustifolius
Swamp Sunflower

SCIENTIFIC NAME: *Helianthus,*
sunflower, from Greek, ηλιος, *(h)ēlios,* the
sun and ανθος, *anthos,* flower, blossom +
angustifolius, Latin for narrow-leaved,
descriptive of the very narrow leaves of
this plant.

COMMON NAME: Swamp, for the habitat; it prefers moist soil. Sunflower, this name was originally used for the genus *Heliotrope*, because the flowers turned with the sun. The genus *Helianthus* was named by Carl Linnaeus (1707-1778) for the type specimen *Helianthus annuus*, because the flower, with its bright yellow rays, reminded him of the sun.

Helianthus annuus Common Sunflower

SCIENTIFIC NAME: *Helianthus + annuus,* Latin for annual, living only one year.

COMMON NAME: Common, most common in its range. Sunflower, see *Helianthus angustifolius.*

Helianthus grosseserratus Sawtooth Sunflower

SCIENTIFIC NAME: *Helianthus + grosseserratus,* Latin for having large saw teeth. Reference is to the serrated leaf edges.

COMMON NAME: Sawtooth, same as species name. Sunflower, see *Helianthus angustifolius.*

Helianthus maximiliani Maximilian Sunflower

SCIENTIFIC NAME: *Helianthus + maximiliani,* for Maximilian A. P. zu Wied-Neuwied (1782-1867), a German prince and naturalist.

COMMON NAME: Maximilian, same as species name. Sunflower, see *Helianthus angustifolius.*

Helianthus mollis Ashy Sunflower

SCIENTIFIC NAME: *Helianthus + mollis,* Latin for soft, tender. Reference is to the soft, white, woolly hairs.

COMMON NAME: Ashy, for the color of the white, woolly hairs. Sunflower, see *Helianthus angustifolius.*

Helianthus petiolaris Plains Sunflower

SCIENTIFIC NAME: *Helianthus + petiolaris,* Latin for having a leaf stalk.

COMMON NAME: Plains, for the habitat. Sunflower, see *Helianthus angustifolius.*

Helianthus salicifolius Willowleaf Sunflower

SCIENTIFIC NAME: *Helianthus + salicifolius,* Latin for willowleaf. The leaves resemble those of the willow.

COMMON NAME: Willow-Leaved, same as species name. Sunflower, see *Helianthus angustifolius.*

Helianthus tuberosus Jerusalem Artichoke

SCIENTIFIC NAME: *Helianthus + tuberosus,* Latin for having tubers.

Reference is to the edible tubers.

COMMON NAME: Jerusalem Artichoke, a corruption of the Italian, *Girasole articiocco,* sunflower artichoke, for the edible tubers.

Heliotropium amplexicaule
Violet Heliotrope

SCIENTIFIC NAME: *Heliotropium,* to turn toward the sun, from Greek, ηλιος, *(h)ēlios,* the sun and τρεπο, *trepo,* to turn toward a thing. Reference is to the flowers following the sun + *amplexicaule,* Latin for stem-clasping, for the leaf bases that encircle the stems.

COMMON NAME: Violet, for the flower color. Heliotrope, same as genus name.

Heliotropium convolvulaceum
Bindweed Heliotrope

SCIENTIFIC NAME: *Heliotropium* + *convolvulaceum,* Latin for to resemble the genus *Convolvulus,* bindweed.

COMMON NAME: Bindweed, for the trailing vinelike stems. Heliotrope, same as genus name.

Heliotropium curassavicum
Seaside Heliotrope

SCIENTIFIC NAME: *Heliotropium* + *curassavicum,* for Curaçao, West Indies, the area of the type specimen.

COMMON NAME: Seaside, for the habitat; it also grows inland on saline soils. Heliotrope, same as genus name.

Heliotropium indicum   Turnsole

SCIENTIFIC NAME: *Heliotropium* + *indicum,* Latin for of India; this name was attached to many plants that came from India, anywhere in the Far East, and even the East Indies.

COMMON NAME: Turnsole, from Spanish, *tornasol,* to turn toward the sun, see *Heliotropium amplexicaule.*

Heliotropium tenellum
Pasture Heliotrope

SCIENTIFIC NAME: *Heliotropium* + *tenellum,* Latin for tender or delicate.

COMMON NAME: Pasture, for the habitat. Heliotrope, same as genus name.

Hesperis matronalis   Dame's Rocket

SCIENTIFIC NAME: *Hesperis,* of the evening, from Greek, εσπερα, *espera,* just at nightfall, the evening. Reference is to the fragrance released in the evening + *matronalis,* Latin for of or befitting a matron, a married woman. Also pertaining to the Roman festival of the matrons, held on March first.

COMMON NAME: Dame's, from the species name. Rocket, from French, *roquette,* their name for cruciferous plants.

Hesperaloe parviflora **Red Yucca**

SCIENTIFIC NAME: *Hesperaloe,*
western aloe, from Greek, εσπερα,
(h)espera, western and the genus *Aloe;*
these plants resemble the old world aloes +
parviflora, Latin for having small flowers.

COMMON NAME: Red, for the flower
color. Yucca, from Carib, *yucca,* their
name for the cassava, inappropriately
applied to this plant.

Heterotheca canescens
Gray Golden Aster

SCIENTIFIC NAME: *Heterotheca,*
different case, from Greek, ετερος,
(h)eteros, different and θηκη, *thēkē,* a case,
a chest. Reference is to the differing sizes
of the achenes of the ray and disk flowers
+ *canescens,* Latin for to become gray.
Reference is to the gray hairs on the
foliage.

COMMON NAME: Gray, same as
species name. Golden Aster, for the gold
color and the star shape of the flower,
from Greek αστερ, *aster,* a star.

Heterotheca stenophylla
Narrowleaf Golden Aster

SCIENTIFIC NAME: *Heterotheca* +
stenophylla, narrow leaves, from Greek,
στενος, *stenos,* narrow and φυλλον,
phullon, leaf.

COMMON NAME: Narrowleaf,
descriptive. Golden Aster, see *Heterotheca
canescens.*

Hibiscus laevis **Scarlet Rose Mallow**

SCIENTIFIC NAME: *Hibiscus,* Latin for
marsh mallow, in turn from Greek,
βλθαξα, *ibiskos,* the hibiscus + *laevis,*
Latin for smooth.

COMMON NAME: Scarlet, for the
flower color. Rose Mallow, for the flower
color and the Latin name for this plant
family, *malva.*

Hibiscus moscheutos **Rose Mallow**

SCIENTIFIC NAME: *Hibiscus* +
moscheutos, Latin for musky, for the scent.

COMMON NAME: Rose Mallow, see
Hibiscus laevis.

Hibiscus trionum **Flower-of-an-Hour**

SCIENTIFIC NAME: *Hibiscus* +
trionum, New Latin, from Greek,
τριονον, *trionon,* a malvaceous plant.

COMMON NAME: Flower-of-the-Hour,
for the short time the flower stays open.

Hoffmannseggia glauca **Pignut**

SCIENTIFIC NAME: *Hoffmannseggia,*
for Johann Centurius Graf von
Hoffmannsegg (1766-1849), a German
entomologist and ornithologist + *glauca,*
Latin for gray-green, having a whitish
bloom. Reference is to the color of the
leaves.

COMMON NAME: Pignut, for the edible tubers, which pigs dig up and eat.

Houstonia humifusa   Mat Bluet

SCIENTIFIC NAME: *Houstonia,* for William Houston (1695-1733), an English surgeon and botanist + *humifusa,* Latin for sprawling on the ground, for the growth pattern.

COMMON NAME: Mat, for the growth pattern. Bluet, for the small, usually blue, flower of this genus.

Houstonia micrantha   Southern Bluet

SCIENTIFIC NAME: *Houstonia* + *micrantha,* small flower, from Greek, μικρος, *micros,* small and ανθος, *anthos,* flower.

COMMON NAME: Southern, for the range in the United States. Bluet see *Houstonia humifusa.*

Houstonia parviflora   Bluet

SCIENTIFIC NAME: *Houstonia* + *parviflora,* Latin for small-flowered.

COMMON NAME: Bluet, see *Houstonia humifusa.*

Houstonia pusilla   Tiny Bluet

SCIENTIFIC NAME: *Houstonia* +

pusilla, Latin for very small, for the flowers.

COMMON NAME: Tiny Bluet, see *Houstonia humifusa.*

Houstonia rosea   Rose Bluet

SCIENTIFIC NAME: *Houstonia* + *rosea,* Latin for rose, for the flower color.

COMMON NAME: Rose, for the rose color of the flowers of this species. Bluet, see *Houstonia humifusa.*

Houstonia subviscosa   Nodding Bluet

SCIENTIFIC NAME: *Houstonia* + *subviscosa,* Latin for a little sticky, for the stems.

COMMON NAME: Nodding, for the nodding flowers. Bluet, see *Houstonia humifusa.*

Hydrolea ovata   Blue Waterleaf

SCIENTIFIC NAME: *Hydrolea,* water olive, from Greek, υδωρ, *udōr,* water and ολεα *olea,* olive tree, olive. Reference is to the habitat in wet areas and the leaves, which are similar in shape to those of the olive tree + *ovata,* Latin for egg-shaped, oval, for the leaf shape.

COMMON NAME: Blue, for the color of the flowers. Waterleaf, from the family name, *Hydrophyllaceae,* waterleaf, for the wet habitat.

Hymenocallis liriosme Spider Lily

SCIENTIFIC NAME: *Hymenocallis,*
beautiful membrane, from Greek, υμην,
(h)umēn, a membrane and καλλ–καλος,
kalli, kalos, beautiful. Reference is to the
appearance of the central cup of the
flower + *liriosme,* lily smell, from Greek,
λειριον, *leirion,* lily and οσμη, *osmē,*
smell, for the fragrance.

COMMON NAME: Spider, for the
appearance of the flower, with long
segments resembling spider legs and the
central cup like the body of a spider. Lily,
for the appearance.

Hymenopappus artemisiifolius
Woolly White

SCIENTIFIC NAME: *Hymenopappus,*
membrane pappus, from Greek, υμην,
umēn, membrane and παππος, *pappos,*
grandfather, down on achenes + *artemisi-*
ifolius, Latin for having leaves like the
genus *Artemisia* (wormwood).

COMMON NAME: Woolly White, for
the soft white hairs on the plant.

Hymenopappus filifolius
Fineleaf Woolly White

SCIENTIFIC NAME: *Hymenopappus +*
filifolius, Latin for threadlike leaves.

COMMON NAME: Fine-Leaf, for the
thin leaves. Woolly White, for the soft
white hairs.

Hymenopappus flavescens
Yellow Hymenopappus

SCIENTIFIC NAME: *Hymenopappus +*
flavescens, Latin for pale yellow. Reference
is to the flower color.

COMMON NAME: Yellow
Hymenopappus, same as scientific name.

Hymenopappus scabiosaeus
Old Plainsman

SCIENTIFIC NAME: *Hymenopappus +*
scabiosaeus, Latin for to resemble the
genus *Scabiosa.*

COMMON NAME: Old Plainsman, for
the woolly hairs and the habitat.

Hymenopappus tenuifolius
Slimleaf Hymenopappus

SCIENTIFIC NAME: *Hymenopappus +*
tenuifolius, Latin for slender or thin-
leaved.

COMMON NAME: Slimleaf,
descriptive. Hymenopappus, same as
genus name.

Hymenoxys odorata Bitterweed

SCIENTIFIC NAME: *Hymenoxys,* sharp
membrane, from Greek, υμην, *(h)umēn,*
membrane and οξυς, *oxus,* sharp.
Reference is to the pappus + *odorata,*
Latin for having a smell, fragrant.

COMMON NAME: Bitterweed, for the resinlike excretions of this genus, which are bitter to the taste.

Hypericum perforatum St. John's Wort

SCIENTIFIC NAME: *Hypericum*, above the picture, from Greek, υπερ, *uper*, above and εικον, *eikon*, picture. Reference is to this plant being hung above pictures to ward off evil spirits + *perforatum*, Latin for pierced with holes. Reference is to the transparent dots on the leaves; it was believed that the devil poked holes in the leaves with a needle in revenge for this plant's properties of warding off evil.

COMMON NAME: St. John's, in Europe this plant blooms on St. John's Day. Wort, from Old English, *wyrt*, root, a plant or herb used for food or medicine.

Hypericum sphaerocarpum Roundfruit St. John's Wort

SCIENTIFIC NAME: *Hypericum* + *sphaerocarpum*, Latin for having rounded fruit.

COMMON NAME: Roundfruit, descriptive. St. John's Wort, see *Hypericum perforatum.*

Hypoxis hirsuta Yellow Star Grass

SCIENTIFIC NAME: *Hypoxis,* sharp below, from Greek, υπο, *(h)upo*, below and οξυς, *oxus,* sharp, for the sharp capsule base + *hirsuta,* Latin for hairy. Reference is to the hairs on the flower stems and buds.

COMMON NAME: Yellow, for the flower color. Star Grass, for the shape of the flowers and the appearance of the leaves.

Ibervillea lindheimeri Globe Berry

SCIENTIFIC NAME: *Ibervillea,* most probably for Iberville Parish Lousiana, the area of the type specimen + *lindheimeri,* for Ferdinand Jacob Lindheimer (1801-1879), a German political exile who collected plants in Texas.

COMMON NAME: Globe Berry, for the spherical red fruit.

Indigofera miniata Scarlet Pea

SCIENTIFIC NAME: *Indigofera,* I bear Indigo, from *indigo,* in turn from Latin, *indicus,* of India and Latin, *fero,* I bear + *miniata,* Latin for having the color of cinnabar, vermilion. Reference is to the flower color.

COMMON NAME: Scarlet, for the flower color. Pea, for the fruit; this plant is a legume.

Ipomoea coccinea Scarlet Creeper

SCIENTIFIC NAME: *Ipomoea,* resembling a vine, from Greek, ιψ, *ips,* vine, worm and ομοιος, *omoios,* resembling, for the growth pattern + *coccinea,* Latin for scarlet, for the flower color.

COMMON NAME: Scarlet, for the flower color. Creeper, for the growth pattern.

Ipomoea cordatotriloba
Wild Morning Glory

SCIENTIFIC NAME: *Ipomoea + cordatotriloba,* Latin for heart-shaped, having three lobes, for the leaves.

COMMON NAME: Wild, for the habitat. Morning Glory, for the pretty bloom that opens in the morning.

Ipomoea hederacea
Ivyleaf Morning Glory

SCIENTIFIC NAME: *Ipomoea + hederacea,* Latin for resembling ivy, for the shape of the leaves.

COMMON NAME: Ivyleaf, descriptive. Morning Glory, see *Ipomoea cordatotriloba.*

Ipomoea leptophylla
Bush Morning Glory

SCIENTIFIC NAME: *Ipomoea + leptophylla,* thin-leaved, from Greek, λεπτος, *leptos,* thin, fine and φυλλον, *phullon,* a leaf.

COMMON NAME: Bush, for the growth pattern. Morning Glory, see *Ipomoea cordatotriloba.*

Ipomoea pandurata   **Wild Potato**

SCIENTIFIC NAME: *Ipomoea + pandurata,* lute shaped, from Greek, πανδουρα, *pandoura,* a three-stringed lute. Reference is to the shape of the leaves.

COMMON NAME: Wild, for the habitat. Potato, for the large starchy root.

Ipomoea pes-caprae
Goat-Foot Morning Glory

SCIENTIFIC NAME: *Ipomoea + pes-caprae,* Latin for goat-footed. Reference is to the shape of the leaves, which resemble the footprint of a goat.

COMMON NAME: Goat-foot, same as species name. Morning Glory, see *Ipomoea cordatotriloba.*

Ipomoea purpurea
Common Morning Glory

SCIENTIFIC NAME: *Ipomoea + purpurea,* Latin for purple, for the flower color.

COMMON NAME: Common, common in its range. Morning Glory, see *Ipomoea cordatotriloba.*

Ipomoea sagittata
Saltmarsh Morning Glory

SCIENTIFIC NAME: *Ipomoea + sagittata,* Latin for arrow-shaped, for the arrowhead-shaped leaves.

COMMON NAME: Saltmarsh, for the preferance of moist, brackish soil. Morning Glory, see *Ipomoea cordatotriloba.*

Ipomoea shumardiana
Narrowleaf Morning Glory

SCIENTIFIC NAME: *Ipomoea + shumardiana,* Latin for pertaining to Shumard, for Benjamin Franklin Shumard (1820-1869), a state geologist for Texas.

COMMON NAME: Narrowleaf, descriptive. Morning Glory, see *Ipomoea cordatotriloba.*

Ipomoea stolonifera
Beach Morning Glory

SCIENTIFIC NAME: *Ipomoea + stolonifera,* Latin for possesing stolons (root runners).

COMMON NAME: Beach, for the habitat. Morning Glory, see *Ipomoea cordatotriloba.*

Ipomopsis aggregata   **Skyrocket**

SCIENTIFIC NAME: *Ipomopsis,* to look like an *Ipomoea,* from the genus *Ipomoea* and the Greek, οψις, *ops,* appearance. Reference is to the flower shape + *aggregata,* Latin for clustered, for the flower distribution on the stem.

COMMON NAME: Skyrocket, for the shape and color of the flower.

Ipomopsis longiflora   **Pale Trumpets**

SCIENTIFIC NAME: *Ipomopsis + longiflora,* Latin for long flower, for the long tube of the flower.

COMMON NAME: Pale, for the white or pale lavender color of the flower. Trumpets, for the trumpet shape of the bloom.

Ipomopsis rubra   **Texas Star**

SCIENTIFIC NAME: *Ipomopsis + rubra,* Latin for red, for the flower color.

COMMON NAME: Texas, for the range. Star, for the shape of the flower.

Iris brevicaulis   **Zigzag Iris**

SCIENTIFIC NAME: *Iris,* from Greek, Ιρις, *Iris,* messenger of the gods, goddess of the rainbow. Reference is to the beautiful hues of the blooms + *brevicaulis,* Latin for short stem.

COMMON NAME: Zigzag, for the shape of the flowering stem. Iris, same as genus name.

Iris pallida   **Pale Blue Flag**

SCIENTIFIC NAME: *Iris + pallida,* Latin for pale, for the pale blue flower.

COMMON NAME: Pale Blue, same as species name. Flag, see *Iris brevicaulis.*

Iris virginica   **Southern Iris**

SCIENTIFIC NAME: *Iris + virginica,* Latin for of Virginia, for the area of the type specimen.

COMMON NAME: Southern, for the range in the United States. Iris, same as genus name.

Isocoma pluriflora   Rayless Goldenrod

SCIENTIFIC NAME: *Isocoma,* equal hair, from Greek, ισος, *isos,* equal and κομη, *kome,* hair of the head. Reference is to the distribution of the leaves on the stem + *pluriflora,* Latin for many flowers.

COMMON NAME: Rayless, the ray flowers are absent. Goldenrod, for the gold flowers on top of the stem.

Jacquemontia tamnifolia
Hairy Cluster Vine

SCIENTIFIC NAME: *Jacquemontia,* for Victor V. Jacquemont (1801-1832), a French naturalist and botanist + *tamnifolia,* Latin for having leaves like the tamus vine, from Latin, *tamus,* a climbing plant.

COMMON NAME: Hairy, for the hairy bracts. Cluster Vine, for the blooms that form in clusters and the growth pattern.

Jacquemontia tamnifolia
Hairy Cluster Vine

Justicia americana   Water Willow

SCIENTIFIC NAME: *Justicia,* for James Justice (1698-1763), a Scottish horticulturist and member of the Royal Society + *americana,* Latin for pertaining to America.

COMMON NAME: Water Willow, for the habitat and the appearance of the leaves.

Kallstroemia californica
California Caltrop

SCIENTIFIC NAME: *Kallstroemia,* for a man named Kallstroem, a friend of Giovanni Antonio Scopoli (1723-1799), who named this genus + *californica,* Latin for of California, for the area of the type specimen.

COMMON NAME: California, same as species name. Caltrop, from Anglo-Saxon, *coltraeppe,* a spiny plant.

Kallstroemia grandiflora   Desert Poppy

SCIENTIFIC NAME: *Kallstroemia* + *grandiflora,* Latin for large flower.

COMMON NAME: Desert, for the habitat. Poppy, for the appearance of the flower.

Kallstroemia hirsutissima   Carpetweed

SCIENTIFIC NAME: *Kallstroemia* + *hirsutissima,* Latin for most hairy, for the hairy stems and leaves.

COMMON NAME: Carpetweed, for the matlike growth pattern.

Kallstroemia parviflora **Warty Caltrop**

SCIENTIFIC NAME: *Kallstroemia* + *parviflora,* Latin for small-flowered.

COMMON NAME: Warty, for the tubercles on the fruit capsule. Caltrop, see *Kallstroemia californica.*

Kosteletzkya virginica **Salt Marshmallow**

SCIENTIFIC NAME: *Kosteletzkya,* for Vincez Franz Kosteletzky (1801-1887), a Czech physician and botanist + *virginica,* Latin for of Virginia, for the area of the type specimen.

COMMON NAME: Salt, prefers brackish wet soil. Marshmallow, from Old English, *merscmealwe,* their name for this plant.

Krameria lanceolata **Trailing Krameria**

SCIENTIFIC NAME: *Krameria,* for Johann Georg Heinrich Kramer (?-1742), an Austrian physician + *lanceolata,* Latin for lance-shaped, for the leaves.

COMMON NAME: Trailing, for the growth pattern. Krameria, same as genus name.

Krigia cespitosa **Dwarf Dandelion**

SCIENTIFIC NAME: *Krigia,* for David Krieg (1670-1710), a German physician and botanist and a fellow of the Royal Society; the Principle of Priority allows the misspelling to stand + *cespitosa,* Latin for growing in tufts.

COMMON NAME: Dwarf, for the small size. Dandelion, for the superficial resemblance to the common dandelion.

Krigia dandelion **Tuber Dwarf Dandelion**

SCIENTIFIC NAME: *Krigia* + *dandelion,* for the appearance, it looks like the true dandelion (*Taraxacum*).

COMMON NAME: Tuber, for the large tubers on the roots. Dwarf Dandelion, see *Krigia cespitosa.*

Krigia occidentalis **Western Dwarf Dandelion**

SCIENTIFIC NAME: *Krigia* + *occidentalis,* Latin for western, for the range in the United States.

COMMON NAME: Western, for the range in the United States. Dwarf Dandelion, see *Krigia cespitosa.*

Krigia virginica
Virginia Dwarf Dandelion

SCIENTIFIC NAME: *Krigia + virginica,*
Latin for of Virginia, for the area of the
type specimen.

COMMON NAME: Virginia, for the
area of the type specimen. Dwarf
Dandelion, see *Krigia cespitosa.*

Krigia wrightii
Wright's Dwarf Dandelion

SCIENTIFIC NAME: *Krigia + wrightii,*
for Charles Wright (1811-1885), a plant
collector in Texas.

COMMON NAME: Wright's, same as
species name. Dwarf Dandelion, see
Krigia cespitosa.

Lactuca canadensis **Wild Lettuce**

SCIENTIFIC NAME: *Lactuca,* Latin for
lettuce, the root word is *lac,* milk, for the

Lamium amplexicaule
Henbit

milky sap + *canadensis,* Latin for belonging to Canada.

COMMON NAME: Wild, for the
habitat. Lettuce, from Old French, *laitue,*
the root is the same as for milk, for the
milky sap.

Lactuca ludoviciana
Western Wild Lettuce

SCIENTIFIC NAME: *Lactuca +
ludoviciana,* Latin for pertaining to
Louisiana, the literal translation is
"pertaining to Louis." Reference is to
Louis XIV (1638-1715), king of France.

COMMON NAME: Western, for the
range in the United States. Wild Lettuce,
see *Lactua canadensis.*

Lactuca serriola **Prickly Lettuce**

SCIENTIFIC NAME: *Lactuca + serriola,*
a litle saw, from Latin, *serra,* a saw and the
diminutive suffix, *-uola.* Reference is to
the spines on the toothed leaf edges.

COMMON NAME: Prickly, for the
spines on the leaves. Lettuce, see *Lactuca
canadensis.*

Lamium amplexicaule **Henbit**

SCIENTIFIC NAME: *Lamium,* Latin
for dead nettle. Reference is to the leaves,
which look like those of the nettle but do
not sting + *amplexicaule,* stem-clasping,
from Latin, *amplexus,* clasping in an
embrace and *caulis,* stalk, stem. Reference

is to the base of the leaves appearing to clasp the stem.

COMMON NAME: Henbit, from Old Low German, *hoenderbeet,* their name for this plant.

Lamium purpureum   **Purple Dead Nettle**

SCIENTIFIC NAME: *Lamium + purpureum,* Latin for purple, for the flower color.

COMMON NAME: Purple Dead Nettle, same as scientific name.

Lantana achyranthifolia **Veinleaf Lantana**

SCIENTIFIC NAME: *Lantana,* the Late Latin name for *Viburnum lantana,* for the flowers, which resemble that plant + *achyranthifolia,* Latin for having leaves like the genus *Achyranthes.*

COMMON NAME: Veinleaf, for the obvious leaf veins. Lantana, same as genus name.

Lantana camara   **Largeleaf Lantana**

SCIENTIFIC NAME: *Lantana + camara,* a South American vernacular name.

COMMON NAME: Largeleaf, has relatively large leaves. Lantana, same as genus name.

Lantana urticoides   **Texas Lantana**

SCIENTIFIC NAME: *Lantana + urticoides,* Latin for resembling the genus *Urtica.*

COMMON NAME: Texas, for the range. Lantana, same as genus name.

Larrea tridentata   **Creosote Bush**

SCIENTIFIC NAME: *Larrea,* for Juan Antonio de Larrea (fl. 1810), a Spanish patron of science + *tridentata,* Latin for three teeth, for the leaves.

COMMON NAME: Creosote Bush, the crushed leaves smell like creosote.

Lepidium austrinum **Southern Pepperweed**

SCIENTIFIC NAME: *Lepidium,* the pepperwort, from Greek, λεπιδιον, *lepidion,* used by Discorides to describe the pepperwort, used to treat scurvy + *austrinum,* Latin for southern, for the range in the United States.

COMMON NAME: Southern, for the range in the United States. Pepperweed, for the fruits, which can be used as a pepper substitute.

Lepidium densiflorum **Prairie Pepperweed**

SCIENTIFIC NAME: *Lepidium + densiflorum,* Latin for densely flowered.

COMMON NAME: Prairie, for the habitat. Pepperweed, see *Lepidium austrinum.*

Lepidium montanum
Mountain Pepperweed

SCIENTIFIC NAME: *Lepidium + montanum,* Latin for pertaining to the mountains.

COMMON NAME: Mountain, for the range. Pepperweed, see *Lepidium austrinum.*

Lespedeza capitata   Bush Clover

SCIENTIFIC NAME: *Lespedeza,* for Vincente Manuel de Cespedes (late 1780s), the Spanish governor of eastern Florida and a patron of botany. His name was misspelled when the book containing this plant's description was being printed; the Principle of Priority allows the misspelling to stand + *capitata,* Latin for having or forming a head. Reference is to the inflorescence.

COMMON NAME: Bush, for the overall appearance. Clover, for the inflorescence, which resembles a large clover inflorescence.

Lespedeza hirta   Hairy Bush Clover

SCIENTIFIC NAME: *Lespedeza + hirta,* Latin for hairy, for the stems.

COMMON NAME: Hairy, for the stems. Bush clover, see *Lespedeza capitata.*

Lespedeza repens   Creeping Bush Clover

SCIENTIFIC NAME: *Lespedeza + repens,* Latin for creeping, for the trailing growth pattern.

COMMON NAME: Creeping, same as species name. Bush Clover, see *Lespedeza capitata.*

Lespedeza texana   Texas Bush Clover

SCIENTIFIC NAME: *Lespedeza + texana,* Latin for pertaining to Texas, for the range.

COMMON NAME: Texas, for the range. Bush Clover, see *Lespedeza capitata.*

Lespedeza violacea   Prairie Lespedeza

SCIENTIFIC NAME: *Lespedeza + violacea,* Latin for violet, for the flower color.

COMMON NAME: Prairie, for the habitat. Lespedeza, same as genus name.

Lespedeza virginica   Slender Lespedeza

SCIENTIFIC NAME: *Lespedeza + virginica,* Latin for of Virginia, for the area of the type specimen.

COMMON NAME: Slender, for the slender stems. Lespedeza, same as genus name.

Lesquerella angustifolia
Narrowleaf Bladderpod

SCIENTIFIC NAME: *Lesquerella,* for Carles Leo Lesquereux (1806-1889), an American paleobotanist + *angustifolia,* Latin for narrow-leaved.

COMMON NAME: Narrowleaf, descriptive. Bladderpod, for the ball-shaped fruits.

Lesquerella densiflora
Denseflower Bladderpod

SCIENTIFIC NAME: *Lesquerella + densiflora,* Latin for densely flowered.

COMMON NAME: Denseflower, descriptive. Bladderpod, see *Lesquerella angustfolia.*

Lesquerella fendleri   **Fendler Bladderpod**

SCIENTIFIC NAME: *Lesquerella + fendleri,* for August Fendler (1813-1883), an American botanist.

COMMON NAME: Fendler, same as species name. Bladderpod, see *Lesquerella angustfolia.*

Lesquerella gracilis   **Cloth-of-Gold**

SCIENTIFIC NAME: *Lesquerella + gracilis,* Latin for slender, graceful.

COMMON NAME: Cloth-of-Gold, the large number of yellow flowers over a large area give the appearance of a gold cloth spread on the ground.

Lesquerella grandiflora
Bigflower Bladderpod

SCIENTIFIC NAME: *Lesquerella + grandiflora,* Latin for large-flowered.

COMMON NAME: Bigflower, has relatively large flowers. Bladderpod, see *Lesquerella angustfolia.*

Lesquerella ovalifolia
Oval-Leaf Bladderpod

SCIENTIFIC NAME: *Lesquerella + ovalifolia,* Latin for oval-leaved, descriptive of the leaf shape.

COMMON NAME: Oval-leaf, descriptive. Bladderpod, see *Lesquerella angustfolia.*

Leucanthemum vulgare
Oxeye Daisy

SCIENTIFIC NAME: *Leucanthemum,* white flower, from Greek, λευκος, *leukos,* of color, white and ανθεον, *antheon,* flower +*vulgare,* Latin for common.

COMMON NAME: Oxeye, for the large size and the eyelike appearance. Daisy, from Anglo-Saxon, *daeges-eage,* day's eye, a daisy, for the eyelike appearance and the opening of the rays in the morning.

Leucophyllum frutescens   **Cenizo**

SCIENTIFIC NAME: *Leucophyllum,*

Latin for white leaves, for the silvery leaves + *frutescens,* Latin for becoming bushy.

COMMON NAME: Cenizo, Spanish for ashy, for the silvery leaves.

Liatris aspera Button Blazing Star

SCIENTIFIC NAME: *Liatris,* a coined New Latin name assigned by Johann Christian Daniel von Schreber (1739-1810), origin is unknown + *aspera,* Latin for rough.

COMMON NAME: Button Blazing Star, for the shape and color of the flowers.

Liatris elegans Gayfeather

SCIENTIFIC NAME: *Liatris + elegans,* Latin for elegant, for the flower spike.

COMMON NAME: Gayfeather, from a distance the inflorescence looks like a bright pink feather.

Liatris mucronata
Narrowleaf Gayfeather

SCIENTIFIC NAME: *Liatris + mucronata,* Latin for having a sharp point. Reference is to the abruptly pointed involucral bracts.

COMMON NAME: Narrowleaf, descriptive, the leaves are 5-10 cm long and 5 mm wide. Gayfeather, see *Liatris elegans.*

Liatris punctata Dotted Gayfeather

SCIENTIFIC NAME: *Liatris + punctata,* Latin for a small hole, a puncture, a dot, a spot. Reference is to the glandular punctuations on the leaves.

COMMON NAME: Dotted, same as species name. Gayfeather, see *Liatris elegans.*

Liatris pycnostachya
Thickspike Gayfeather

SCIENTIFIC NAME: *Liatris + pycnostachya,* thick spike, thick ear of corn, from Greek, πυκνος, *puknos,* thick and στακυς, *stakhus,* spike, ear of corn. Reference is to the thick inflorescences.

COMMON NAME: Thickspike, same as species name. Gayfeather, see *Liatris elegans.*

Liatris squarrosa Blazing Star

SCIENTIFIC NAME: *Liatris + squarrosa,* Latin for scurfy, scaly. Reference is to the spreading tips of the bracts.

COMMON NAME: Blazing Star, for the color and shape of the flowers.

Liatris squarrosa
Blazing Star

Linaria texana   Texas Toadflax

SCIENTIFIC NAME: *Linaria,* New Latin, from Latin, *linum,* the flax plant, a thread or cord. Reference is to the leaf shape of some species, which resemble those of the flax + *texana,* Latin for pertaining to Texas.

COMMON NAME: Texas, for the range. Toadflax, not a true flax, but the leaves look like those of flax. The toad part of the name is believed to be from mistaking the Latin, *bubonium,* a plant used medicinally for swelling of the groin (buboes), for *bufonis,* of or belonging to a toad, in an early translation of Dodoen's Latin description of this plant.

Linaria vulgaris   **Common Toadflax**

SCIENTIFIC NAME: *Linaria + vulgaris,* Latin for common.

COMMON NAME: Common, common in its range. Toadflax, see *Linaria texana.*

Lindernia dubia
Clasping False Pimpernel

SCIENTIFIC NAME: *Lindernia,* for Franz Balthasa von Lindern (1682-1755), a German physician and botanist + *dubia,* Latin for dubious, doubtful, it looks like a pimpernel but is not.

COMMON NAME: Clasping, for the leaf bases of the middle and upper leaves. False Pimpernel, for the appearance.

Lindheimera texana   **Texas Yellow Star**

SCIENTIFIC NAME: *Lindheimera,* for Ferdinand Jacob Lindheimer (1801-1879), a German botanist who made a large collection of plants in Texas + *texana,* Latin for pertaining to Texas.

COMMON NAME: Texas, for the range. Yellow Star, for the color and shape of the flowers.

Linum grandiflorum   **Flowering Flax**

SCIENTIFIC NAME: *Linum,* Latin for flax + *grandiflorum,* Latin for large-flowered.

COMMON NAME: Flowering, for the prominent flowers. Flax, from Old Teutonic, *flah,* to plait, for its use in making thread and cloth.

Linum hudsonioides   **Flax**

SCIENTIFIC NAME: *Linum + hudsonioides,* to resemble *Hudsonia,* from the genus *Hudsonia* and Greek, ειδος, *eidos,* resembling.

COMMON NAME: Flax, see *Linum grandiflorum.*

Linum lewisii   **Prairie Flax**

SCIENTIFIC NAME: *Linum + lewisii,* for Captain Meriwether Lewis (1774-1809), of the Lewis and Clark Expedition.

COMMON NAME: Prairie, for the habitat. Flax, see *Linum grandiflorum.*

Linum pratense   Meadow Flax

SCIENTIFIC NAME: *Linum + pratense,* Latin for belonging to meadows, for the habitat.

COMMON NAME: Meadow Flax, same as scientific name.

Linum rigidum   Stiffstem Flax

SCIENTIFIC NAME: *Linum + rigidum,* Latin for rigid. Reference is to the stiff stems.

COMMON NAME: Stiffstem, descriptive. Flax, see *Linum grandiflorum.*

Linum sulcatum   Yellow Prairie Flax

SCIENTIFIC NAME: *Linum + sulcatum,* Latin for a furrow. Reference is to the grooved stem.

COMMON NAME: Yellow, for the flower color. Prairie, for the habitat. Flax, see *Linum rigidum.*

Linum usitatissimum   Common Flax

SCIENTIFIC NAME: *Linum + usitatissimum,* Latin for most useful; this is the flax that is cultivated and has many uses.

COMMON NAME: Common, common in range. Flax, see *Linum grandiflorum.*

Lithospermum arvense   Corn Gromwell

SCIENTIFIC NAME: *Lithospermum,* stone seed, the Greek name for gromwell, from Greek, λιθος, *lithos,* stone and σπερμα, *sperma,* seed. Reference is to the hard mericarps + *arvensis,* Latin for belonging to a field, for the habitat.

COMMON NAME: Corn, for the large seeds. Gromwell, old form is *grommel,* or *gromel,* the "w" is a late intrusion. Thought to have come from Latin, *granummilii,* grain or millet, with reference to the seeds. Exact derivation is uncertain.

Lithospermum canescens   Hoary Puccoon

SCIENTIFIC NAME: *Lithospermum + canescens,* Latin for to become covered with white. Reference is to the soft, white hairs on the stems and leaves.

COMMON NAME: Hoary, same as species name. Puccoon, an American Indian name for this type of plant.

Lithospermum carolinense   Puccoon

SCIENTIFIC NAME: *Lithospermum + carolinense,* Latin for belonging to Carolina.

COMMON NAME: Puccoon, see *Lithospermum canescens.*

Lithospermum incisum　**Fringed Puccoon**

SCIENTIFIC NAME: *Lithospermum + incisum,* Latin for an incision or cut. Reference is to the fringed flower petals.

COMMON NAME: Fringed, same as species name. Puccoon, see *Lithospermum canescens.*

Lobelia appendiculata　**Pale Lobelia**

SCIENTIFIC NAME: *Lobelia,* for Mathias de L'Obel (1538-1616), a Flemish physician and botanist + *appendiculata,* Latin for having appendages. Reference is to the two upper petals on the flower, which were thought to stand up like the tufts of feathers (appendages) above the eyes of an owl.

COMMON NAME: Pale, for the white to light blue flowers. Lobelia, same as genus name.

Lobelia cardinalis　**Cardinal Flower**

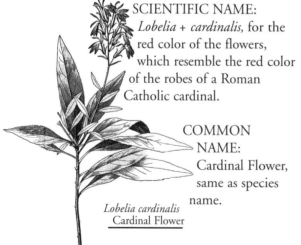

SCIENTIFIC NAME: *Lobelia + cardinalis,* for the red color of the flowers, which resemble the red color of the robes of a Roman Catholic cardinal.

COMMON NAME: Cardinal Flower, same as species name.

Lobelia cardinalis
Cardinal Flower

Lobelia siphilitica　**Blue Cardinal Flower**

SCIENTIFIC NAME: *Lobelia + siphilitica,* for its former use in treating syphilis.

COMMON NAME: Blue Cardinal Flower, a somewhat contradictory name, it came about from the blue flowers and the fact that this plant is in the same genus as the cardinal flower, see *Lobelia cardinalis.*

Lobelia spicata　**Palespike Lobelia**

SCIENTIFIC NAME: *Lobelia + spicata,* Latin for spiked. Reference is to the terminal inflorescences.

COMMON NAME: Palespike, for the pale blue flowers and the spikelike terminal inflorescences. Lobelia, same as genus name.

Lomatium foeniculaceum　**Wild Parsley**

SCIENTIFIC NAME: *Lomatium,* a small fringe, a diminutive of the Greek, λωμα, *lōma,* a fringe or border. Reference is to the winged fruit + *foeniculaceum,* Latin for resembling fennel.

COMMON NAME: Wild, for the habitat. Parsley, from Old French, *peresil,* their name for this type of plant.

Lomatium orientale　**Wild Parsley**

SCIENTIFIC NAME: *Lomatium + orientale,* Latin for eastern.

COMMON NAME: Wild Parsley, see *Lomatium foeniculaceum.*

Lonicera albiflora **White Honeysuckle**

SCIENTIFIC NAME: *Lonicera,* for Adam Lonitzer (Lonicer) (1528-1586), a German botanist + *albiflora,* Latin for white-flowered.

COMMON NAME: White, for the flower color. Honeysuckle, for the "honey-sucking" of bees that feed on the sweet nectar.

Lonicera fragrantissima
Sweet-Breath-of-Spring

SCIENTIFIC NAME: *Lonicera* + *fragrantissima,* Latin for the most fragrant.

COMMON NAME: Sweet-Breath-of-Spring, for the pleasant scent.

Lonicera sempervirens
Coral Honeysuckle

SCIENTIFIC NAME: *Lonicera* + *sempervirens,* Latin for always green, for the leaves.

COMMON NAME: Coral, for the coral-red flowers. Honeysuckle, see *Lonicera albiflora.*

Ludwigia alternifolia **Bushy Seedbox**

SCIENTIFIC NAME: *Ludwigia,* for Christian Gottlieb Ludwig (1709-1773), a German physician and botanist + *alternifolia,* Latin for alternate leaves. Reference is to the leaves being alternate and not opposite on the stem.

COMMON NAME: Bushy, for the appearance. Seedbox, for the square-shaped fruits, which contain many small seeds.

Ludwigia leptocarpa **Water Primrose**

SCIENTIFIC NAME: *Ludwigia* + *leptocarpa,* thin-fruited, from Greek, λεπτος, *lepto,* thin, slender and καρπος, *karpos,* fruit.

COMMON NAME: Water, for the habitat. Primrose, for the appearance of the flower.

Ludwigia linearis **Narrowleaf Seedbox**

SCIENTIFIC NAME: *Ludwigia* + *linearis,* Latin for having sides nearly parallel, narrow, for the leaves.

COMMON NAME: Narrowleaf, descriptive. Seedbox, see *Ludwiga alternifolia.*

Ludwigia peploides
Floating Evening Primrose

SCIENTIFIC NAME: *Ludwigia* + *peploides,* to look like *Peplis,* from the genus *Peplis* and Greek, ειδος, *eidos,* resembling.

COMMON NAME: Floating, the plant will float on water when aquatic. Evening Primrose, for the flower, which looks like that of an Evening Primrose.

Lupinus concinnus Annual Lupine

SCIENTIFIC NAME: *Lupinus,* the Latin name for this plant, root word means of or belonging to a wolf. Reference is to the old belief that this plant took the good parts out of the soil + *concinnus,* Latin for neat, elegant.

COMMON NAME: Annual, completes its life cycle in one year. Lupine, same as genus name.

Lupinus havardii Big Bend Bluebonnet

SCIENTIFIC NAME: *Lupinus +
havardii,* for Valery Harvard (1846-1927), an American physician and botanist. The name was misspelled when assigned. The Principle of Priority allows the misspelling to stand.

COMMON NAME: Big Bend, for the range in the Big Bend area of Texas. Bluebonnet, for the color and shape of the flowers.

Lupinus plattensis Dune Bluebonnet

SCIENTIFIC NAME: *Lupinus +
plattensis,* Latin for belonging to the platte, for the Platte River, for the area of the type specimen.

COMMON NAME: Dune, for the habitat on sand dunes. Bluebonnet, see *Lupinus havardii.*

Lupinus subcarnosus
Sandyland Bluebonnet

SCIENTIFIC NAME: *Lupinus +
subcarnosus,* Latin for somewhat fleshy. Reference is to the inflated side petals of the young blooms.

COMMON NAME: Sandyland, for the habitat. Bluebonnet, see *Lupinus havardii.*

Lupinus texensis Texas Bluebonnet

SCIENTIFIC NAME: *Lupinus + texensis,* Latin for belonging to Texas.

COMMON NAME: Texas, for the habitat. Bluebonnet, see *Lupinus havardii.*

Lycopus americanus
American Bugleweed

SCIENTIFIC NAME: *Lycopus,* wolf's foot, from Greek, λυκος, *lukos,* wolf and πους, *pous,* foot, for the shape of the rhizomes + *americanus,* Latin for pertaining to America.

COMMON NAME: American, for the range. Bugleweed, origin unknown, possibly for the shape of the flowers.

Lycopus virginicus Virginia Bugleweed

SCIENTIFIC NAME: *Lycopus + virgincus,*

Latin for of Virginia, for the area of the type specimen.

COMMON NAME: Virginia, for the area of the type specimen. Bugleweed, see *Lycopus americanus.*

Lygodesmia juncea Rush Skeletonplant

SCIENTIFIC NAME: *Lygodesmia,* like a willow bond, from Greek, λυγωδης, *lugōdēs,* like a willow and δεσμος, *desmos,* a band, a bond, anything used for tying. Reference is to the thin stems that resemble thin willow branches used to tie bundles + *juncea,* from *iuncus,* Latin for a rush, for the appearance of the stems.

COMMON NAME: Rush, same as species name. Skeletonplant, for the appearance of the branching leafless stems.

Lygodesmia texana Skeletonplant

SCIENTIFIC NAME: *Lygodesmia* + *texana,* Latin for pertaining to Texas.

COMMON NAME: Skeletonplant, see *Lygodesmia juncea.*

Lythrum californicum
California Loosestrife

SCIENTIFIC NAME: *Lythrum,* from Greek, λυθρον, *luthron,* defilement by blood, of blood in general. Reference is to the color of the flowers + *californicum,* Latin for of California, for the area of the type specimen.

COMMON NAME: California, for the area of the type specimen. Loosestrife, from Greek, λυσιμαχια, *lusimakhia,* their name for this plant.

Lythrum lanceolatum
Lanceleaf Loosestrife

SCIENTIFIC NAME: *Lythrum* + *lanceolatum,* Latin for spearlike. Reference is to the lance-shaped leaves.

COMMON NAME: Lanceleaf, same as species name. Loosestrife, see *Lythrum californicum.*

Machaeranthera gracilis
Slender Goldenweed

SCIENTIFIC NAME: *Machaeranthera,* dagger anther, from Greek, μαχαιρα, *makhaira,* a dirk, a dagger, and *anther,* a New Latin formation from Greek, ανθρος, *anthros,* anther + *gracilis,* Latin for slender, graceful, for the thin stems.

COMMON NAME: Slender, for the stems. Goldenweed, for the flower color.

Machaeranthera pinnatifida
Cutleaf Ironplant

SCIENTIFIC NAME: *Machaeranthera* + *pinnatifida,* Latin for pinnately cut, like a feather, for the deeply cut leaves.

COMMON NAME: Cutleaf, for the deeply cut leaves. Ironplant, for the hard stems.

Machaeranthera tanacetifolia
Tansy Aster

SCIENTIFIC NAME: *Machaeranthera* + *tanacetifolia,* Latin for having leaves like *Tanacetum,* a tansy, from the genus *Tanacetum* and Latin, *folia,* leaves.

COMMON NAME: Tansy, for the leaves, which look like those of the true tansy. Aster, Latin for a star, for the shape of the inflorescence.

Macrosiphonia lanuginosa
Longtube Trumpet Flower

SCIENTIFIC NAME: *Macrosiphonia,* long tube, from Greek, μακρος, *makro,* long and σιφονια, *siphonia,* tube, for the trumpet-shaped flowers + *lanuginosa,* Latin for woolly or downy.

COMMON NAME: Longtube Trumpet Flower, for the trumpet-shaped flowers with a long tubular base.

Malva neglecta   **Common Mallow**

SCIENTIFIC NAME: *Malva,* Latin for the mallow + *neglecta,* Latin for not cared for, neglected.

COMMON NAME: Common, common in its range. Mallow, from the genus name.

Malva parviflora   **Little Mallow**

SCIENTIFIC NAME: *Malva* + *parviflora,* Latin for small-flowered.

COMMON NAME: Little, for the flower size. Mallow, same as genus name.

Malva rotundifolia   **Roundleaf Mallow**

SCIENTIFIC NAME: *Malva* + *rotundifolia,* Latin for having round leaves.

COMMON NAME: Roundleaf Mallow, same as scientific name.

Malvastrum aurantiacum   **False Mallow**

SCIENTIFIC NAME: *Malvastrum,* Latin for little *Malva,* for the appearance + *aurantiacum,* Latin for orange-red, for the flower color.

COMMON NAME: False Mallow, for the resemblance to the genus *Malva.*

Malvaviscus arboreus   **Turk's Cap**

SCIENTIFIC NAME: *Malvaviscus,* either a combination of the genus names *Malva* and *Hibiscus* or, more probably from Latin, *malva,* mallow and *viscus,* glue, for the sticky pulp around the seeds, either derivation is unclear + *arboreus,* Latin for tree-like.

COMMON NAME: Turk's Cap, the flower was thought to resemble a Turkish turban.

Malvella leprosa   **Malvella**

SCIENTIFIC NAME: *Malvella,* little *malva,* a diminutive of the Latin, *malva,* for the appearance and size + *leprosa,* scales, from Greek, λεπος, λεπις, *lepos, lepis,* a scale. Reference is to the small scales on the stems and leaves.

COMMON NAME: Malvella, same as genus name.

Malvella sagittifolia Arrowleaf Malvella

SCIENTIFIC NAME: *Malvella + sagittifolia,* Latin for having arrowhead-shaped leaves.

COMMON NAME: Arrowleaf, for the arrowhead-shaped leaves. Malvella, same as genus name.

Marshallia caespitosa
White Barbara's Buttons

SCIENTIFIC NAME: *Marshallia,* for Moses Marshall (1758-1813), an American botanist + *caespitosa,* Latin for growing in clumps.

COMMON NAME: White, for the flower color. Barbara's Buttons, the flowers resemble a round lacy button used on women's dresses.

Maurandya antirrhiniflora
Snapdragon Vine

SCIENTIFIC NAME: *Maurandya,* for Catalina Pancratia Maurandy (fl. late eighteenth century), a Spanish botanist + *antirrhiniflora,* to have flowers like the genus *Antirrhinum,* from the genus *Antirrhinum* (snapdragon) and *flora,* Latin for flower.

COMMON NAME: Snapdragon, the flowers resemble those of the Snapdragon. Vine, for the climbing behavior.

Melampodium leucanthum
Blackfoot Daisy

SCIENTIFIC NAME: *Melampodium,* black foot, from Greek, μελας, *melas,* black and πους, *pous,* foot. Reference is to the small bract, shaped like a foot, at the base of each ray flower. It turns black at maturity + *leucanthum,* white flower, from Greek, λευκος, *leukos,* of color, white and ανθος, *anthos,* flower, blossom.

COMMON NAME: Blackfoot, same as genus name. Daisy, from Anglo-Saxon, *daeges-eage,* day's eye, daisy, for the eyelike appearance and the rays that open in the morning.

Melilotus alba White Sweet Clover

SCIENTIFIC NAME: *Melilotus,* honey lotus, from Greek, μελι, *meli,* honey, and Latin for lotus + *alba,* Latin for white, for the flower color.

COMMON NAME: White, for the flower color. Sweet, for the fragrance. Clover, from Old English, *clafre,* in turn from Old Teutonic, *klaibron,* their name for this type of plant.

Melilotus indicus   Sour Clover

SCIENTIFIC NAME: *Melilotus + indicus,* Latin for of India, this name was attached to many plants that came in from India, the far east, and even the East Indies.

COMMON NAME: Sour, for the taste. Clover, see *Melilotus alba.*

Melilotus officinalis   Yellow Sweet Clover

SCIENTIFIC NAME: *Melilotus + officinalis,* Latin for a place where something is made, sold in shops. Used here to mean sold in apothecary shops, having medicinal value.

COMMON NAME: Yellow, for the flower color. Sweet Clover, see *Melilotus alba.*

Menodora heterophylla   Redbud

SCIENTIFIC NAME: *Menodora,* moon gift, from Greek, μηνη, *mēnē,* moon and δορον, *doron,* a gift + *heterophylla,* different leaves, from Greek, ετρος, *(h)etros* one or the other of two, different and φυλλον, *phullon,* leaf. The leaves may be entire or lobed.

COMMON NAME: Redbud, for the red buds, which forms before the yellow bloom.

Menodora longiflora   Showy Menodora

SCIENTIFIC NAME: *Menodora +*

longiflora, Latin for long-flowered.

COMMON NAME: Showy, for the flowers. Menodora, same as genus name.

Mentzelia decapetala
Tenpetal Mentzelia

SCIENTIFIC NAME: *Mentzelia,* for Christian Mentzel (1622-1701), a German physician and botanist + *decapetala,* ten petals, from Greek, δεκα, *deka,* ten and πεταλον, *petalon,* a leaf, a petal. Reference is to the ten flower petals.

COMMON NAME: Tenpetal Mentzelia, same as scientific name.

Mentzelia multiflora   Blazing Star

SCIENTIFIC NAME: *Mentzelia + multiflora,* Latin for many flowers.

COMMON NAME: Blazing Star, for the bright yellow, star-shaped flower.

Mentzelia nuda   Sand Lily

SCIENTIFIC NAME: *Mentzelia + nuda,* Latin for naked or bare. Reference is to the absence of bracts.

COMMON NAME: Sand, for the habitat. Lily, for the appearance.

Mentzelia oligosperma Stickleaf

SCIENTIFIC NAME: *Mentzelia +
oligosperma,* few seeds, from Greek,
ολιγος, *oligos,* few and σπερμα, *sperma,*
seed.

COMMON NAME: Stickleaf, for the
short barbs on the leaves, common to this
family of plants. The leaves are easily
detached and stick to clothing or animals.

Mentzelia reverchonii Prairie Stickleaf

SCIENTIFIC NAME: *Mentzelia +
reverchonii,* for Julien Reverchon (1834-
1905), a French botanist.

COMMON NAME: Prairie, for the
habitat. Stickleaf, see *Mentzelia
oligosperma.*

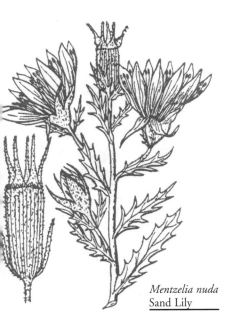

Mentzelia nuda
Sand Lily

Microseris cuspidata False Dandelion

SCIENTIFIC NAME: *Microseris,* little
chicory, from Greek, μικρος, *mikros,*
small, little and σερις, *seris,* chicory.
Reference is to the tuberous roots + *cuspidata,* Latin for having a sharp point, a
lance, a spear, for the lance-shaped leaves.

COMMON NAME: False Dandelion,
for the resemblance to the true dandelion,
Taraxacum officinale.

Mikania scandens Climbing Hempweed

SCIENTIFIC NAME: *Mikania,* for
Joseph Gottfried Mikan (1743-1814), a
Bohemian botanist + *scandens,* Latin for
climbing, for the growth pattern.

COMMON NAME: Climbing, for the
growth pattern. Hempweed, for the
appearance, the allusion is to a rope.

Mimosa borealis Fragrant Mimosa

SCIENTIFIC NAME: *Mimosa,* from
Latin, *mimus,* an actor in mimes, a mimic.
Reference is to the collapse of the sensitive
leaves when they are touched + *borealis,*
Latin for northern.

COMMON NAME: Fragrant, for the
scent. Mimosa, same as genus name.

Mimosa hystricina Bristly Sensitive Briar

SCIENTIFIC NAME: *Mimosa + hystricina,*
Latin for bristly, to be like a porcupine,
for the small thorns.

COMMON NAME: Bristly, for the small thorns. Sensitive, the leaves fold up when stroked. Briar, for the small thorns.

Mimosa nuttallii **Catclaw Sensitive Briar**

SCIENTIFIC NAME: *Mimosa + nuttallii,* for Thomas Nuttall (1786-1859), an English botanist, explorer, printer, ornithologist, and plant collector. He was a fellow of the Linnaean Society.

COMMON NAME: Catclaw, for the small thorns. Sensitive Briar, see *Mimosa hystricina.*

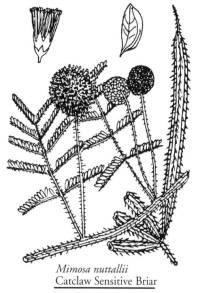

Mimosa nuttallii
Catclaw Sensitive Briar

Mimosa strigillosa **Powderpuff**

SCIENTIFIC NAME: *Mimosa + strigillosa,* Latin for having short bristles. Reference is to the bristles on the stems.

COMMON NAME: Powderpuff, for the appearance of the infloresence.

Mimulus alatus
Sharpwing Monkey Flower

SCIENTIFIC NAME: *Mimulus,* Latin for a little mime. Reference is to the shape of the flowers, thought to resemble the face of a monkey + *alatus,* Latin for winged, for the shape of the leaves.

COMMON NAME: Sharpwing Monkey Flower, same as scientific name.

Mimulus glabratus
Roundleaf Monkey Flower

SCIENTIFIC NAME: *Mimulus + glabratus,* Latin for lacking hair, smooth. Reference is to the lack of hairs on the stems and leaves.

COMMON NAME: Roundleaf, descriptive. Monkey Flower, see *Mimulus alatus.*

Mimulus ringens
Allegheny Monkey Flower

SCIENTIFIC NAME: *Mimulus + ringens,* Latin for gaping, for the open flower.

COMMON NAME: Allegheny, for the range of the type specimen. Monkey Flower, see *Mimulus alatus.*

Minuartia drummondii
Drummond's Sandwort

SCIENTIFIC NAME: *Minuartia,* for Juan Minuart (1693-1768), a Spanish botanist and apothecary + *drummondii,* for Thomas Drummond (1780-1835), a Scottish plant collector.

COMMON NAME: Drummond's, same as species name. Sand, for the habitat. Wort, from Anglo-Saxon, *wyrt,* a plant used in food or medicine.

Minuartia michauxii Rock Sandwort

SCIENTIFIC NAME: *Minuartia + michauxii,* for Andre Michaux (1746-1803), a French botanist.

COMMON NAME: Rock, for the common habitat among rocks. Sandwort, see *Minuartia drummondii.*

Mirabilis albida White Four O'Clock

SCIENTIFIC NAME: *Mirabilis,* Latin for marvelous. Reference is to the flowers + *albida,* Latin for white or whitish, for the glaucous or whitened underside of the leaves.

COMMON NAME: White, same as species name. Four O'Clock, the flowers open in the late afternoon.

Mirabilis gigantea Giant Four O'Clock

SCIENTIFIC NAME: *Mirabilis + gigantea,* gigantic, from Greek, γιγας, *gigas,* giant. Reference is to the size of the overall plant, may grow to two meters in height.

COMMON NAME: Giant, for the size. Four O'Clock, see *Mirabilis albida.*

Mirabilis linearis
Narrowleaf Four O'Clock

SCIENTIFIC NAME: *Mirabilis + linearis,* Latin for narrow, with sides nearly parallel. Reference is to the thin leaves.

COMMON NAME: Narrowleaf, descriptive. Four O'Clock, see *Mirabilis albida.*

Mirabilis nyctaginea
Wild Four O'Clock

SCIENTIFIC NAME: *Mirabilis + nyctaginea,* night plant, from Greek, νυξ, νυκτος, *nux, nuktos,* night and Latin -*agin,* used for some plant names. The original intent was to mean night blooming. Reference is to the flower opening in late afternoon.

COMMON NAME: Wild, occurs naturally in nature. Four O'Clock, see *Mirabilis albida.*

Mollugo verticillata Carpetweed

SCIENTIFIC NAME: *Mollugo,* Latin, used by Pliny for the lappago plant. The root is Latin, *mollis,* soft, for the soft leaves of the lappago + *verticillata,* Latin for whirlpool, whorl. Reference is to the whorls of leaves surrounding the stem.

COMMON NAME: Carpetweed, for the low, spreading growth pattern that carpets the ground.

Monarda citriodora Lemon Mint

SCIENTIFIC NAME: *Monarda,* for Nicolas Bautista Mondardes (1493-1588), a Spanish physician and botanist + *citriodora,* Latin for to smell like a lemon, from, *citrus,* the citron (citrus) tree and *odoro,* to make fragrant, perfume.

COMMON NAME: Lemon, for the fragrance of the entire plant. Mint, from Latin, *menta,* mint.

Monarda fistulosa Wild Bergamont

SCIENTIFIC NAME: *Monarda* + *fistulosa,* Latin for full of holes, pipe-shaped, tubular. Reference is to the tubular flowers.

COMMON NAME: Wild, occurs naturally in nature. Bergamont, for the fragrance, which is similar to essence of bergamont.

Monarda lindheimeri
Lindheimer Beebalm

SCIENTIFIC NAME: *Monarda* + *lindheimeri,* for Ferdinand Jacob Lindheimer (1801-1879), a German political exile who collected plants in Texas.

COMMON NAME: Lindheimer, same as species name. Beebalm, for the aromatic fragrance that attracts bees.

Monarda pectinata Spotted Beebalm

SCIENTIFIC NAME: *Monarda* + *pectinata,* Latin for like a comb.

COMMON NAME: Spotted, for the gland dots on the leaves. Beebalm, see *Monarda lindheimeri.*

Monarda punctata Dotted Beebalm

SCIENTIFIC NAME: *Monarda* + *punctata,* Latin for a small hole, a dot. Reference is to the gland dots on the leaves.

COMMON NAME: Dotted, for the gland dots on the leaves. Beebalm, see *Monarda lindheimeri.*

Nama hispidum Sand Bell

SCIENTIFIC NAME: *Nama,* from Greek, ναμα, *nama,* anything flowing, running water. Many of this genus grow by streams + *hispidum,* Latin for bristly, hairy, for the rough hairs on the stems.

COMMON NAME: Sand Bell, for the habitat and the shape of the flower.

Nama jamaicense Fiddleleaf

SCIENTIFIC NAME: *Nama* + *jamaicense,* Latin for belonging to Jamaica, for the area of the type specimen.

COMMON NAME: Fiddleleaf, for the leaf shape.

Nemastylis geminiflora **Prairie Iris**

SCIENTIFIC NAME: *Nemastylis,* thread column, from Greek, νημα, *nēma,* thread and στυλος, *stulos,* a pillar, column. Reference is to the slender style + *geminiflora,* twin-flowered, from Latin, *geminus,* twins and *flora,* flower.

COMMON NAME: Prairie, for the habitat. Iris, from Greek, Ιρις, *Iris,* messenger among the gods, goddess of the rainbow. Reference is to the beautiful hues of the flowers.

Nemophila phacelioides **Baby Blue Eyes**

SCIENTIFIC NAME: *Nemophila,* glade-loving, from Greek, νεμος, *nemos,* a glade and φιλο, *philo,* loving. Reference is to the habitat + *phacelioides,* like a *Phacelia,* from the genus *Phacelia* and Greek, ειδος, *eidos,* resembling.

COMMON NAME   Baby Blue Eyes, for the flower color.

Neolloydia conoidea **Cone Cactus**

SCIENTIFIC NAME: *Neolloydia,* for Francis Ernest Lloyd (1868-1947), an American plant physiologist and professor of botany at Montreal. The prefix neo-was used because the genus name *Lloydia* was already in use + *conoidea,* Latin for conelike, for the overall shape.

COMMON NAME: Cone, for the over-all shape. Cactus, from Greek, κακτος, *kaktos,* a prickly plant.

Neptunia lutea **Yellow Puff**

SCIENTIFIC NAME: *Neptunia,* for Neptune, the Roman god of water. Many plants of the genus grow around water + *lutea,* Latin for yellow, especially bright reddish or orange-yellow. Reference is to the flower color.

COMMON NAME: Yellow, for the flower color. Puff, the inflorescence shape resembles a powder puff.

Nerisyrenia camporum
Velvety Nerisyrenia

SCIENTIFIC NAME: *Nerisyrenia,* fresh plant, from Greek, νηρος, *nēros,* fresh and συρεον, *sureon,* a name used by Pliny for an unidentified plant + *camporum,* to bend, from Greek, καμπη, *kampē,* to bend, turn, wind.

COMMON NAME: Velvety, for the soft hairs on the leaves. Nerisyrenia, same as genus name.

Nicotiana glauca **Tobacco Tree**

SCIENTIFIC NAME: *Nicotiana,* Latin for pertaining to Nicot, for Jean Nicot (1530-1600), a French diplomat who introduced tobacco into France + *glauca,* Latin for gray-green, for the leaf color.

COMMON NAME: Tobacco Tree, the leaves were smoked for various rituals by the Cahuilla Indians.

Nicotiana obtusifolia **Desert Tobacco**

SCIENTIFIC NAME: *Nicotiana* + *obtusifolia,* Latin for blunt-leaved.

COMMON NAME: Desert, for the habitat. Tobacco, the Carib Indian (Haiti) name for this plant.

Nicotiana repanda **Fiddleleaf Tobacco**

SCIENTIFIC NAME: *Nicotiana* + *repanda,* Latin for bent backward, turned up, undulate. Reference is to the wavy leaf margins.

COMMON NAME: Fiddleleaf, descriptive of the shape of the leaves. Tobacco, see *Nicotiana obtusifolia.*

Nothoscordum bivalve **False Garlic**

SCIENTIFIC NAME: *Nothoscordum,* false garlic, from Greek, νοθος, *nothos,* false and σκορδον, *skordon,* garlic. This plant looks like garlic but does not smell or taste like it + *bivalve,* Latin for two folding doors. Reference is to the leaves, which have a deep central groove.

COMMON NAME: False Garlic, same as genus name.

Nuphar lutea **Yellow Cow Lily**

SCIENTIFIC NAME: *Nuphar,* from *ninufar,* the Persian name for this type of plant + *lutea,* Latin for yellow, for the flower color.

COMMON NAME: Yellow, for the flower color. Cow Lily, for the habitat in cow ponds and the appearance.

Nymphaea elegans **Blue Water Lily**

SCIENTIFIC NAME: *Nymphaea,* from Greek, νυμφαια, *numphaia,* a water nymph, for the habitat in water + *elegans,* Latin for elegant.

COMMON NAME: Blue Water Lily, for the flower color and the habitat.

Nymphaea mexicana **Banana Water Lily**

SCIENTIFIC NAME: *Nymphaea* + *mexicana,* Latin for pertaining to Mexico.

COMMON NAME: Banana, for the yellow flower. Water Lily, for the habitat and the appearance.

Nymphaea odorata **Fragrant Water Lily**

SCIENTIFIC NAME: *Nymphaea* + *odorata,* Latin for having a fragrance.

COMMON NAME: Fragrant, for the scent. Water Lily, see *Nymphaea mexicana.*

Oenothera albicaulis
Pale Evening Primrose

SCIENTIFIC NAME: *Oenothera,* named by Carolus Linnaeus (1707-1778) to mean a plant with roots that smell like wine. From Greek, οινοθηρας, *oinothēras,* from οινος, *oinos,* wine and θεραν, *theran,* hunting, seeker, therefore the literal translation is "wine seeker" + *albicaulis,* Latin for white stem, from *albus,* white and *caulis,* stalk, stem.

COMMON NAME: Pale, for the pale flower color. Evening, the flower opens in the evening. Primrose, first rose, from Medieval Latin, *prima,* first and *rosa,* rose.

Oenothera biennis
Common Evening Primrose

SCIENTIFIC NAME: *Oenothera + biennis,* Latin for biennial, this plant lives two years and only flowers in the second year.

COMMON NAME: Common, abundant in its range. Evening Primrose, see *Oenothera albicaulis.*

Oenothera coryi
Cory's Evening Primrose

SCIENTIFIC NAME: *Oenothera + coryi,* for Victor Louis Cory (1880-1964), an American botanist.

COMMON NAME: Cory's, same as species name. Evening Primrose, see *Oenothera albicaulis.*

Oenothera drummondii
Beach Evening Primrose

SCIENTIFIC NAME: *Oenothera + drummondii,* for Thomas Drummond (c. 1790-1831), a British plant collector who worked in North America.

COMMON NAME: Beach, for the habitat. Evening Primrose, see *Oenothera albicaulis.*

Oenothera engelmannii
Engelmann Evening Primrose

SCIENTIFIC NAME: *Oenothera + engelmannii,* for George Engelmann (1809-1884), a German-born physician and botanist who worked in North America.

COMMON NAME: Engelmann, same as species name. Evening Primrose, see *Oenothera albicaulis.*

Oenothera jamesii
Trumpet Evening Primrose

SCIENTIFIC NAME: *Oenothera + jamesii,* for Edwin James (1797-1861), an American surgeon and plant collector.

COMMON NAME: Trumpet, for the flower shape. Evening Primrose, see *Oenothera albicaulis.*

Oenothera laciniata
Cutleaf Evening Primrose

SCIENTIFIC NAME: *Oenothera + laciniata,* Latin for torn, for the deeply lobed leaves.

COMMON NAME: Cutleaf, for the deeply lobed leaves. Evening Primrose, see *Oenothera albicaulis.*

Oenothera latifolia
Pale Evening Primrose

SCIENTIFIC NAME: *Oenothera +
latifolia,* Latin for broad leaves.

COMMON NAME: Pale Evening
Primrose, see *Oenothera albicaulis.*

Oenothera macrocarpa
Missouri Primrose

SCIENTIFIC NAME: *Oenothera +
macrocarpa,* large fruit, from Greek,
μακρος, *macros,* long, large and καρπος,
karpos, fruit.

COMMON NAME: Missouri, for the
area of the type specimen. Primrose, see
Oenothera albicaulis

Oenothera rhombipetala
Fourpoint Evening Primrose

SCIENTIFIC NAME: *Oenothera +
rhombipetala,* Latin for having rhomboid
or diamond-shaped petals.

COMMON NAME: Fourpoint, for the
four diamond-shaped petals of the flower.
Evening Primrose, see *Oenothera
albicaulis.*

Oenothera speciosa
Showy Evening Primrose

SCIENTIFIC NAME: *Oenothera +
speciosa,* Latin for attractive in appearance,
showy, for the flower.

COMMON NAME: Showy, for the
flower. Evening Primrose, see *Oenothera
albicaulis.*

Oenothera triloba
Stemless Evening Primrose

SCIENTIFIC NAME: *Oenothera + triloba,* Latin for having three lobes.
Reference is to the lobed leaves.

COMMON NAME: Stemless, descriptive. Evening Primrose, see *Oenothera
albicaulis.*

Oenothera triloba
Stemless Evening Primrose

Onosmodium helleri   **Heller's Marbleseed**

SCIENTIFIC NAME: *Onosmodium,*
Latin for to be like the genus *Onosma +
helleri,* for Amos Arthur Heller (1867-
1844), the American botanist who discovered the plant.

COMMON NAME: Heller's, same as
species name. Marbleseed, for the appearance of the mericarps.

Opuntia engelmannii
Engelmann's Prickly Pear

SCIENTIFIC NAME: *Opuntia,* from the ancient Greek town Opus or Opuntis (town of figs), it got transferred to this cactus for the figlike fruit + *engelmannii,* for Georg Engelmann (1809-1884), a German physician and botanist.

COMMON NAME: Engelmann's, same as species name. Prickly Pear, for the spines on the pear-shaped fruit.

Opuntia fragilis **Little Prickly Pear**

SCIENTIFIC NAME: *Opuntia + fragilis,* Latin for liable to break. Reference is to the stem segments easily breaking off.

COMMON NAME: Little, for the relative size. Prickly Pear, see *Opuntia engelmannii.*

Opuntia grahamii
Graham's Prickly Pear

SCIENTIFIC NAME: *Opuntia + grahamii,* for Robert Graham (1786-1845), a Scottish physician and botanist.

COMMON NAME: Graham, same as species name. Prickly Pear, see *Opuntia engelmannii.*

Opuntia humifusa **Low Prickly Pear**

SCIENTIFIC NAME: *Opuntia + humifusa,* Latin for sprawling on the ground, for the low spreading growth pattern.

COMMON NAME: Low, for the low growth pattern. Prickly Pear, see *Opuntia fragilis.*

Optunia imbricata **Tree Cholla**

SCIENTIFIC NAME: *Opuntia,* ancient Greek town Opus, which originally meant "town of figs." see *Opuntia engelmannii,* + *imbricata,* Latin for shaped like an imbrex, a semi-cylindrical tile placed over the joints between roof tiles. Reference is to the pattern on the stems.

COMMON NAME: Tree, for the appearance. Cholla, the Mexican Spanish name for this type of plant.

Opuntia leptocaulis **Christmas Cactus**

SCIENTIFIC NAME: *Opuntia + leptocaulis,* thin stemmed, from Greek, λεπτος, *leptos,* thin and καυλος, *kaulis,* stem.

COMMON NAME: Christmas, for the red fruits that look like Christmas tree balls. Cactus, from Greek, κακτος, *kaktos,* a prickly plant.

Opuntia macrorhiza **Plains Prickly Pear**

SCIENTIFIC NAME: *Opuntia + macrorhiza,* large roots, from Greek, μακρος, *makros,* long, large and ριζα, *riza,* root.

COMMON NAME: Plains, for the habitat. Prickly Pear, see *Opuntia engelmannii.*

Opuntia rufida   **Blind Prickly Pear**

SCIENTIFIC NAME: *Opuntia + rufida,* Latin for somewhat red, for the multiple reddish glochids.

COMMON NAME: Blind, the glochids are very loose on this cactus and will blow away in a strong wind. They have lodged in the eyes of cattle and blinded them, hence the common name. Prickly Pear, see *Opuntia engelmannii.*

Oxalis articulata
Windowbox Wood Sorrel

SCIENTIFIC NAME: *Oxalis,* from Greek, οξαλις, *oxalis,* the sorrel, sour wine. Reference is to the sour taste + *articulata,* Latin for jointed.

COMMON NAME: Windowbox, commonly cultivated in windowboxes. Wood, for the habitat. Sorrel, used for plants with a sour taste, from German, *sur,* sour.

Oxalis corniculata
Creeping Ladies Sorrel

SCIENTIFIC NAME: *Oxalis +* *corniculata,* Latin for having small horns. Reference is to the seed capsules.

COMMON NAME: Creeping, for the growth pattern. Ladies, a pet name. Sorrel, see *Oxalis articulata.*

Oxalis drummondii
Drummond's Oxalis

SCIENTIFIC NAME: *Oxalis + drummondii,* for Thomas Drummond (1780-1835), a British plant collector.

COMMON NAME: Drummond's Oxalis, same as scientific name.

Oxalis stricta   **Yellow Wood Sorrel**

SCIENTIFIC NAME: *Oxalis + stricta,* Latin for closely packed, dense, for the flower clusters.

COMMON NAME: Yellow, for the flower color. Wood Sorrel, see *Oxalis articulata.*

Oxalis stricta
Yellow Wood Sorrel

Oxalis violacea   Violet Wood Sorrel

SCIENTIFIC NAME: *Oxalis* + *violacea,* Latin for violet, for the flower color.

COMMON NAME: Violet, for the flower color. Wood Sorrel, see *Oxalis articulata.*

Oxytropis lambertii   Locoweed

SCIENTIFIC NAME: *Oxytropis,* sharp keel, from Greek, οξυς, *oxus,* sharp, brought to a point and τροπις, *tropis,* a keel. Reference is to the flower shape + *lambertii,* for Aylmer Bourke Lambert (1761-1842), an English botanist.

COMMON NAME: Locoweed, for the neurologic effects of this plant's toxin; it accumulates selenium from the soil.

Oxytropis sericea   White Locoweed

SCIENTIFIC NAME: *Oxytropis* + *sericea,* Latin for silky.

COMMON NAME: White, for the flower color. Locoweed, see *Oxytropis lambertii.*

Packera glabella   Yellowtop

SCIENTIFIC NAME: *Packera,* for John G. Packer (1929-) + *glabella,* Latin for hairless, smooth.

COMMON NAME: Yellowtop, for the yellow flowers, which are produced at the top of the plant.

Packera plattensis   Prairie Groundsel

SCIENTIFIC NAME: *Packera* + *platensis,* Latin for belonging to the Platte, for the Platte River, the area of the type specimen.

COMMON NAME: Prairie, for the habitat. Groundsel, etymology is uncertain, thought to come from an Old English word for pus absorber. This plant was used as a wound poultice.

Palafoxia callosa   Small Palafoxia

SCIENTIFIC NAME: *Palafoxia,* for an unspecified Spaniard, there are two possibilites: (1) General Jose de Rebolledo Palafox y Melei (or Melzi) (c. 1776-1847) or (2) Prelate Jaun de Palafox y Mendoza (1600-1659) + *callosa,* Latin for hardskinned, tough. Reference is to the leaves, which are rough to the touch.

COMMON NAME: Small, for the relative size. Palafoxia, same as genus name.

Palafoxia hookeriana   Hooker Palafoxia

SCIENTIFIC NAME: *Palafoxia* + *hookeriana,* Latin for pertaining to Hooker, for William Jackson Hooker (1785-1865), an English botanist and director of the Royal Botanic Gardens at Kew.

COMMON NAME: Hooker Palafoxia, same as scientific name.

Palafoxia rosea   Rose Palafoxia

SCIENTIFIC NAME: *Palafoxia + rosea,* Latin for rose, for the flower color.

COMMON NAME: Rose Palafoxia, same as scientific name.

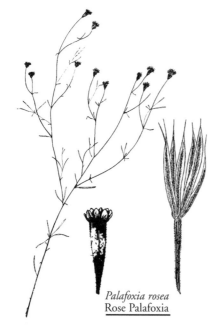

Palafoxia rosea
Rose Palafoxia

Palafoxia sphacelata   Sand Palafoxia

SCIENTIFIC NAME: *Palafoxia + sphacelata,* from Greek, σφακηλος, *sphakēlos,* gangrene, rot, withered. Reference is to the overall withered appearance of this plant.

COMMON NAME: Sand, for the habitat. Palafoxia, same as genus name.

Parkinsonia aculeata   Paloverde

SCIENTIFIC NAME: *Parkinsonia,* for John Parkinson (1567-1650), a London

apothecary + *aculeata,* Latin for prickly, for the thorns on the stems.

COMMON NAME: Paloverde, Mexican Spanish for green tree, for the green bark.

Paronychia drummondii
Drummond's Nailwort

SCIENTIFIC NAME: *Paronychia,* a whitlow, from Greek, παρα, *para,* beside and ονυξ, *onukhos,* a claw or nail. A whitlow is a soft tissue infection on the end of the finger or around the nail; this plant was used in the past to treat this problem + *drummondii,* for Thomas Drummond (1780-1835), a British plant collector.

COMMON NAME: Drummond's, same as species name. Nailwort, nail, for its use in treating whitlow and wort, from Old English, *wyrt,* root, a plant used for food or medicine.

Paronychia fastigata
Clusterstem Nailwort

SCIENTIFIC NAME: *Paronychia + fastigata,* Latin for crowded with erect branches.

COMMON NAME: Clusterstem, same as species name. Nailwort, see *Paronychia drummondii.*

Paronychia jamesii   James' Nailwort

SCIENTIFIC NAME: *Paronychia + jamesii,* for Edwin James (1797-1861), an American explorer and plant collector.

COMMON NAME: James', same as species name. Nailwort, see *Paronychia drummondii.*

Paronychia lindheimeri
Lindheimer's Nailwort

SCIENTIFIC NAME: *Paronychia + lindheimeri,* for Ferdinand Jacob Lindheimer (1801-1879), a German political exile who collected plants in Texas.

COMMON NAME: Lindheimer's, same as species name. Nailwort, see *Paronychia drummondii.*

Paronychia virginica
Broom Whitlow Wort

SCIENTIFIC NAME: *Paronychia + virginica,* Latin for of Virginia, for the area of the type specimen.

COMMON NAME: Broom, for the appearance. Whitlow Wort, see *Paronychia drummondii.*

Parthenium hysterophorus
False Ragweed

SCIENTIFIC NAME: *Parthenium,* from Greek, παρθενος, *parthenos,* maiden, girl, virgin. Reference is to only the pistillate ray flowers producing seeds + *hysterophorus,* to bear a uterus, from Greek, υστερα, *(h)istera,* uterus and φορος, *phoros,* to bear, for the seed capsule, this was an old genus name.

COMMON NAME: False Ragweed, for the resemblance of the leaves to those of ragweed.

Passiflora incarnata   Passion Flower

SCIENTIFIC NAME: *Passiflora,* Latin for passion flower, from *passio,* to suffer, passion and *floris,* a flower. This flower was named by the early missionaries to South America, who believed it showed various signs of the crucifixion of Christ + *incarnata,* Latin for flesh-colored.

COMMON NAME: Passion Flower, same as genus name.

Passiflora lutea   Yellow Passion Flower

SCIENTIFIC NAME: *Passiflora + lutea,* Latin for yellow, for the flower color.

COMMON NAME: Yellow, for the flower color. Passion Flower, see *Passiflora incarnata.*

Passiflora tenuiloba
Birdwing Passion Flower

SCIENTIFIC NAME: *Passiflora + tenuiloba,* Latin for narrow lobes, for the leaves.

COMMON NAME: Birdwing, for the shape of the leaves. Passion Flower, see *Passiflora incarnata.*

Pavonia lasiopetala Rock Rose

SCIENTIFIC NAME: *Pavonia*, for José Antonio Pavon y Jiménez (1754-1844), a Spanish botanist who explored in Chile and Peru + *lasiopetala*, Latin for woolly leaved, from Greek, λασιος, *lasios*, shaggy, woolly and πεταλον, *petalon*, leaf.

COMMON NAME: Rock, for the habitat among rocks. Rose, for the appearance and color of the flower.

Pectis angustifolia Pectis

SCIENTIFIC NAME: *Pectis*, Latin for comb, for the serrated leaf margins + *angustifolia*, Latin for narrow leaves.

COMMON NAME: Pectis, same as genus name.

Pedicularis canadensis Wood Betony

SCIENTIFIC NAME: *Pedicularis*, Latin for relating to lice. This name came from the belief that if sheep ate this plant is would cause them to develop lice + *canadensis*, Latin for belonging to Canada, for the area of the type specimen.

COMMON NAME: Wood, for the habitat. Betony, a name for a plant used by Pliny, who said it was discovered by a Spanish tribe called the Vettones, of which betony is a corruption.

Pediomelum argophyllum
Silverleaf Scurf Pea

SCIENTIFIC NAME: *Pediomelum*, plain melon, from Greek, πεδιον, *pedion*, plain and Latin, *melo*, a short form of *melopepo*, a melon-shaped fruit. Reference is to the character and shape of the fruit + *argophyllum*, white leaves, from Greek, αργος, *argo*, white, shining and φυλλον, *phullon*, leaf.

COMMON NAME: Silverleaf, descriptive of the leaf color. Scurf Pea, for the glandular dots and the fruit.

Pediomelum cuspidatum
Tall-Bread Scurf Pea

SCIENTIFIC NAME: *Pediomelum* + *cuspidatum*, Latin for having a point, for the beaked seed.

Pediomelum hypogaeum
Indian Breadroot

COMMON NAME: Tall-bread, for the relative height and the root used for making flour. Scurf Pea, see *Pediomelum argophylla.*

Pediomelum cyphocalyx
Turniproot Scurf Pea

SCIENTIFIC NAME: *Pediomelum + cyphocalyx,* Latin for a curved calyx.

COMMON NAME: Turniproot, for the large turnip-shaped root. Scurf Pea, see *Pediomelum argophylla.*

Pediomelum esculentum
Breadroot Scurf Pea

SCIENTIFIC NAME: *Pediomelum + esculentum,* Latin for good to eat, for the root.

COMMON NAME: Breadroot, for the large root that is used in making flour. Scurf Pea, see *Pediomelum argophylla.*

Pediomelum hypogaeum
Indian Breadroot

SCIENTIFIC NAME: *Pediomelum + hypogaeum,* below the earth, from Greek, υπο, *upo,* below and γαια, *gaia,* earth, for the edible root.

COMMON NAME: Indian Breadroot, the American Indians used the root of this genus for making flour for bread.

Penstemon albidus   **White Beardtongue**

SCIENTIFIC NAME: *Penstemon,* five stamens, from Greek, πεντε, *pente,* five and στημων, *stēmōn,* stamen of a flower. Reference is to the four stamens and one staminode + *albidus,* Latin for white, for the flower color.

COMMON NAME: White, for the flower color. Beardtongue, for the hairy staminode.

Penstemon ambiguus
Pink Plains Penstemon

SCIENTIFIC NAME: *Penstemon + ambiguus,* Latin for doubtful. Reference is to the difficulty in correctly identifying this plant.

COMMON NAME: Pink, for one of the flower colors. Plains, for the habitat. Penstemon, same as genus name.

Penstemon buckleyi   **Buckley's Penstemon**

SCIENTIFIC NAME: *Penstemon + buckleyi,* for Samuel Botsford Buckley (1809-1884), an American botanist and state geologist of Texas.

COMMON NAME: Buckley's Penstemon, same as scientific name.

Penstemon cobaea   **Cobaea Beardtongue**

SCIENTIFIC NAME: *Penstemon + cobaea,* for its resemblance to the genus

Cobaea, in turn for Bernardo Cobo (1572-1659), a Jesuit priest in Mexico and Peru.

COMMON NAME: Cobaea , same as species. Beardtongue, see *Penstemon albidus.*

Penstemon digitalis
Smooth Beardtongue

SCIENTIFIC NAME: *Penstemon + digitalis,* Latin for measuring a finger breadth, of the finger. A Latinized form of the common German name for foxglove (fingerhut), so called because the flowers looked like the fingers of a glove. The flowers of many penstemons look like those of the foxglove.

COMMON NAME: Smooth, for the smooth stems. Beardtongue, see *Penstemon albidus.*

Penstemon fendleri   Fendler's Penstemon

SCIENTIFIC NAME: *Penstemon + fendleri,* for August Fendler (1813-1883), a German botanist.

COMMON NAME: Fendler's Penstemon, same as scientific name.

Penstemon grandiflorus
Large Beardtongue

SCIENTIFIC NAME: *Penstemon + grandiflorus,* Latin for large-flowered, from *grandis,* large and *floris,* flower.

COMMON NAME: Large, for the large flowers. Beardtongue, see *Penstemon albidus.*

Penstemon havardii   Havard Penstemon

SCIENTIFIC NAME: *Penstemon + havardii,* for Valery Harvard (1846-1927), an American physician and botanist. The name was misspelled when assigned. The Principle of Priority allows the misspelling to stand.

COMMON NAME: Havard Penstemon, same as scientific name.

Penstemon laxiflorus
Looseflower Penstemon

SCIENTIFIC NAME: *Penstemon + laxiflorus,* Latin for loose-flowered, from *laxus,* relaxed, loose and *floris,* flower. Reference is to the sprawling appearance.

COMMON NAME: Looseflower Penstemon, same as scientific name.

Penstemon murrayanus
Scarlet Penstemon

SCIENTIFIC NAME: *Penstemon + murrayanus,* Latin for pertaining to Murray, for Johann Andreas Murray (1740-1791), a Swedish physician and botanist.

COMMON NAME: Scarlet, for the flower color. Penstemon, same as genus name.

Penstemon triflorus **Penstemon**

SCIENTIFIC NAME: *Penstemon + triflorus,* Latin for three-flowered.

COMMON NAME: Penstemon, same as genus name.

Penstemon tubiflorus **Tube Penstemon**

SCIENTIFIC NAME: *Penstemon + tubiflous,* Latin for trumpet flower, from *tuba,* a trumpet with a straight tube and *floris,* flower. Reference is to the flower shape.

COMMON NAME: Tube Penstemon, same as scientific name.

Penthorum sedoides **Ditch Stonecrop**

SCIENTIFIC NAME: *Penthorum,* five pillars, from Greek, πεντε, *pente,* five and ορος, *oros,* pillar, boundary, mark. Reference is to the five symmetrical petals + *sedoides,* to look like *Sedum,* form the genus *Sedum* and Greek ειδος, *eidos,* resembling.

COMMON NAME: Ditch, for the habitat. Stonecrop, commonly grows among rocks.

Phacelia congesta **Spike Phacelia**

SCIENTIFIC NAME: *Phacelia,* from Greek, φακελος, *phakelos,* a bundle. Reference is to the flower clusters + *congesta,* Latin for congested, arranged close together. Reference is again to the flower clusters.

COMMON NAME: Spike, for the flower spike. Phacelia, same as genus name.

Phacelia glabra **Smooth Phacelia**

SCIENTIFIC NAME: *Phacelia + glabra,* Latin for hairless, smooth, for the smooth stems.

COMMON NAME: Smooth Phacelia, same as scientific name.

Phacelia hirsuta **Hairy Phacelia**

SCIENTIFIC NAME: *Phacelia + hirsuta,* Latin for hairy, for the hairy stems.

COMMON NAME: Hairy Phacelia, same as scientific name.

Phacelia integrifolia **Gyp Blue Curls**

SCIENTIFIC NAME: *Phacelia + integrifolia,* Latin for whole leaves, entire leaves, a leaf without any indentations.

COMMON NAME: Gyp, this flower is commonly found in gypsum-rich soil. Blue curls, for the blue, coiled spike of flowers.

Phacelia patuliflora **Purple Phacelia**

SCIENTIFIC NAME: *Phacelia + patuliflora,* spreading flower, from Latin, *patulus,* wide-open, gaping, spreading and *flora,* flower. For the wide open flowers.

COMMON NAME: Purple, for the

flower color. Phacelia, same as genus name.

Phacelia strictiflora   Phacelia

SCIENTIFIC NAME: *Phacelia + strictiflora,* Latin for upright flower.

COMMON NAME: Phacelia, same as genus name.

Phlox cuspidata   Pointed Phlox

SCIENTIFIC NAME: *Phlox,* from Greek, φλοξ, *phlox,* a flame. Reference is to the flower color; this genus name was originally used for the current genus *Lychnis + cuspidata,* Latin for having a sharp point. Reference is to the pointed flower petals.

COMMON NAME: Pointed Phlox, same as scientific name.

Phlox divaricata   Blue Phlox

SCIENTIFIC NAME: *Phlox + divaricata,* Latin for spread out, splayed. Reference is to the growth pattern.

COMMON NAME: Blue, for the flower color. Phlox, same as genus name.

Phlox drummondii   Drummond Phlox

SCIENTIFIC NAME: *Phlox + drummondii,* for Thomas Drummond (1780-1835), a British plant collector who worked in the United States.

COMMON NAME: Drummond Phlox, same as scientific name.

Phlox oklahomensis   Oklahoma Phlox

SCIENTIFIC NAME: *Phlox + oklahomensis,* Latin for belonging to Oklahoma, for the area of the type specimen.

COMMON NAME: Oklahoma Phlox, same as scientific name.

Phlox pilosa   Prairie Phlox

SCIENTIFIC NAME: *Phlox + pilosa,* Latin for covered with hair. Reference is to the soft hairs on the stems.

COMMON NAME: Prairie, for the habitat. Phlox, same as genus name.

Phlox roemeriana   Roemer's Phlox

SCIENTIFIC NAME: *Phlox + roemeriana,* Latin for pertaining to Roemer for Ferdinand Roemer (1818-1891), an American geologist and paleontologist.

COMMON NAME: Roemer's Phlox, same as scientific name.

Phyla nodiflora   Frog Fruit

SCIENTIFIC NAME: *Phyla,* from Greek, φυλη, *phulē,* a tribe. Reference is to the grouped flowers + *nodiflora,* Latin for flowering at the nodes.

COMMON NAME: Frog Fruit, a corruption of Fog Fruit, for the natural habitat in low-lying moist areas.

Physalis angulata
Cutleaf Ground Cherry

SCIENTIFIC NAME: *Physalis,* from Greek, φυσα, *phusa,* a bladder. Reference is to the inflated calyx that encloses the fruit + *angulata,* Latin for angled, for the leaf edges.

COMMON NAME: Cutleaf, for the sharply angled leaves. Ground Cherry, for the size and shape of the fruit and the low-growing habit.

Physalis cinerascens
Beach Ground Cherry

SCIENTIFIC NAME: *Physalis* + *cineracens,* Latin for to become ashy, for the color of the leaves.

COMMON NAME: Beach, for the common habitat. Ground Cherry, see *Physalis angulata.*

Physalis longifolia
Common Ground Cherry

SCIENTIFIC NAME: *Physalis* + *longifolia,* Latin for having long leaves.

COMMON NAME: Common, abundant in its range. Ground Cherry, see *Physalis angulata.*

Physalis pubescens
Downy Ground Cherry

SCIENTIFIC NAME: *Physalis* + *pubescens,* Latin for to become downy, for the soft hairs on the stems.

COMMON NAME: Downy, for the soft hairs on the stems. Ground Cherry, see *Physalis angulata.*

Physalis pumila   Low Ground Cherry

SCIENTIFIC NAME: *Physalis* + *pumila,* Latin for dwarf, for the small size.

COMMON NAME: Low, for the small size. Ground Cherry, see *Physalis angulata.*

Physalis virginiana
Virginia Ground Cherry

SCIENTIFIC NAME: *Physalis* + *virginiana,* Latin for pertaining to Virginia, for the area of the type specimen.

COMMON NAME: Virginia, same as scientific name. Ground Cherry, see *Physalis angulata.*

Physostegia angustifolia
Narrowleaf Dragonhead

SCIENTIFIC NAME: *Physostegia,* bladder roof, from Greek, φυσα, *phusa,* a bladder and στεγη, *stegē,* a roof or covering. Reference is to the inflated calyx that covers the fruit + *angustifolia,* Latin for narrow leaves.

COMMON NAME: Narrowleaf, descriptive. Dragonhead, for the shape of the flowers, which look like those of the *Dracocephalum*, the true dragonhead.

Physostegia digitalis False Dragonhead

SCIENTIFIC NAME: *Physostegia* + *digitalis,* a Latinized form of the common German name for foxglove (fingerhut), so called because the flowers looked like the finger of a glove. This plant was named for its resemblance to foxglove.

COMMON NAME: False Dragonhead, see *Physostegia angustifolia.*

Physostegia intermedia Intermediate False Dragonhead

SCIENTIFIC NAME: *Physostegia* + *intermedia,* Latin for an intermediate form.

COMMON NAME: Intermediate, same as species name. False Dragonhead, see *Physostegia angustifolia.*

Physostegia pulchella Beautiful False Dragonhead

SCIENTIFIC NAME: *Physostegia* + *pulchella,* meant to be Latin for "little pretty," literally translated it is a condescending diminutive of *pulcher,* beautiful, pretty.

COMMON NAME: Beautiful, for the showy flowers. False Dragonhead, see *Physostegia angustifolia.*

Phytolacca americana Pokeweed

SCIENTIFIC NAME: *Phytolacca,* plant dye, from Greek, φυτον, *phuton,* a plant and *lacca,* a Latinization of the Hindi, *lakh,* which refers to a dye extracted from the lac insect. Reference here is to the berries of pokeweed having the properties of a dye + *americana,* Latin for pertaining to America.

COMMON NAME: Pokeweed, Poke is from Algonquian Indian, *puccoon,* any plant used for dyeing.

Pinaropappus roseus White Dandelion

SCIENTIFIC NAME: *Pinaropappus,* dirty fluff, from Greek, πιναρος, *pinaros,* dirty and παππος, *pappos,* grandfather, down on the achenes + *roseus,* Latin for rose-colored. Reference is to the rose color of the underside of the flower petals.

COMMON NAME: White, for the color of the upper sides of the flower petals. Dandelion, for the resemblance of the bloom to that of the dandelion.

Plantago patagonica Patagonia Plantain

SCIENTIFIC NAME: *Plantago,* Latin name for plantain, so named by Pliny, from Latin, *planta,* the sole of the foot. Reference was to the shape of the leaves + *patagonica,* Latin for of Patagonia, for the area of the type specimen.

COMMON NAME: Patagonia Plantain, same as scientific name.

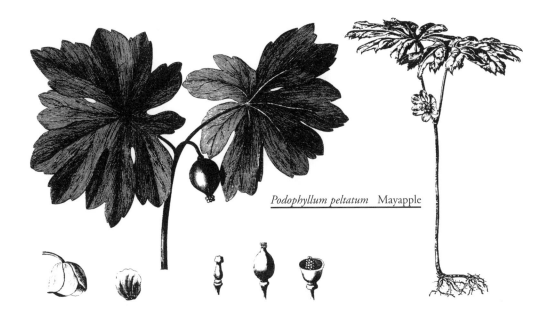

Podophyllum peltatum Mayapple

Pluchea camphorata **Camphor Weed**

SCIENTIFIC NAME: *Pluchea,* for Noel-Antoine Pluche (1688-1761), a French abbot and naturalist + *camphorata,* Latin for possessing camphor, for the camphor odor of the leaves.

COMMON NAME: Camphor Weed, for the camphor odor of the leaves.

Pluchea foetida **Stinking Pluchea**

SCIENTIFIC NAME: *Pluchea* + *foetida,* Latin for bad smelling.

COMMON NAME: Stinking Pluchea, same as scientific name.

Pluchea odorata **Purple Pluchea**

SCIENTIFIC NAME: *Pluchea* + *odorata,* Latin for having an odor, fragrant.

COMMON NAME: Purple, for the flower color. Pluchea, same as genus name.

Podophyllum peltatum **Mayapple**

SCIENTIFIC NAME: *Podophyllum,* (duck)foot leaf, from *Anapodophyllum,* the original name. From Latin, *anas,* duck, from Greek, πους, *pous,* foot and φυλλον, *phullon,* leaf. Reference is to the shape of the leaves + *peltatum,* from Greek, πελτη, *peltē,* a small shield. Reference is to the leaf shape and to the attachment of the stem away from the leaf margin, toward the center of the leaf as where the handle of a small shield would be.

COMMON NAME: Mayapple, for the appearance of the fruit that forms in the spring, in many areas during the month of May.

Polanisia dodecandra **Clammy Weed**

SCIENTIFIC NAME: *Polanisia,* many unequal, from Greek, πολυς, *polus,* many, αγ, *an,* not, and ισος, *isos,* equal. Reference is to how the stamens differ from a closely related genus, *Cleome* + *dodecandra,* twelve stamens, from Greek, δοδεκα, *dodeka,* twelve and ανδρος, *andros,* man, the root for stamen. The stamen number actually ranges from ten to twenty.

COMMON NAME: Clammy Weed, for the sticky exudate on the stems and leaves.

Polanisia jamesii Cristatella

SCIENTIFIC NAME: *Polanisia + jamesii,* for Edwin James (1797-1861), an American physician and botanist.

COMMON NAME: Cristatella, little crest, a diminutive of the Latin, *cristata,* a crest. Reference is to the fringed flower petals.

Polanisia uniglandulosa Clammy Weed

SCIENTIFIC NAME: *Polanisia + uniglandulosa,* Latin for one gland, for the resinous leaf gland.

COMMON NAME: Clammy Weed, for the sticky exudate on the stems and leaves.

Polycarpon tetraphyllum Fourleaf Manyseed

SCIENTIFIC NAME: *Polycarpon,* many fruited, from Greek, πολυς, *polus,* many and καρπος, *karpos,* fruit + *tetraphyllum,* Latin for four-leaved; the leaves occur in groups of four in whorls around the stem.

COMMON NAME: Fourleaf Manyseed, same as genus name.

Polygala alba White Milkwort

SCIENTIFIC NAME: *Polygala,* much milk, from Greek, πολυς, *polus,* many, much and γαλα, *gala,* milk. It was believed that this plant increased milk production in nursing mothers and cows + *alba,* Latin for white, for the flower color.

COMMON NAME: White Milkwort, same as scientific name.

Polygala cruciata Marsh Milkwort

SCIENTIFIC NAME: *Polygala + cruciata,* Latin for like a cross.

COMMON NAME: Marsh, for the habitat in moist areas. Milkwort, same as genus name.

Polygala incarnata Slender Milkwort

SCIENTIFIC NAME: *Polygala + incarnata,* Latin for flesh-colored. Reference is to the flower color.

COMMON NAME: Slender, for the thin stems. Milkwort, same as genus name.

Polygala lindheimeri Lindheimer's Milkwort

SCIENTIFIC NAME: *Polygala + lindheimeri,* for Ferdinand Jacob Lindheimer (1809-1879), a German political exile who collected plants in Texas.

COMMON NAME: Lindheimer's Milkwort, same as scientific name.

Polygala polygama Pink Milkwort

SCIENTIFIC NAME: *Polygala + polygama,* many marriage, from Greek, πολυς, *polus,* many and γαμος, *gamos,* marriage. Reference here is to having two types of flowers, see common name.

COMMON NAME: Pink, for the above ground (chasmogamous, or open-pollinated) flowers, there are also underground (cleistogamous, or self-pollinating) flowers that are white. Milkwort, same as genus name.

Polygala sanguinea Blood Milkwort

SCIENTIFIC NAME: *Polygala + sanguinea,* Latin for blood-colored, for the flower color.

COMMON NAME: Blood Milkwort, same as scientific name.

Polygala verticillata Whorled Milkwort

SCIENTIFIC NAME: *Polygala + verticillata,* Latin for having whorls. Reference is to the leaf whorls.

COMMON NAME: Whorled Milkwort, same as scientific name.

Polygonatum biflorum
Great Solomon's Seal

SCIENTIFIC NAME: *Polygonatum,* many knees, from Greek, πολυς, *polus,* many, much and γονυ, *gonu,* knee. Reference is to the jointed appearance of the rhizome + *biflorum,* Latin for two flowers. Reference is to the blooms occurring in pairs.

COMMON NAME: Great Solomon's Seal, the scar formed by the stems breaking off the rhizome was thought to resemble the seal of King Solomon.

Polygonella americana
Southern Jointweed

SCIENTIFIC NAME: *Polygonella,* little *Polygonum,* from the genus *Polygonum* and the diminutive-*ella.* Reference is to the swollen nodes on the stems + *americana,* Latin for pertaining to America.

COMMON NAME: Southern, for the range in the United States. Jointweed, for the multiple nodes on the stems.

Polygonum amphibium
Water Smartweed

SCIENTIFIC NAME: *Polygonum,* many knees, from Greek, πολυς, *polus,* many, much and γονυ, *gonu,* knee. Reference is to the swellings on the stems that resemble joints or knots + *amphibium,* from Greek, αμφιβιος, *amphibios,* living a double life. Reference is to this plant growing both on land and in the water.

COMMON NAME: Water, for part of the habitat. Smartweed, the sap will irritate the skin (make it "smart").

Polygonum aviculare Knotweed

SCIENTIFIC NAME: *Polygonum + aviculare,* Latin for pertaining to small birds, in this case they eat the seeds of this plant.

COMMON NAME: Knotweed, same as genus name.

Polygonum convolvulus Cornbind

SCIENTIFIC NAME: *Polygonum + convolvulus,* Latin for convoluted, to twist around, for the growth pattern of twisting around other plants.

COMMON NAME: Cornbind, this plant will twine around crop plants.

Polygonum densiflorum
Snout Smartweed

SCIENTIFIC NAME: *Polygonum + densiflorum,* Latin for densely flowered.

COMMON NAME: Snout, for the flower shape. Smartweed, see *Polygonum amphibium.*

Polygonum lapathifolium
Pale Smartweed

SCIENTIFIC NAME: *Polygonum + lapathifolium,* to have leaves like a dock or sorrel, from Greek, λαπαθον, *lapathon,* dock and Latin, *folium,* leaf.

COMMON NAME: Pale, for the pale flowers. Smartweed, see *Polygonum amphibium.*

Polygonum pensylvanicum
Pennsylvania Smartweed

SCIENTIFIC NAME: *Polygonum + pensylvanicum,* Latin for of Pennsylvania, the Principle of Priority allows the misspelling to stand.

COMMON NAME: Pennsylvania Smartweed, same as scientific name.

Polygonum punctatum
Dotted Smartweed

SCIENTIFIC NAME: *Polygonum + punctatum,* Latin for dotted, for the glands on the flowers.

COMMON NAME: Dotted, same as species name. Smartweed, see *Polygonum amphibium.*

Polygonum ramosissimum
Bushy Knotweed

SCIENTIFIC NAME: *Polygonum + ramosissimum,* Latin for most branched, for the overall appearance.

COMMON NAME: Bushy Knotweed, same as scientific name.

Polygonum scandens
Thicket Knotweed

SCIENTIFIC NAME: *Polygonum* + *scandens,* Latin for climbing, for the growth pattern.

COMMON NAME: Thicket, for the habitat. Knotweed, same as genus name.

Polytaenia nuttallii   Prairie Parsley

SCIENTIFIC NAME: *Polytaenia,* many ribbons, from Greek, πολυς, *polus,* many, much and ταινια, *tainia,* ribbon, band. Reference is to oil tubes in the fruit + *nuttallii,* for Thomas Nuttall (1786-1859), an English botanist, explorer, printer, ornithologist, and plant collector. He was a fellow of the Linnaean Society.

COMMON NAME: Prairie, for the habitat. Parsley, from Greek, ετροσελινον, *petroselinon,* rock parsley, the name for this type of plant.

Pontederia cordata   Pickerelweed

SCIENTIFIC NAME: *Pontederia,* for Guilio Pontedera (1688-1757), an Italian physician and botanist. He was prefect of the botanical garden of Padua + *cordata,* Latin for heart-shaped. Reference is to the shape of the leaf.

COMMON NAME: Pickerelweed, a pickerel is a small pike. This aquatic plant grows where pike spawn. In the past this plant was thought to have been produced by the pike.

Portulaca pilosa   Shaggy Portulaca

SCIENTIFIC NAME: *Portulaca,* the Latin name for this plant, it is a diminutive of the Latin, *porta,* a door or gate. Reference is to the lid on the fruit + *pilosa,* Latin for long, soft hairs, for the woolly leaf axils.

COMMON NAME: Shaggy Portulaca, same as scientific name.

Portulaca umbraticola
Wingpod Portulaca

SCIENTIFIC NAME: *Portulaca* + *umbraticola,* Latin for living in the shade.

COMMON NAME: Wingpod, for the winged seedpods. Portulaca, same as genus name.

Potentilla recta   Cinquefoil

SCIENTIFIC NAME: *Potentilla,* little powerful, a diminutive of Latin, *potentis,* powerful, mighty. Reference is to the medicinal properties of some in this genus + *recta,* Latin for upright.

COMMON NAME: Cinquefoil, Old French for five leaves, the leaves of this genus are made up of five to seven leaflets.

Potentilla simplex   Oldfield Cinquefoil

SCIENTIFIC NAME: *Potentilla* + *simplex,* Latin for simple, in this case unbranched.

COMMON NAME: Oldfield, for the habitat in abandonded fields. Cinquefoil, see *Potentilla recta.*

Proboscidea louisianica Devil's Claw

SCIENTIFIC NAME: *Proboscidea,* from Greek, προβοσκιδος, *proboskidos,* a form of προβοσκις, *proboskis,* an elephant's trunk. Reference is to the shape of the unopened fruit + *louisianica,* Latin for of Louisana, for the area of the type specimen.

COMMON NAME: Devil's Claw, for the hooked shape of the opened fruit capsule and the black color.

Prosopis glandulosa Honey Mesquite

SCIENTIFIC NAME: *Prosopis,* from Greek, προσωπις, *prosōpis,* an unidentified plant. Carolus Linnaeus (1707-1778) selected this genus name in 1767, the reason is not clear + *glandulosa,* Latin for glandular.

COMMON NAME: Honey, the seeds are sweet, used by many American Indian tribes as food, drink, and animal fodder. Mesquite, from Mexican Spanish, *mesquite,* in turn from Nahuatl, *mizquitil,* their name for this tree.

Prunella vulgaris Self-Heal

SCIENTIFIC NAME: *Prunella,* a corruption of the German vernacular, *brunella,* their name for this herb + *vulgaris,* Latin for common, usual.

COMMON NAME: Self-Heal, also called All-Heal, reference is to the use in treating wounds.

Prunus angustifolia Sandhill Plum

SCIENTIFIC NAME: *Prunus,* Latin for a plum tree + *angustifolia,* Latin for narrow-leaved.

COMMON NAME: Sandhill, for the common habitat. Plum, from Old English, *plume,* their name for this fruit.

Prunus americana Wild Plum

SCIENTIFIC NAME: *Prunus + americana,* Latin for pertaining to America.

COMMON NAME: Wild, occuring naturally, not domesticated. Plum, see *Prunus angustifolia.*

Prunus caroliniana Laurel Cherry

SCIENTIFIC NAME: *Prunus + caroliniana,* Latin for pertaining to Carolina, for the area of the type specimen.

COMMON NAME: Laurel, for the leaves, which are evergreen and resemble those of the laurel, which is also evergreen. Cherry, adopted into English from Old French, *cherise,* originally from Greek, κερασος, *kerasos,* cherry.

Prunus gracilis Oklahoma Plum

SCIENTIFIC NAME: *Prunus* + *gracilis,* Latin for graceful, slender.

COMMON NAME: Oklahoma, for part of the range. Plum, see *Prunus angustifolia.*

Prunus mexicana Mexican Plum

SCIENTIFIC NAME: *Prunus* + *mexicana,* Latin for pertaining to Mexico, for the area of the type specimen.

COMMON NAME: Mexican, same as species name. Plum, see *Prunus angustifolia.*

Prunus rivularis Creek Plum

SCIENTIFIC NAME: *Prunus* + *rivularis,* Latin for brook-loving, for the habitat by streams.

COMMON NAME: Creek Plum, same as scientific name.

Prunus serotina Blackcherry

SCIENTIFIC NAME: *Prunus* + *serotina,* Latin for to ripen late.

COMMON NAME: Blackcherry, for the dark purple fruit, which sometimes does approach black.

Psilostrophe tagetina
Woolly Paper Flower

SCIENTIFIC NAME: *Psilostrophe,* bare twist, from Greek, ψιλος, *psilos,* bare and τροφε, *trophe,* twisting. Reference is to the many-branched stems + *tagetina,* to look like a *Tagetes,* a marigold.

COMMON NAME: Woolly, for the woolly white hairs on the leaves and stems. Paper Flower, the blooms stay on the plant and dry, taking on the character and appearance of paper.

Psoralidium tenuiflorum Scurfy Pea

SCIENTIFIC NAME: *Psoralidium,* little scabby, a diminutive of the Greek, πσοραλεος, *psōraleos* scabby, mangy. Reference is to the glandular dots on the leaves + *tenuiflorum,* Latin for slender flowers.

COMMON NAME: Scurfy Pea, for the glandular dots on the leaves and the fruit.

Ptilimnium capillaceum
Threadleaf Mock Bishop's Weed

SCIENTIFIC NAME: *Ptilimnium,* little marsh feather, from Greek, πτιλον, *ptilon,* feather, wing and a diminutive of λιμνιον, *limnion,* marsh or a marshy lake, mud. Reference is to the habitat and to the featherlike leaves + *capillaceum,* Latin for being thin or hairlike.

COMMON NAME: Threadleaf, for the thin leaves. Mock Bishop's Weed, because it resembles Bishop's Weed.

Ptilimnium nuttallii
Mock Bishop's Weed

SCIENTIFIC NAME: *Ptilimnium +
nuttallii,* for Thomas Nuttall (1786-1859),
an English botanist, explorer, printer,
ornithologist, and plant collector. He was
a fellow of the Linnaean Society.

COMMON NAME: Mock Bishop's
Weed, see *Ptilimnium capillaceum.*

Pycnanthemum albescens
Whiteleaf Mountain Mint

SCIENTIFIC NAME: *Pycnanthemum,*
dense flower, from Greek, πυκνος, *puknos,*
dense and ανθεμον, *anthemon,* flower.
Reference is to the tightly clustered
flowers + *albescens,* Latin for becoming
white, for the leaves.

COMMON NAME: White-Leaf, for the
whitish color of the top of the leaves.
Mountain, for the habitat. Mint, from
Latin, *mentha,* in turn from Greek, μινθη,
minthē, mint.

Pycnanthemum tenuifolium
Slender Mountain Mint

SCIENTIFIC NAME: *Pycnanthemum +
tenuifolium,* Latin for slender leaves.

COMMON NAME: Slender, for the
thin leaves. Mountain Mint, see
Pycnanthemum albescens.

Pyrrhopappus carolinianus
False Dandelion

SCIENTIFIC NAME: *Pyrrhopappus,*
flame colored fluff, from Greek, πυρρος,
pyrrhos, flame-colored and παππος,
pappos, grandfather, down on the achenes
+ *carolinianus,* Latin for pertaining to
Carolina, for the area of the type
specimen.

COMMON NAME: False Dandelion,
for its resemblance to the dandelion.

Pyrrhopappus grandiflorus
Tuber False Dandelion

SCIENTIFIC NAME: *Pyrrhopappus +
grandiflorus,* Latin for large-flowered.

COMMON NAME: Tuber, for the
swollen structure at the end of the tap-
root. False Dandelion, for its resemblance
to the dandelion.

Pyrrhopappus pauciflorus
Texas Dandelion

SCIENTIFIC NAME: *Pyrrhopappus +
pauciflorus,* Latin for few flowers.

COMMON NAME: Texas, for the area
of the type specimen. Dandelion, for the
resemblance to the dandelion.

Quincula lobata   **Purple Ground Cherry**

SCIENTIFIC NAME: *Quincula,* Latin
for little five, for the five spots on the
corolla of the type specimen + *lobata,*

Latin for having lobes. Some of the leaves are lobed.

COMMON NAME: Purple, for the flower color. Ground Cherry, for the low-growing habit and for the cherry-sized fruit.

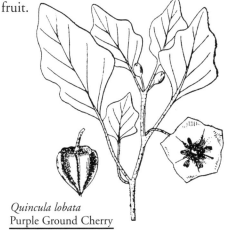

Quincula lobata
Purple Ground Cherry

Rafinesquia neomexicana   Plume Seed

SCIENTIFIC NAME: *Rafinesquia,* for Constantine Samuel Rafinesque (1783-1840), a Turkish-born botanist, conchologist, and archaeologist. He lived many years in the United States + *neomexicana,* Latin for pertaining to New Mexico, for the area of the type specimen.

COMMON NAME: Plume Seed, for the feathery hairs on the achenes.

Ranunculus abortivus
Littleleaf Buttercup

SCIENTIFIC NAME: *Ranunculus,* Latin for little frog, for the habitat in damp places + *abortivus,* Latin for with parts missing, reduced parts, abortive, for the small stem leaves.

COMMON NAME: Littleleaf, descriptive. Buttercup, for the yellow color and the shape of the flower.

Ranunculus hispidus   Buttercup

SCIENTIFIC NAME: *Ranunculus + hispidus,* Latin for bristly, for the hairs on the stems.

COMMON NAME: Buttercup, see *Ranunculus abortivus.*

Ranunculus macranthus
Large Buttercup

SCIENTIFIC NAME: *Ranunculus + macranthus,* large flower, from Greek, μακρος, *macros,* large and ανθος, *anthos,* flower; this plant has the largest flower in the genus.

COMMON NAME: Large, same as species name. Buttercup, see *Ranunculus abortivus.*

Ranunculus macranthus
Large Buttercup

Ranunculus sceleratus
Celeryleaf Buttercup

SCIENTIFIC NAME: *Ranunculus + sceleratus,* Latin for cursed, wicked, hurtful; the sap of this plant will blister the skin.

COMMON NAME: Celeryleaf, the leaves resemble those of celery. Buttercup, see *Ranunculus abortivus.*

Ratibida columnifera **Mexican Hat**

SCIENTIFIC NAME: *Ratibida,* listed by Constantine Samuel Rafinesque (1783-1840) without comment, most probably a local vernacular name + *columnifera,* Latin for column bearing. Reference is to the column-shaped central receptacle.

COMMON NAME: Mexican Hat, for the hat-shaped inflorescence and the brightly colored petals.

Ratibida columnifera Mexican Hat

Ratibida pinnata
Grayhead Prairie Coneflower

SCIENTIFIC NAME: *Ratibida + pinnata,* Latin for featherlike. Reference is to the leaves.

COMMON NAME: Grayhead, for the central gray disk. Prairie, for the habitat. Coneflower, for the columnar central receptacle.

Ratibida tagetes
Short-ray Prairie Coneflower

SCIENTIFIC NAME: *Ratibida + tagetes,* from the genus *Tagetes,* the marigold, for the appearance. *Tagetes* was named for Tages, an Etruscan god who sprung from the earth as it was being tilled.

COMMON NAME: Short-ray, for the short ray petals. Prairie Coneflower, see *Ratibida pinnata.*

Rhexia lutea **Yellow Meadow Beauty**

SCIENTIFIC NAME: *Rhexia,* from Greek, rexis, *rexis,* a breaking, a rupture, burst forth. This name was used by Pliny for an unidentified plant + *lutea,* Latin for yellow, for the flower color.

COMMON NAME: Yellow, for the flower color. Meadow Beauty, for the habitat and the appearance.

Rhexia mariana
Maryland Meadow Beauty

SCIENTIFIC NAME: *Rhexia* + *mariana,*
Latin for pertaining to Mary, in this case,
pertaining to Maryland, for the area of the
type specimen.

COMMON NAME: Maryland, for the
area of the type specimen. Meadow
Beauty, for the habitat and the appearance.

Rhexia virginica
Common Meadow Beauty

SCIENTIFIC NAME: *Rhexia* + *virginica,*
Latin for of Virginia, for the area of the
type specimen.

COMMON NAME: Common,
common in its range. Meadow Beauty, for
the habitat and the appearance.

Rhododendron canescen **Wild Azalea**

SCIENTIFIC NAME: *Rhododendron,*
rose tree, from Greek, ροδοδενδρον,
r(h)ododendron, for the rose-flowered
oleander + *canescens,* Latin for becoming
greyed, for the grayish hairs on most parts
of the plant.

COMMON NAME: Wild, for the habitat. Azalea, from Greek, azalea, *azalea,*
dry. Reference is either to the dry soil in
which it grows or to the dry, brittle wood.

Rivina humilis **Rouge Plant**

SCIENTIFIC NAME: *Rivina,* for
Augustus Quirinus Rivinus (1652-1723), a
German physician and botanist + *humilis,*
Latin for low-growing.

COMMON NAME: Rouge Plant, for
the red dye produced from the berries.

Robinia hispida **Bristly Locust**

SCIENTIFIC NAME: *Robinia,* for Jean
Robin (1550-1629), a French gardener for
Henri IV and Louis XIII, and his son
Vespasian Robin (1579-1662), who was
the first to cultivate locust in France +
hispida, Latin for bristly, for the bristly
stems and branches.

COMMON NAME: Bristly, same as
species name. Locust, used as a common
name for this tree in the United States
area since 1550, origin is obscure.

Robinia pseudoacacia **Black Locust**

SCIENTIFIC NAME: *Robinia* +
pseudoacacia, false acacia, from Greek,
ψευδης, *pseudēs,* false and the genus
Acacia, for the appearance.

COMMON NAME: Black, for the dark
bark. Locust, see *Robinia hispida.*

Rorippa microphylla **Watercress**

SCIENTIFIC NAME: *Rorippa,* from
Old Saxon, *rorippen,* their name for this
type of plant + *microphylla,* small leaves,

from Greek, μικρος, *micros,* small and
φυλλον, *phullon,* leaf.

COMMON NAME: Watercress, water,
for the habitat and cress, from Old High
German, *chresan,* to creep, for the growth
pattern.

Rorippa palustris   Bog Yellowcress

SCIENTIFIC NAME: *Rorippa + palustris,* Latin for marsh-loving, for the habitat
in damp places.

COMMON NAME: Bog, for the habitat.
Yellowcress, for the flower color, see
Rorippa microphylla for cress.

Rosa arkansana   Prairie Wild Rose

SCIENTIFIC NAME: *Rosa,* Latin for
rose + *arkansana,* Latin for pertaining to
Arkansas, for the area of the type specimen.

COMMON NAME: Prairie, for the
habitat. Wild Rose, occurring naturally
in nature.

Rosa carolina   Carolina Rose

SCIENTIFIC NAME: *Rosa + carolina,*
Latin for of Carolina, for the area of the
type specimen.

COMMON NAME: Carolina Rose,
same as scientific name.

Rosa foliolosa   Leafy Rose

SCIENTIFIC NAME: *Rosa + foliolosa,*
Latin for full of leaves.

COMMON NAME: Leafy Rose, same as
scientific name.

Rosa micrantha   Smallflower Rose

SCIENTIFIC NAME: *Rosa + micrantha,*
small-flowered, from Greek, μικρος,
micros, small and ανθος, *anthos,* flower.

COMMON NAME: Smallflower Rose,
same as scientific name.

Rosa setigera   Climbing Prairie Rose

SCIENTIFIC NAME: *Rosa + setigera,*
Latin for bearing bristles, for the thorns.

COMMON NAME: Climbing, for the
growth pattern. Prairie, for the habitat.
Rose, same as genus name.

Rosa multiflora   Multiflora Rose

SCIENTIFIC NAME: *Rosa + multiflora,*
Latin for many flowers.

COMMON NAME: Multiflora Rose,
same as scientific name.

Rubus aboriginum   Northern Dewberry

SCIENTIFIC NAME: *Rubus,* Latin for
bramble or blackberry + *aboriginum,* Latin
for aboriginal, native.

COMMON NAME: Northern, the type specimen was found in the northern United States. Dewberry, a berry associated with the dew.

Rubus allegheniensis **Common Blackberry**

SCIENTIFIC NAME: *Rubus + allegheniensis,* Latin for belonging to the Alleghenies, for the area of the type specimen.

COMMON NAME: Common, abundant. Blackberry, descriptive of the ripe berry.

Rubus oklahomus **Oklahoma Blackberry**

SCIENTIFIC NAME: *Rubus + oklahomus,* Latin for of Oklahoma, for the area of the type specimen.

COMMON NAME: Oklahoma for the area of the type of specimen; Blackberry, descriptive of the fruit.

Rubus trivialis **Southern Dewberry**

SCIENTIFIC NAME: *Rubus + trivialis,* Latin for trivial, ordinary, for its common occurance.

COMMON NAME: Southern, for the range in the United States. Dewberry, see *Rubus aboriginum.*

Rudbeckia grandiflora **Tall Coneflower**

SCIENTIFIC NAME: *Rudbeckia,* for Olaf Rudbeck (1630-1702) and his son Olaf Rudbeck (1660-1740), both were professors at Uppsala. Carolus Linnaeus (1707-1778) was the student of the son + *grandiflora,* Latin for large flower.

COMMON NAME: Tall, may grow up to five feet tall. Coneflower, for the cone-shaped central receptacle.

Rudbeckia hirta **Black-Eyed Susan**

SCIENTIFIC NAME: *Rudbeckia + hirta,* Latin for hairy, for the hairs on the bracts, stems, and leaves.

COMMON NAME: Black-eyed, for the black central disk. Susan, a pet name.

Rudbeckia laciniata **Golden Glow**

SCIENTIFIC NAME: *Rudbeckia + laciniata,* Latin for slashed or torn. Reference is to the three- to five-lobed leaves.

COMMON NAME: Golden Glow, for the yellow central disk and petals.

Rudbeckia triloba **Brown-Eyed Susan**

SCIENTIFIC NAME: *Rudbeckia + triloba,* Latin for having three lobes. Reference is to the leaves.

COMMON NAME: Brown-Eyed, for the brown central disk. Susan, a pet name.

Ruellia humilis   Fringeleaf Ruellia

SCIENTIFIC NAME: *Ruellia,* for Jean Ruel (1474-1537), a French physician and botanist + *humilis,* Latin for low-growing.

COMMON NAME: Fringeleaf, for the hairy leaf margins. Ruellia, same as genus name.

Ruellia malacosperma   Softseed Ruellia

SCIENTIFIC NAME: *Ruellia* + *malacosperma,* soft seed, from Greek, μαλακος, *malakos* and σπερμα, *sperma, seed*

COMMON NAME: Softseed Ruellia, same as scientific name.

Ruellia nudiflora   Violet Ruellia

SCIENTIFIC NAME: *Ruellia* + *nudiflora,* Latin for naked flower. Reference is to the flowers appearing on the plant before the leaves.

COMMON NAME: Violet, for the flower color. Ruellia, same as genus name.

Ruellia pedunculata   Stalked Ruellia

SCIENTIFIC NAME: *Ruellia* + *pedunculata,* Latin for stalked, for the flower stalk.

COMMON NAME: Stalked Ruellia, same as scientific name.

Ruellia strepens   Limestone Ruellia

SCIENTIFIC NAME: *Ruellia* + *strepens,* Latin for rattling, clattering, for the seeds that rattle in the capsule.
COMMON NAME: Limestone, for the habitat. Ruellia, same as genus name.

Rumex altissimus   Smooth Dock

SCIENTIFIC NAME: *Rumex,* Latin for sorrel + *altissimus,* Latin for the tallest.

COMMON NAME: Smooth, for the leaves. Dock, from Anglo-Saxon, *docce,* their name for this plant.

Rumex crispus   Curly Dock

SCIENTIFIC NAME: *Rumex* + *crispus,* Latin for crisped, curled, for the leaves.

COMMON NAME: Curly, same as species name. Dock, see *Rumex altissimus.*

Rumex hymenosepalus   Canaigre

SCIENTIFIC NAME: *Rumex* + *hymenosepalus,* membranous sepals, from Greek, υμεν, *(h)umen,* a thin membrane and Modern Latin, *sepalum,* sepal.

COMMON NAME: Canaigre, the Mexican Spanish name for this plant.

Rumex pulcher   Fiddle Dock

SCIENTIFIC NAME: *Rumex* + *pulcher,* Latin for pretty, handsome.

COMMON NAME: Fiddle, for the leaf shape. Dock, see *Rumex altissimus.*

Sabatia campestris
Prairie Rose Gentian

SCIENTIFIC NAME: *Sabatia,* for Liberato Sabbati (1714-?), an Italian botanist and surgeon + *campestris,* Latin for growing in fields.

COMMON NAME: Prairie, for the habitat. Rose, for the flower color. Gentian, from Latin, *gentiana,* their name for this type of plant.

Sagittaria brevirostra **Arrowhead**

SCIENTIFIC NAME: *Sagittaria,* Latin for formed like an arrow, for the arrowhead-shaped leaves + *brevirostra,* Latin for short-beaked, for the beaked achenes.

COMMON NAME: Arrowhead, for the arrowhead-shaped leaves.

Sagittaria lancifolia
Scythe-Fruit Arrowhead

SCIENTIFIC NAME: *Sagittaria +
lancifolia,* Latin for lance-shaped leaves.

COMMON NAME: Scythe-fruit, for the curved fruit. Arrowhead, see *Sagittaria brevirostra.*

Sagittaria latifolia **Common Arrowhead**

SCIENTIFIC NAME: *Sagittaria +*

latifolia, Latin for having broad leaves.

COMMON NAME: Common, abundant in its range. Arrowhead, see *Sagittaria brevirostra.*

Salvia azurea **Blue Sage**

SCIENTIFIC NAME: *Salvia,* Latin for sage, in turn from *salvare,* to save, for its medicinal properties + *azurea,* Latin for sky blue, for the flower color.

COMMON NAME: Blue Sage, same as scientific name.

Salvia coccinea **Indian Fire**

SCIENTIFIC NAME: *Salvia + coccinea,* Latin for scarlet-dyed, for the flower color.

COMMON NAME: Indian Fire, for the bright red flowers.

Salvia farinacea **Mealy Sage**

SCIENTIFIC NAME: *Salvia + farinacea,* Latin for mealy, powdered. Reference is to the white hairs on the calyx.

COMMON NAME: Mealy Sage, same as scientific name.

Salvia lycioides **Canyon Sage**

SCIENTIFIC NAME: *Salvia + lycioides,* referring to Lycia in Asia Minor, for the area of the type specimen and Greek, ειδος, *eidos,* resembling.

COMMON NAME: Canyon, for the habitat. Sage, see *Salvia azurea.*

Salvia lyrata Lyreleaf Sage

SCIENTIFIC NAME: *Salvia* + *lyrata,* Latin for shaped like a lyre, for the shape of the leaves.

COMMON NAME: Lyreleaf Sage, same as scientific name.

Salvia reflexa Lanceleaf Sage

SCIENTIFIC NAME: *Salvia* + *reflexa,* Latin for bent backward.

COMMON NAME: Lanceleaf, for the leaf shape. Sage, see *Salvia azurea.*

Salvia texana Texas Sage

SCIENTIFIC NAME: *Salvia* + *texana,* Latin for pertaining to Texas, for the range.

COMMON NAME: Texas Sage, same as scientific name.

Sambucus nigra Elderberry

SCIENTIFIC NAME: *Sambucus,* a form of Latin, *sabucus,* the Elder tree + *nigra,* Latin for black, for the fruit color.

COMMON NAME: Elderberry, for the berries on the Elder.

Sanguinaria canadensis Bloodroot

SCIENTIFIC NAME: *Sanguinaria,* Latin for belonging to blood. Reference is to the yellowish-red sap + *canadensis,* Latin for belonging to Canada.

COMMON NAME: Bloodroot, for the yellowish-red sap.

Saponaria officinalis Soapwort

SCIENTIFIC NAME: *Saponaria,* Latin for possessing soap, for the mucilaginous sap that will form suds with water + *officinalis,* Latin for sold in shops, usually apothecaries. Reference is to real or supposed medicinal value.

COMMON NAME: Soapwort, same as scientific name.

Saururus cernuus Lizard's Tail

SCIENTIFIC NAME: *Saururus,* lizard tail, from Greek, σαυρος, *sauros,* lizard and ουρα, *oura,* tail. Reference is to the shape of the flower spike + *cernuus,* Latin for head first, drooping, nodding, for the drooping flower spike.

COMMON NAME: Lizard's Tail, same as genus name.

Schoenocaulon drummondii Green Lily

SCIENTIFIC NAME: *Schoenocaulon,* reed stem, from Greek, σχοινος, *skhoinos,* rush, reed, and καυλος, *kaulos,* stem of a plant + *drummondii,* for Thomas

Drummond (1780-1835), a British plant collector.

COMMON NAME: Green, for the flower color. Lily, from Latin, *lilium,* a lily.

Schoenocaulon texanum Texas Sabadilla

SCIENTIFIC NAME: *Schoenocaulon + texanum,* Latin for pertaining to Texas.

COMMON NAME: Texas, for the range. Sabadilla, little barley, a diminutive of the Spanish word for barley, *cebada.*

Schoenolirion croceum Yellow Sunnybell

SCIENTIFIC NAME: *Schoenolirion,* reed lily, from Greek, σχοινος, *skhoinos,* rush, reed, and λειρον, *leiron,* a lily. Reference is to the appearance + *croceum,* Latin for saffron-colored, yellow, for the flower color.

COMMON NAME: Yellow, for the flower color. Sunnybell, for the yellow color and shape of the buds just before opening.

Scutellaria drummondii Skullcap

SCIENTIFIC NAME: *Scutellaria,* Latin for possessing a small shield or dish. Reference is to the disk-shaped calyx appendage; it persists after flowering + *drummondii,* for Thomas Drummond (1780-1835), a British plant collector.

COMMON NAME: Skullcap, same as genus name.

Scutellaria lateriflora Sideflower Skullcap

SCIENTIFIC NAME: *Scutellaria + lateriflora,* Latin for having flowers on the sides of the stems.

COMMON NAME: Sideflower, descriptive. Skullcap, see *Scutellaria drummondii.*

Scutellaria ovata Eggleaf Skullcap

SCIENTIFIC NAME: *Scutellaria + ovata,* Latin for oval, egg-shaped, for the leaves.

COMMON NAME: Eggleaf, same as species name. Skullcap, see *Scutellaria drummondii.*

Scutellaria parvula Small Skullcap

SCIENTIFIC NAME: *Scutellaria + parvula,* Latin for very small, for the relative size.

COMMON NAME: Small Skullcap, same as scientific name.

Scutellaria resinosa Resinous Skullcap

SCIENTIFIC NAME: *Scutellaria + resinosa,* Latin for having resin, for the resin-dotted stems.

COMMON NAME: Resinous Skullcap, same as scientific name.

Scutellaria wrightii **Wright's Skullcap,**

SCIENTIFIC NAME: *Scutellaria + wrightii,* for Charles Wright (1811-1885), a Texas plant collector.

COMMON NAME: Wright's Skullcap, same as scientific name.

Sedum nuttallianum **Yellow Stonecrop**

SCIENTIFIC NAME: *Sedum,* Latin for stonecrop, from *sedo,* to set, for their attachment to rocks + *nuttallianum,* Latin for pertaining to Nuttall, for Thomas Nuttall (1786-1839), an English botanist, explorer, printer, ornithologist, and plant collector. He was a fellow of the Linnaean Society.

COMMON NAME: Yellow, for the flower color. Stonecrop, for the typically rocky habitat.

Sedum pulchellum **Texas Stonecrop**

SCIENTIFIC NAME: *Sedum + pulchellum,* Latin for little pretty, a dimunitive of *pulcher,* pretty.

COMMON NAME: Texas, for the range. Stonecrop, see *Sedum nuttallianum.*

Selenia dissecta **Texas Selenia**

SCIENTIFIC NAME: *Selenia,* the moon, from Greek, σεληνη, *selēnē,* the moon. Reference is most probably to the mound of yellow flowers, the shape of the

seeds is another possibility + *dissecta,* Latin for deeply cut. Reference is to the deeply lobed leaves.

COMMON NAME: Texas, for the range. Selenia, same as genus name.

Selenia jonesii **Jones Selenia**

SCIENTIFIC NAME: *Selenia + jonesii,* for Marcus Eugene Jones (1852-1934), an American botanist and mining engineer.

COMMON NAME: Jones Selenia, same as scientific name.

Senecio ampullaceus **Texas Groundsel**

SCIENTIFIC NAME: *Senecio,* Latin for old man, also for groundsel. Reference is to the white pappus on the achenes + *ampullaceus,* Latin for shaped like a flask, for the inflorescence shape.

COMMON NAME: Texas, for the range. Groundsel, etymology is uncertain, thought to come from an Old English word for pus absorber. This plant was used as a wound poultice.

Senecio vulgaris **Common Groundsel**

SCIENTIFIC NAME: *Senecio + vulgaris,* Latin for common, unremarkable.

COMMON NAME: Common, common in its range. Groundsel, see *Senecio ampullaceus.*

Senna alata Emperor's Candlesticks

SCIENTIFIC NAME: *Senna,* from Arabic, *sana,* their name for this type of plant + *alata,* Latin for winged, for the fruits; this is the only American *Senna* that has winged fruit.

COMMON NAME: Emperor's Candlesticks, for the seed capsules.

Senna lindheimeriana Lindheimer's Senna

SCIENTIFIC NAME: *Senna* + *lindheimeriana.* Latin for pertaining to Lindheimer, for Ferdinand Jacob Lindheimer (1801-1879), a German political exile who collected plants in Texas.

COMMON NAME: Lindheimer's Senna, same as scientific name.

Senna obtusifolia Sickle Pod

SCIENTIFIC NAME: *Senna* + *obtusifolia,* Latin for blunt leaves.

COMMON NAME: Sickle Pod, for the shape of the seed capsule.

Senna roemeriana Twoleaf Senna

SCIENTIFIC NAME: *Senna* + *roemeriana,* Latin for pertaining to Roemer, for Ferdinand Roemer (1818-1891), an American geologist and paleontologist.

COMMON NAME: Twoleaf, each leaf is made up of two leaflets. Senna, same as genus name.

Sesbania drummondii Rattlebush

SCIENTIFIC NAME: *Sesbania,* from Arabic, *sisaban,* their name for this plant + *drummondii,* for Thomas Drummond (1780-1835), a British plant collector.

COMMON NAME: Rattlebush, for the rattling sound the dried seed pods make.

Sesbania herbacea Coffee Bean

SCIENTIFIC NAME: *Sesbania* + *herbacea,* Latin for not woody, herbaceous.

COMMON NAME: Coffee Bean, for the seeds, which resemble coffee beans but are poisonous.

Sida abutifolia Spreading Sida

SCIENTIFIC NAME: *Sida,* from Greek, σιδη, *sidē,* a type of water lily, a pomegranate, this name was used by Theophrastus for a similar plant + *abutifolia,* Latin for having leaves like the genus *Abutilon.*

COMMON NAME: Spreading, for the growth pattern. Sida, same as genus name.

Sida spinosa Prickly Sida

SCIENTIFIC NAME: *Sida* + *spinosa,* Latin for spiny.

COMMON NAME: Prickly, for the spines. Sida, same as genus name.

Silene laciniata   Fire Pink

SCIENTIFIC NAME: *Silene,* for the Greek god, Silēnus (Σιληνος), a companion of Bacchus (Βακκος) + *laciniata,* Latin for having a fringe, cut into small divisions. Reference is to the fringed petals.

COMMON NAME: Fire Pink, for the shape and color of the flower.

Silene stellata   Whorled Silene

SCIENTIFIC NAME: *Silene* + *stellata,* Latin for starry, for the flowers.

COMMON NAME: Whorled, for the whorls of basal leaves. Silene, same as genus name.

Silphium albiflorum
Whiteflower Rosinweed

SCIENTIFIC NAME: *Silphium,* from Greek, σιλφιον, *silphion,* the laserwort, used as food and medicine + *albiflorum,* Latin for white-flowered.

COMMON NAME: Whiteflower, descriptive. Rosinweed, for the sticky secretions on the stems and leaves.

Silphium gracile   Slender Rosinweed

SCIENTIFIC NAME: *Silphium* + *gracile,*

Latin for graceful, slender.

COMMON NAME: Slender, for the stems. Rosinweed, see *Silphium albiflorum.*

Silphium laciniatum   Compass Plant

SCIENTIFIC NAME: *Silphium* + *laciniatum,* Latin for slashed into narrow divisions. Reference is to the leaves.

COMMON NAME: Compass Plant, the blade edges of the leaves tend to be oriented north and south.

Silphium perfoliatum   Cup Rosinweed

SCIENTIFIC NAME: *Silphium* + *perfoliatum,* Latin for having leaves that surround the stem.

COMMON NAME: Cup, the joined leaf bases form a cup around the stem. Rosinweed, see *Silphium albiflorum.*

Silphium radula
Roughstem Rosinweed

SCIENTIFIC NAME: *Silphium* + *radula,* Latin for a rasp or file, for the rough stems.

COMMON NAME: Roughstem, descriptive. Rosinweed, see *Silphium albiflorum.*

Silybum marianum
Blessed Milk Thistle

SCIENTIFIC NAME: *Silybum*, from Greek, σιλυβον, *silubon*, their name for this type of plant + *marianum*, Latin for pertaining to Mary, for the Virgin Mary; the white spots on the leaves were believed to represent drops of milk from the Virgin Mary.

COMMON NAME: Blessed Milk Thistle, same as species name.

Siphonoglossa pilosella   **Tube Tongue**

SCIENTIFIC NAME: *Siphonoglossa*, tube tongue, from Greek, σιφων, *siphōn*, tube and γλωσσα, *glōssa*, tongue. Reference is to the lipped corolla, which is tube-shaped + *pilosella*, Latin for little hairy or shaggy one.

COMMON NAME: Tube Tongue, same as scientific name.

Sisymbrium altissimum
Tumble Mustard

SCIENTIFIC NAME: *Sisymbrium*, from Greek, σισυμβριον, *sisumbrion*, bergamont mint + *altissimum*, Latin for the tallest.

COMMON NAME: Tumble, the dried plant breaks at the base and is blown (tumbled) by the wind. Mustard, from Spanish, *mostaza*, mustard. The name came from the condiment, prepared by grinding the seeds of the plant with must (new wine), not from the plant. This plant is in the mustard family.

Sisymbrium irio   **Rocket Mustard**

SCIENTIFIC NAME: *Sisymbrium* + *irio*, Latin for a mustard or mustardlike plant.

COMMON NAME: Rocket, from French, *roquette*, a brassicaceous plant, used in salads. Mustard, see *Sisymbrium altissimum*.

Sisymbrium officinale   **Hedge Mustard**

SCIENTIFIC NAME: *Sisymbrium* + *officinale*, Latin for sold in shops, used as food or medicine, usually pertains to apothecaries.

COMMON NAME: Hedge, for the growth pattern. Mustard, see *Sisymbrium altissimum*.

Sisyrinchium angustifolium
Blue-Eyed Grass

SCIENTIFIC NAME: *Sisyrinchium*, from Greek, σισυριγχιον, *sisurigkhion*, Iris *sisyrinchium*; this plant is in the iris family + *angustifolium*, Latin for having narrow leaves.

COMMON NAME: Blue-Eyed Grass, for the blue flowers and the thin, grasslike leaves.

Sisyrinchium campestre
White-Eyed Grass

SCIENTIFIC NAME: *Sisyrinchium* + *campestre*, Latin for flat country, the plains, for the habitat.

COMMON NAME: White-Eyed Grass, for the white flowers and the thin, grass-like leaves.

Sisyrinchium langloisii
Pale Blue-Eyed Grass

SCIENTIFIC NAME: *Sisyrinchium + langloisii*, for A. B. Langlois (1832-1900), a French botanist and clergyman.

COMMON NAME: Pale, for the light blue flowers. Blue-Eyed Grass, see *Sisyrinchium angustifolium*.

Sisyrinchium sagittiferum
Blue-Eyed Grass

SCIENTIFIC NAME: *Sisyrinchium + sagittiferum*, Latin for arrow bearing, for the long pointed leaves.

COMMON NAME: Blue-Eyed Grass, see *Sisyrinchium angustifolium*.

Solanum carolinense
Carolina Horse Nettle

SCIENTIFIC NAME: *Solanum*, thought to be Latin for nightshade, listed as of dubious origin in the *Oxford Latin Dictionary + carolinense*, Latin for belonging to Carolina, for the area of the type specimen.

COMMON NAME: Carolina, for the area of the type specimen. Horse Nettle, Horse, for the large size and Nettle, from Old English, *netele*, their name for this type of plant.

Solanum citrullifolium
Melonleaf Nightshade

SCIENTIFIC NAME: *Solanum + citrullifolium*, Latin for having leaves like the genus *Citrullus* (watermelon).

COMMON NAME: Melonleaf, same as species name. Nightshade, an allusion to the poisonous or narcotic action of the berries.

Solanum elaeagnifolium
Silverleaf Nightshade

SCIENTIFIC NAME: *Solanum + elaeagnifolium*, Latin for having leaves resembling those of the genus *Elaeagnus* (olive).

COMMON NAME: Silverleaf, for the gray-green scales covering the leaves, which give the appearance of silver dust. Nightshade, see *Solanum citrullifolium*.

Solanum rostratum   **Buffalo Bur**

SCIENTIFIC NAME: *Solanum + rostratum*, Latin for having a beak. Reference is to the brown stamen, which is longer than the yellow ones and is curved like a hook.

COMMON NAME: Buffalo Bur, for the large, spine-covered calyx.

Solidago canadensis   **Canada Goldenrod**

SCIENTIFIC NAME: *Solidago*, Latin for to make firm or whole. Reference is to its medicinal use on wounds + *canadensis,* Latin for belonging to Canada, for the area of the type specimen.

COMMON NAME: Canada, same as species name. Goldenrod, for the color and shape of the inflorescence panicle.

Solidago gigantea Giant Goldenrod

SCIENTIFIC NAME: *Solidago + gigantea,* Latin for giant, for the relative size.

COMMON NAME: Giant, same as species name. Goldenrod, see *Solidago canadensis.*

Solidago missouriensis Missouri Goldenrod

SCIENTIFIC NAME: *Solidago + mis- souriensis,* Latin for belonging to Missouri.

COMMON NAME: Missouri, same as species name. Goldenrod, see *Solidago canadensis.*

Solidago mollis Soft Goldenrod

SCIENTIFIC NAME: *Solidago + mollis,* Latin for soft, for the soft hairs on the stems.

COMMON NAME: Soft, same as species name. Goldenrod, see *Solidago canadensis.*

Solidago nemoralis Old-Field Goldenrod

SCIENTIFIC NAME: *Solidago + nemoralis,* Latin for growing in groves or woods.

COMMON NAME: Old-field, for the habitat. Goldenrod, see *Solidago Canadensis.*

Solidago odora Fragrant Goldenrod

SCIENTIFIC NAME: *Solidago + odora,* Latin for fragrant.

COMMON NAME: Fragrant, descriptive. Goldenrod, see *Solidago canadensis.*

Solidago petiolaris Downy Goldenrod

SCIENTIFIC NAME: *Solidago + petiolaris,* Latin for having a leaf stalk.

COMMON NAME: Downy, for the fine hairs on the stem. Goldenrod, see *Solidago canadensis.*

Solidago rigida Rigid Goldenrod

SCIENTIFIC NAME: *Solidago + rigida,* Latin for rigid. Reference is to the straight, unbranched stems.

COMMON NAME: Rigid, same as species name. Goldenrod, see *Solidago canadensis.*

Solidago speciosa
Showy-Wand Goldenrod

SCIENTIFIC NAME: *Solidago* + *speciosa,* Latin for showy, attractive in appearance, for the showy inflorescence.

COMMON NAME: Showy-Wand, for the appearance and shape of the inflorescence. Goldenrod, see *Solidago canadensis.*

Sonchus asper   **Sow Thistle**

SCIENTIFIC NAME: *Sonchus,* from Greek, σογκος, *sogkos,* their name for this type of plant + *asper,* Latin for rough, harsh, for the spiny leaves.

COMMON NAME: Sow Thistle, a corruption of the earlier name for this plant, Thow Thistle. Thow, from Anglo-Saxon, *theaw,* a custom or habit, having properties that indicate strength. Thistle, from Old Teutonic, *pistil-o,* their name for this type of plant.

Sonchus oleraceus   **Common Sow Thistle**

SCIENTIFIC NAME: *Sonchus* + *oleraceus,* Latin for of the vegetable garden.

COMMON NAME: Common, common in its range. Sow Thistle, see *Sonchus asper.*

Sophora affinis   **Texas Sophora**

SCIENTIFIC NAME: *Sophora,* from Arabic, *sophera,* for a tree with pea like flowers + *affinis,* Latin for related, similar.

COMMON NAME: Texas, for the range. Sophora, same as genus name.

Sophora nuttalliana   **White Loco**

SCIENTIFIC NAME: *Sophora* + *nuttalliana,* Latin for pertaining to Nuttall, for Thomas Nuttall (1786-1839), an English botanist, explorer, printer, ornithologist, and plant collector. He was a fellow of the Linnaean Society.

COMMON NAME: White, for the flower color. Loco, for the effect the toxic properties have on animals that eat it, from Spanish, *loco,* crazy.

Sophora secundiflora
Texas Mountain Laurel

SCIENTIFIC NAME: *Sophora* + *secundiflora,* Latin for having flowers on only one side of the stem.

COMMON NAME: Texas, for the range. Mountain, for the habitat, common in the Guadalupe Mountains. Laurel, the Modern Spanish name for the Bay tree, which the leaves of this plant resemble.

Sphaeralcea angustifolia
Narrowleaf Globe Mallow

SCIENTIFIC NAME: *Sphaeralcea,* from Greek, σφαιρα, *sphaira,* a ball, any globe, and the genus *Alcea,* αλκαια, *alkaia,* a mallow. Reference is to the globular fruit + *angustifolia,* Latin for narrow leaves.

Sphaeralcea angustifolia
Narrowleaf Globe Mallow

COMMON NAME: Narrowleaf, descriptive. Globe, for the globular fruit. Mallow, from Latin, *malva*, mallow.

Sphaeralcea coccinea
Scarlet Globe Mallow

SCIENTIFIC NAME: *Sphaeralcea + coccinea,* Latin for scarlet-dyed, for the flower color.

COMMON NAME: Scarlet, for the flower color. Globe Mallow, see *Sphaeralcea angustifolia.*

Spiranthes cernua Ladies' Tresses

SCIENTIFIC NAME: *Spiranthes,* twisted flower, from Greek, σπειρα, *speira,* any-thing twisted or wound and ανθος, *anthos,* flower. Reference is to the spiraling inflorescence + *cernua,* Latin for head

foremost, in this case drooping. Reference is to the flowers pointing downward.

COMMON NAME: Ladies' Tresses, the inflorescence was thought to resemble a woman's braids or curls.

Spiranthes lacera Slender Ladies' Tresses

SCIENTIFIC NAME: *Spiranthes + acera,* Latin for to tear or lacerate. Reference is to the wavy lip of the flower.

COMMON NAME: Slender, the inflo-rescence is more slender than the others of this genus. Ladies' Tresses, see *Spiranthes cernua.*

Spiranthes magnicamporum
Great Plains Ladies' Tresses

SCIENTIFIC NAME: *Spiranthes + magnicamporum,* Latin for belonging to the Great Plains, from *magnus,* large, great, *campus,* flat, open country, plains, and the suffix, *-orius, orum,* belonging to. Reference is to the habitat.

COMMON NAME: Great Plains, for the range. Ladies' Tresses, see *Spiranthes cernua.*

Spiranthes tuberosa Little Ladies' Tresses

SCIENTIFIC NAME: *Spiranthes + tuberosa,* Latin for having a tuber.

COMMON NAME: Little, for the relative size. Ladies' Tresses, see *Spiranthes cernua.*

Stachys drummondii **Pink Mint**

SCIENTIFIC NAME: *Stachys,* from Greek, σταχυς, *stakhus,* an ear of corn, a spike. Reference is to the shape of the inflorescence + *drummondii,* for Thomas Drummond (c. 1790-1831), a British plant collector.

COMMON NAME: Pink, for the flower color. Mint, from Latin, *mentha,* mint.

Stachys tenuifolia **Slenderleaf Betony**

SCIENTIFIC NAME: *Stachys + tenuifolia,* Latin for ribbon or slender leaves.

COMMON NAME: Slenderleaf, descriptive. Betony, from Latin, *vettonica,* said by Pliny to be a Gaulish name for a plant discovered by a tribe called the Vettones.

Stellaria media **Chickweed**

SCIENTIFIC NAME: *Stellaria,* Latin for starlike, for the flower shape + *media,* Latin for intermediate (in form).

COMMON NAME: Chickweed, the plants are eaten by wild and domesticated birds.

Stellaria pallida **Lesser Chickweed**

SCIENTIFIC NAME: *Stelleria + pallida,* Latin for pale, for the flowers.

COMMON NAME: Lesser, for the size. Chickweed, see *Stellaria media.*

Stenosiphon linifolius **False Gaura**

SCIENTIFIC NAME: *Stenosiphon,* narrow siphon, from Greek, στενος, *stenos,* narrow and σιφων, *siphōn,* a siphon, tube. Reference is to the tube-shaped flowers + *linifolius,* Latin for having leaves like flax.

COMMON NAME: False Gaura, so named because the flowers look like those of the genus *Gaura.* Actually, recent DNA testing has shown this plant to be a true *Gaura,* the genus *Stenosiphon* will soon be extinct.

Stillingia sylvatica **Queen's Delight**

SCIENTIFIC NAME: *Stillingia,* for Benjamin Stillingfleet (1702-1771), a British botanist + *sylvatica,* Latin for growing in the forest.

COMMON NAME: Queen's Delight, in honor of the queen of England.

Stillingia texana **Texas Stillingia**

SCIENTIFIC NAME: *Stillingia + texana,* Latin for pertaining to Texas.

COMMON NAME: Texas Stillingia, same as scientific name.

Streptanthus carinatus
Lyreleaf Twistflower

SCIENTIFIC NAME: *Streptanthus,* twisted flower, from Greek, στρεπτος, *streptos,* twisted and ανθος, *anthos,* flower, bloom. Reference is to the twisted, wavy petals + *carinatus,* Latin for having a keel, for the keeled sepals.

COMMON NAME: Lyreleaf, for the shape of some of the leaves. Twistflower, descriptive, same as genus name.

Streptanthus hyacinthoides
Smooth Twistflower

SCIENTIFIC NAME: *Streptanthus + hyacinthoides,* to look like a *Hyacinthus,* from the genus *Hyacinthus* and Greek, ειδος, *eidos,* resembling.

COMMON NAME: Smooth, for the hairless stems and leaves. Twistflower, see *Streptanthus carinatus.*

Streptanthus playtcarpus
Broadpod Twistflower

SCIENTIFIC NAME: *Streptanthus + platycarpus,* broad fruit, from Greek, πλατυς, *platus,* broad and καρπος, *karpos,* fruit, for the broad seed pod.

COMMON NAME: Broadpod, same as species name. Twistflower, see *Streptanthus carinatus.*

Strophostyles helvula   Trailing Wildbean

SCIENTIFIC NAME: *Strophostyles,* twisted pillar, from Greek, στροφειον, *stropheion,* twisted and στυλος, *stulos,* a pillar. Reference is to the twisted flower keel + *helvula,* Latin for a dull yellow, for the color of the seeds.

COMMON NAME: Trailing, for the growth pattern. Wildbean, descriptive of the fruit.

Strophostyles leiosperma
Slickseed Wildbean

SCIENTIFIC NAME: *Strophostyles + leiosperma,* smooth seed, from Greek, λειος, *leios,* smooth and σπερμα, *sperma,* seed. This is to contrast it with *Strophostyles helvula,* which has hairy seeds.

COMMON NAME: Slickseed, same as species name. Wildbean, descriptive of the fruit.

Stylisma humistrata   White Stylisma

SCIENTIFIC NAME: *Stylisma,* from Greek, στυλος, *stulos,* a pillar, for the style + *humistrata,* Latin for spread out on the ground.

COMMON NAME: White, for the flower color. Stylisma, same as genus name.

Symphyotrichum boreale
Northern Bog Aster

SCIENTIFIC NAME: *Symphyotrichum* from Greek, συμφυω, *sumphuo,* to make; to grow together, and, θριξ, *thrix* hair + *boreale,* Latin for northern; for the range in the United States.

COMMON NAME: Northern, for the range in the United States. Bog, for the habitat in moist places. Aster, from Greek, αστερ, *aster*, a star; for the flower shape.

Symphyotrichum ciliolatum
Leafy Aster

SCIENTIFIC NAME: *Symphyotrichum + ciliolatum*, Latin for fringed.

COMMON NAME: Leafy, for the leafy stems. Aster, see *Symphyotrichum boreale*.

Symphyotrichum cordifolius
Common Blue Wood Aster

SCIENTIFIC NAME: *Symphyotrichum + cordifolius*, Latin for having heart-shaped leaves.

COMMON NAME: Common, common in its range. Blue, for the flower color. Wood, for the habitat. Aster, see *Symphyotrichum boreale*.

Symphyotrichum divaricatum
Southern Annual Saltmarsh Aster

SCIENTIFIC NAME: *Symphyotrichum + divaricatum*, Latin for spreading or straggling growth.

COMMON NAME: Southern for the range in the United States. Annual, grows each year from seed. Saltmarsh, for the habitat. Aster, see *Symphyotrichum boreale*.

Symphyotrichum drummondii
Drummond's Aster

SCIENTIFIC NAME: *Symphyotrichum + drummondii*, for Thomas Drummond (1780-1835), a Scottish Botanist.

COMON NAME: Drummond's, same as species name. Aster, see *Symphyotrichum boreale*.

Symphyotrichum dumosus Bushy Aster

SCIENTIFIC NAME: *Aster + dumosus*, Latin for bushy, for the growth pattern.

COMMON NAME: Bushy, for the growth pattern. Aster, see *Symphyotrichum boreale*.

Symphyotrichum ericoides
White Heath Aster

SCIENTIFIC NAME: *Symphyotrichum + ericoides*, to resemble *Erica*, from the genus for heath, *Erica* and the Greek suffix, ειοδος, *eiodos*, to resemble.

COMMON NAME: White, for the flower color. Heath, for the leaf pattern. Aster, see *Symphyotrichum boreale*.

Symphyotrichum falcatum
White Prairie Aster

SCIENTIFIC NAME: *Symphyotrichum + falcatum*, Latin for curved like a scythe, for the curved leaves.

COMMON NAME: White, for the

flower color. Prairie, for the habitat. Aster, see *Symphyotrichum boreale*.

Symphyotrichum frondrosum   Leafy Aster

SCIENTIFIC NAME: *Symphyotrichum + frondrosum,* Latin for leafy, for the leafy stems.

COMMON NAME: Leafy, for the leafy stems. Aster, see *Symphyotrichum boreale*.

Symphyotrichum lanceolatum
White Panicle Aster

SCIENTIFIC NAME: *Symphyotrichum + lanceolatum,* Latin for lance-shaped, for the leaves.

COMMON NAME: White Panicle, for the flowers. Aster, see *Symphyotrichum boreale*.

Symphyotrichum lateriflorum
Calico Aster

SCIENTIFIC NAME: *Symphyotrichum +*

Symphyotrichum patens
Late Purple Aster

lateriflorum, Latin for having flowers on one side.

COMMON NAME: Calico, for the flower color. Aster, see *Symphyotrichum boreale*.

Symphyotrichum oblongifolium
Aromatic Aster

SCIENTIFIC NAME: *Symphyotrichum + oblongifolium,* Latin for having leaves of oblong shape.

COMMON NAME: Aromatic, for the scent. Aster, see *Symphyotrichum boreale*.

Symphyotrichum oolentangiensis
Skyblue Aster

SCIENTIFIC NAME: *Symphyotrichum + oolentangiensis,* Latin for belonging to Olentangy, for the Olentangy River in Ohio, the area of the type specimen.

COMMON NAME: Skyblue, for the flower color. Aster, see *Symphyotrichum boreale*.

Symphyotrichum patens
Late Purple Aster

SCIENTIFIC NAME: *Symphyotrichum + patens,* Latin for spreading, for the growth pattern.

COMMON NAME: Late, blooms later than other species. Purple, for the flower color. Aster, see *Symphyotrichum boreale*.

Symphyotrichum pilosum   **Heath Aster**

SCIENTIFIC NAME: *Symphyotrichum + pilosum,* Latin for covered with fine hair.

COMMON NAME: Heath, for the leaf pattern. Aster, see *Symphyotrichum boreale.*

Symphyotrichum praealtum
Willowleaf Aster

SCIENTIFIC NAME: *Symphyotrichum + praealtus,* Latin for very tall.

COMMON NAME: Willowleaf, the leaves resemble those of the willow. Aster, see *Symphyotrichum boreale.*

Symphyotrichum sericeum
Western Silver Aster

SCIENTIFIC NAME: *Symphyotrichum + sericeum,* Latin for silky. Reference is to the silky hairs on the leaves.

COMMON NAME: Western, for the range, although in this case the range is in the middle of the United States. Silver, for the leaves. Aster, see *Symphyotrichum boreale.*

Symphyotrichum subulatum
Eastern Annual Saltmarsh Aster

SCIENTIFIC NAME: *Symphyotrichum + subulatum,* to be shaped like an awl, from Latin, *subula,* a shoemaker's awl. Reference is to the shape of the leaves.

COMMON NAME: Eastern, for the range in the United States. Annual, grows each year from seed. Saltmarsh for the habitat. Aster, see *Symphyotrichum boreale.*

Talinum aurantiacum
Orange Flameflower

SCIENTIFIC NAME: *Talinum,* most probably from Greek, θαλεια, *thaleia,* rich, plentiful, full of bloom + *aurantiacum,* Latin for orange, orange-red, for the flower color.

COMMON NAME: Orange, for the flower color. Flameflower, for the color and appearance.

Talinum calycinum   **Rockpink**

SCIENTIFIC NAME: *Talinum + calycinum,* Latin for calyxlike, for the flowers.

COMMON NAME: Rockpink, for the color of the flowers and the habitat on sandstone outcrops.

Talinum parviflorum
Prairie Flameflower

SCIENTIFIC NAME: *Talinum + parviflorum,* Latin for having small flowers.

COMMON NAME: Prairie, for the habitat. Flameflower, see *Talinum aurantiacum.*

Taraxacum laevigatum
Redseed Dandelion

SCIENTIFIC NAME: *Taraxacum,* bitter herb, from Persian, *tarashqum* or *talkh chakok* + *laevigatum,* Latin for smooth.

COMMON NAME: Redseed, for the red-brown achenes. Dandelion, from French, *dent de lion,* tooth of the lion. Reference is to the leaves.

Taraxacum officinale
Common Dandelion

SCIENTIFIC NAME: *Taraxacum* + *officinale,* Latin for official, used to designate plants sold in shops that were used for food or medicine, usually referring to apothecaries.

COMMON NAME: Common, abundant. Dandelion, see *Taraxacum laevigatum.*

Tephrosia lindheimeri
Lindheimer Tephrosia

SCIENTIFIC NAME: *Tephrosia,* from Greek, τεφρος, *tephros,* ash-colored. Reference is to the hoary leaves of some of this genus + *lindheimeri,* for Ferdinand Jacob Lindheimer (1801-1879), a German political exile who collected plants in Texas.

COMMON NAME: Lindheimer Tephrosia, same as scientific name.

Tephrosia onobrychoides
Multibloom Tephrosia

SCIENTIFIC NAME: *Tephrosia* + *onobrychoides,* to look like *Onobrychis,* from the genus *Onobrychis,* and Greek, ειοδος, *eiodos,* resembling.

COMMON NAME: Multibloom, for the multiple blooms on a single spike. Tephrosia, same as genus name.

Tephrosia virginiana   Goat's Rue

SCIENTIFIC NAME: *Tephrosia* + *virginiana,* Latin for pertaining to Virginia, for the area of the type specimen.

COMMON NAME: Goat's Rue, this plant was fed to goats to increase milk production. Rue comes from Greek, ρυτη, *rutē,* their name for this plant.

Tetragonotheca texana
Squarebud Daisy

SCIENTIFIC NAME: *Tetragonotheca,* four-cornered box, from Greek, τετρα, *tetra,* four, γωνια, *gōnia,* corner, angle and θηκη, *thēkē,* a money chest, a tomb, a box. Reference is to the four sepals that cover the flower bud + *texana,* Latin for pertaining to Texas.

COMMON NAME: Squarebud, same as genus name. Daisy, from Anglo-Saxon, *daeges-eage,* day's eye, a daisy. For the eyelike appearance and the opening of the rays in the morning.

Teucrium canadense
American Germander

SCIENTIFIC NAME: *Teucrium,* from Greek, Τευκρως, *Teukrōs,* the son of Scamander, (Σχαμανδρος), a river and Idaea (Ιδαεα), a nymph of Mount Ida (Ιδα). He was the most ancient of the kings of Troy + *canadense,* Latin for belonging to Canada, for the area of the type specimen.

COMMON NAME: American, for the range in North America. Germander, a corruption of the Greek, χαμανδρυα, *khamandrua,* a ground oak.

Teucrium cubense   Coast Germander

SCIENTIFIC NAME: *Teucrium* + *cubense,* Latin for belonging to Cuba, for the area of the type specimen.

COMMON NAME: Coast, for the habitat of the type specimen. Germander, see *Teucrium canadense.*

Teucrium laciniatum
Cutleaf Germander

SCIENTIFIC NAME: *Teucrium* + *laciniatum,* Latin for cut or torn, for the leaves that have deep, narrow lobes.

COMMON NAME: Cutleaf, same as species name. Germander, see *Teucrium canadense.*

Thalictrum arkansanum
Arkansas Meadow Rue

SCIENTIFIC NAME: *Thalictrum,* from Greek, ταλικτρον, *taliktron,* used by Dioscoridēs (Διοσκοριδες) for a plant with leaves resembling the coriander + *arkansanum,* Latin for belonging to Arkansas, for the area of the type specimen.

COMMON NAME: Arkansas, for the area of the type specimen. Meadow, for the habitat. Rue, for its resemblance to European rue (ruta).

Thalictrum dasycarpum
Purple Meadow Rue

SCIENTIFIC NAME: *Thalictrum* + *dasycarpum,* thick-fruited, from Greek, δασυ, *dasu,* thick, hairy and καρπος, *karpos,* fruit.

COMMON NAME: Purple, stems are often purple. Meadow-Rue, see *Thalictrum arkansanum.*

Thelesperma filifolium   Greenthread

SCIENTIFIC NAME: *Thelesperma,* from Greek, θηλη, *thēlē,* a nipple and σπερμα, *sperma,* seed, for the bumps on the achenes + *filifolium,* Latin for threadlike leaves.

COMMON NAME: Greenthread, for the thin leaves.

Thelesperma flavodiscum
East Texas Greenthread

SCIENTIFIC NAME: *Thelesperma* + *flavodiscum,* Latin for yellow disk, for the yellow central disk.

COMMON NAME: East Texas, for the range. Greenthread, for the threadlike leaves.

Thelesperma megapotamicum
Slender Greenthread

SCIENTIFIC NAME: *Thelesperma* + *megapotamicum,* of the big river, from Greek, μεγα, *mega,* big and ποταμιος, *potamios,* of or from a river. Reference is to the range along the Rio Grande.

COMMON NAME: Slender Greenthread, for the thin leaves.

Thelocactus setispinus   **Hedgehog Cactus**

SCIENTIFIC NAME: *Thelocactus,* nipple cactus, from Greek, θηλη, *thēlē,* nipple, the ribs of some in this genus look like nipples, and κακτος, *kaktos,* a prickly plant + *setispinus,* Latin for bristly spines.

COMMON NAME: Hedgehog, for the shape and the spines. Cactus, see genus name.

Thymophylla acerosa
Prickleleaf Dogweed

SCIENTIFIC NAME: *Thymophylla,* thyme leaf, from Greek, θυμον, *thumon,*

thyme, and φυλλον, *phullon,* leaf + *acerosa,* Latin for needlelike, for the prickly leaves.

COMMON NAME: Prickleleaf, for the spines on the leaves. Dogweed, a depreciatory moniker, probably for the disagreeable scent.

Towndsendia exscapa   **Easter Daisy**

SCIENTIFIC NAME: *Towndsendia,* for David Towndsend (1787-1858) an American amateur botanist + *exscapa,* Latin for without a scape, a scape is a leafless stem, therefore, stemless.

COMMON NAME: Easter, for the timing of the bloom. Daisy, from Anglo-Saxon, *daeges-eage,* day's eye, a daisy. For the eyelike appearance and the opening of the rays in the morning.

Tradescantia bracteata
Bracted Spiderwort

SCIENTIFIC NAME: *Tradescantia,* for John Tradescant (1608-1662), a British botanist and gardener to Charles I + *bracteata,* Latin for having bracts.

COMMON NAME: Bracted, for the prominent bracts. Spiderwort, this plant was used for the treatment of spider bites.

Tradescantia edwardsiana
Plateau Spiderwort

SCIENTIFIC NAME: *Tradescantia* + *edwardsiana,* Latin for belonging to

Edwards, for the habitat on the Edwards Plateau of Texas, named for Haden (or Hayden) Edwards (1771-1849), an early settler in the area.

COMMON NAME: Plateau, same as species name. Spiderwort, see *Tradescantia bracteata*.

Tradescantia gigantea Giant Spiderwort

SCIENTIFIC NAME: *Tradescantia + gigantea*, Latin for gigantic, for the relative size.

COMMON NAME: Giant, for the relative size. Spiderwort, see *Tradescantia bracteata*.

Tradescantia hirtsutiflora
Hairyflower Spiderwort

SCIENTIFIC NAME: *Tradescantia +*

Tradescantia ohiensis Ohio Spiderwort

hirsutiflora, Latin for hairy flower, for the hairs on the floral bracts.

COMMON NAME: Hairyflower, same as species name. Spiderwort, see *Tradescantia bracteata*.

Tradescantia humilis
Texas Spiderwort

SCIENTIFIC NAME: *Tradescantia + humilis*, Latin for low-growing.

COMMON NAME: Texas, for the range. Spiderwort, see *Tradescantia bracteata*.

Tradescantia occidentalis
Prairie Spiderwort

SCIENTIFIC NAME: *Tradescantia + occidentalis*, Latin for western, of the west, for the range in the United States.

COMMON NAME: Prairie, for the habitat. Spiderwort, see *Tradescantia bracteata*.

Tradescantia ohiensis Ohio Spiderwort

SCIENTIFIC NAME: *Tradescantia + ohiensis*, Latin for belonging to Ohio, for the area of the type specimen.

COMMON NAME: Ohio, same as species name. Spiderwort, see *Tradescantia bracteata*.

Tradescantia reverchonii
Reverchon's Spiderwort

SCIENTIFIC NAME: *Tradescantia* + *reverchonii,* for Julien Reverchon (1837-1905), a French immigrant to Texas, who was a plant collector.

COMMON NAME: Reverchon's, same as species name. Spiderwort, see *Tradescantia bracteata.*

Tradescantia subacaulis
Stemless Spiderwort

SCIENTIFIC NAME: *Tradescantia* + *subacaulis,* Latin for almost stemless, for the short stem of this species.

COMMON NAME: Stemless, actually has a stem but it is much shorter than the others of this genus. Spiderwort, see *Tradescantia bracteata.*

Tradescantia tharpii   Tharp's Spiderwort

SCIENTIFIC NAME: *Tradescantia* + *tharpii,* for Benjamin Carroll Tharp (1885-1964), an American botanist.

COMMON NAME: Tharp's, same as species name. Spiderwort, see *Tradescantia bracteata.*

Tragopogon dubius   Goat's Beard

SCIENTIFIC NAME: *Tragopogon,* he-goat beard, from Greek, τραγος, *tragos,* he-goat and πωγων, *pōgōn,* beard. Reference is to the hairy pappus on the achenes + *dubius,* Latin for doubtful, does not conform to the usual pattern.

COMMON NAME: Goat's Beard, same as genus name.

Tragopogon porrifolius   Oyster Plant

SCIENTIFIC NAME: *Tragopogon* + *porrifolius,* Latin for having leaves like a leek.

COMMON NAME: Oyster Plant, for the edible root.

Tribulus terrestris   Goat Head

SCIENTIFIC NAME: *Tribulus,* three points, from Greek, τριβολος, *tribolos,* three-pointed. Reference is to the fruits, which break into five triangular segments + *terrestris,* Latin for of the ground, growing on the ground, for the sprawling growth pattern.

COMMON NAME: Goat Head, for the shape of the triangular fruit segments.

Trichostema brachiatum
False Pennyroyal

SCIENTIFIC NAME: *Trichostema,* hair stamen, from Greek, θριξ, *thrix,* hair and στεμμα, *stema,* stamen, for the long hairlike filaments + *brachiatum,* Latin for branching at right angles armlike, for the stems.

COMMON NAME: False Pennyroyal, for its resemblance to pennyroyal.

Trichostema dichotomum
Forked Blue Curls

SCIENTIFIC NAME: *Trichostema* + *dichotomum,* Latin for forked in pairs, for the stems.

COMMON NAME: Forked, for the stems. Blue-Curls, for the blue flowers with long curled stamen filaments.

Trifolium campestre **Low Hop Clover**

SCIENTIFIC NAME: *Trifolium,* Latin for three-leaved, for the three leaflets that make up the leaf + *campestre,* Latin for belonging to open fields.

COMMON NAME: Low, for the sprawling growth pattern. Hop, the flowers resemble those of hops. Clover, from Old English, *clafre,* their name for this type of plant.

Trifolium incarnatum **Crimson Clover**

SCIENTIFIC NAME: *Trifolium* + *incarnatum,* Latin for blood-colored, for the crimson flowers.

COMMON NAME: Crimson, for the flower color. Clover, see *Trifolium campestre.*

Trifolium pratense **Red Clover**

SCIENTIFIC NAME: *Trifolium* + *pratense,* Latin for meadows, for the habitat.

COMMON NAME: Red, for the flower color. Clover, see *Trifolium campestre.*

Trifolium repens **White Clover**

SCIENTIFIC NAME: *Trifolium* + *repens,* Latin for creeping, for the growth pattern.

COMMON NAME: White, for the flower color. Clover, see *Trifolium campestre.*

Triodanis perfoliata
Venus' Looking Glass

SCIENTIFIC NAME: *Triodanis,* three-toothed, from Greek, τρεις, *treis,* three and οδοντ,-*odont,* tooth. Reference is to the shape of the calyx + *perfoliata,* Latin for having a leaf base that surrounds the stem.

COMMON NAME: Venus' Looking-Glass, for the black shiny mirrorlike seeds.

Utricularia radiata
Floating Bladderwort

SCIENTIFIC NAME: *Utricularia,* Latin for possessing a sac. Reference is to the bladders, which trap small aquatic animals + *radiata,* Latin for radiating, having rays, for the floating leaf rosette.

COMMON NAME: Floating, descriptive. Bladderwort, for the bladders.

Vaccaria hispanica   **Cowherb**

SCIENTIFIC NAME: *Vaccaria,* from Latin, *vacca,* cow, for its use as cow fodder + *hispanica,* Latin for Spanish.

COMMON NAME: Cowherb, for its use as cow fodder.

Valerianella amarella   **Corn Salad**

SCIENTIFIC NAME: *Valerianella,* little valeriana, from the genus *Valeriana* and the Latin diminutive, *-ella* + *amaros,* Latin for bitter; the leaves have a bitter taste.

COMMON NAME: Corn Salad, commonly found in grain fields and used in salads.

Valerianella radiata   **Beaked Corn Salad**

SCIENTIFIC NAME: *Valerianella* + *radiata,* Latin for having rays.

COMMON NAME: Beaked, for the beaked fruits. Corn Salad, see *Valerianella amarelle.*

Verbascum blattaria   **Moth Mullein**

SCIENTIFIC NAME: *Verbascum,* Latin name for this plant, used by Pliny + *blattaria,* Latin for associated with moths; the flowers attract moths.

COMMON NAME: Moth, same as spcies name. Mullein, most probably from French, *mol,* soft, for the soft leaves.

Verbascum thapsus   **Common Mullein**

SCIENTIFIC NAME: *Verbascum* + *thapsus,* from the name of a town in Sicily, now known as Magnisi.

COMMON NAME: Common, most common mullein in its range. Mullein, see *Verbascum blattaria.*

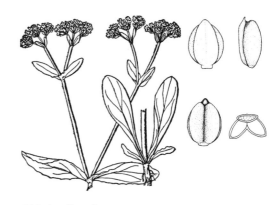

Valerianella radiata
Beaked Corn Salad

Verbena bipinnatifida Dakota Verbena

SCIENTIFIC NAME: *Verbena,* Latin name for plants used in ceremony or sacred rites + *bipinnatifida,* Latin for two feathers, used for a leaf that is bipinnately lobed.

COMMON NAME: Dakota, for the area of the type specimen. Verbena, same as genus name.

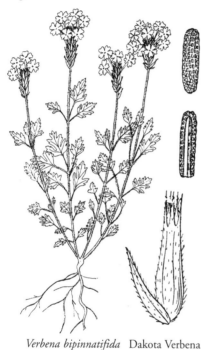

Verbena bipinnatifida Dakota Verbena

Verbena bracteata Prostrate Verbena

SCIENTIFIC NAME: *Verbena + bracteata,* Latin for having bracts.

COMMON NAME: Prostrate, for the low, sprawling growth pattern.

Verbena halei Texas Vervain

SCIENTIFIC NAME: *Verbena + halei,* for J. P. Hale (fl. 1889) a California plant collector.

COMMON NAME: Texas, for the area of the type specimen. Vervain, a form of verbena, same as genus name.

Verbena hastata Blue Verbena

SCIENTIFIC NAME: *Verbena + hastata,* Latin for spear-shaped, for the flower spike.

COMMON NAME: Blue, for the flower color. Verbena, same as genus name.

Verbena neomexicana Hillside Vervain

SCIENTIFIC NAME: *Verbena + neomexicana,* Latin for of New Mexico, for the area of the type specimen.

COMMON NAME: Hillside, for the common habitat. Vervain, a form of verbena, same as genus name.

Verbena plicata Fanleaf Vervain

SCIENTIFIC NAME: *Verbena + plicata,* Latin for folded like a fan, for the leaves.

COMMON NAME: Fanleaf, for the folds and shape of the leaves. Vervain, a form of verbena, same a genus name.

Verbena simplex
Narrowleaf Verbena

SCIENTIFIC NAME: *Verbena +simplex,* Latin for simple, in this case, unbranched.

COMMON NAME: Narrowleaf, descriptive. Verbena, same as genus name.

Verbena stricta **Hoary Verbena**

SCIENTIFIC NAME: *Verbena + stricta,* Latin for erect, standing up.

COMMON NAME: Hoary, for the white hairs on the stems. Verbena, same as genus name.

Verbena urticifolia **Nettleleaf Vervain**

SCIENTIFIC NAME: *Verbena + urticifolia,* Latin for having leaves like the genus *Urtica* (nettle).

COMMON NAME: Nettleleaf, same as species name. Vervain, a form of verbena, same as genus name.

Verbesina alternifolia **Wingstem**

SCIENTIFIC NAME: *Verbesina,* Latin for resembling verbena, although this plant does not resemble the genus *Verbena.* Reference is to the leaves resembling some species of *Verbena + alternifolia,* Latin for having alternate leaves.

COMMON NAME: Wingstem, for the leafy wings extending from the base of the leaves.

Verbesina encelioides
Golden Crownbeard

SCIENTIFIC NAME: *Verbesina + encelioides,* to look like *Encelia,* from the genus *Encelia,* and the Greek, ειδος, *eidos,* resembling.

COMMON NAME: Golden, for the flower color. Crownbeard, for the appearance of the disk flowers.

Verbesina nana **Dwarf Crownbeard**

SCIENTIFIC NAME: *Verbesina + nana,* Latin for dwarf, for the low growth pattern.

COMMON NAME: Dwarf, same as species name. Crownbeard, see *Verbesina enclioides.*

Verbesina virginica **Frostweed**

SCIENTIFIC NAME: *Verbesina + virginica,* Latin for of Virginia, for the area of the type specimen.

COMMON NAME: Frostweed, at first freeze the stems of this plant split and release a sap that expands and then freezes to look like frost.

Vernonia baldwinii **Western Ironweed**

SCIENTIFIC NAME: *Vernonia,* for William Vernon (c. 1666-1711), an English botanist and Fellow of the Royal Society who collected plants in North

America + *baldwinii,* for William Baldwin (1779-1819), an American physician and botantist who collected the plant.

COMMON NAME: Western, for the range in the United States. Ironweed, for the tough stems and roots.

Vernonia fasciculata   Ironweed

SCIENTIFIC NAME: *Vernonia + fasciculata,* Latin for clustered, for the flower arrangement.

COMMON NAME: Ironweed, see *Vernonia baldwinii.*

Vernonia gigantea   Tall Ironweed

SCIENTIFIC NAME: *Vernonia + gigantea,* Latin for gigantic, for the relative size.

COMMON NAME: Tall, for the relative height. Ironweed, see *Vernonia baldwinii.*

Vernonia lindheimeri   Woolly Ironweed

SCIENTIFIC NAME: *Vernonia + lindheimeri,* for Ferdinand Jacob Lindheimer (1801-1879), a German political exile who collected plants in Texas.

COMMON NAME: Woolly, for the gray woolly hairs. Ironweed, see *Vernonia baldwinii.*

Vernonia marginata   Plains Ironweed

SCIENTIFIC NAME: *Vernonia + marginata,* Latin for having margins. Reference is to the white leaf margins.

COMMON NAME: Plains, for the habitat. Ironweed, see *Vernonia baldwinii.*

Vernonia texana   Texas Ironweed

SCIENTIFIC NAME: *Vernonia + texana,* Latin for pertaining to Texas, for the range.

COMMON NAME: Texas, for the range. Ironweed, see *Vernonia baldwinii.*

Vicia ludoviciana   Deer Pea Vetch

SCIENTIFIC NAME: *Vicia,* Latin for vetch, from *vincire,* to bind, for the winding tendrils + *ludoviciana,* Latin for pertaining to Louisiana.

COMMON NAME: Deer Pea, deer will graze on this plant. Vetch, same as genus name.

Vicia minutiflora   Smallflower Vetch

SCIENTIFIC NAME: *Vicia + minutiflora,* Latin for small-flowered.

COMMON NAME: Smallflower, for the relatively small flowers. Vetch, same as genus name.

Vicia sativa **Common Vetch**

SCIENTIFIC NAME: *Vicia* + *sativa*, Latin for cultivated.

COMMON NAME: Common, most common in its range. Vetch, same as genus name.

Vicia villosa **Winter Vetch**

SCIENTIFIC NAME: *Vicia* + *villosa*, Latin for soft hair, for the hairy fruit and vegetative parts.

COMMON NAME: Winter, gows in the winter. Vetch, same as genus name.

Viguiera cordifolia **Heartleaf Goldeneye**

SCIENTIFIC NAME: *Viguiera*, for L. G. Alexander Viguier (1790-1867), a French physician and botanist + *cordifolia*, Latin for heart-shaped leaves.

COMMON NAME: Heartleaf, for the heart-shaped leaves. Goldeneye, for the yellow flowers.

Viguiera dentata **Golden Eye**

SCIENTIFIC NAME: *Viguiera* + *dentata*, Latin for having teeth. Reference is to the toothed leaf edges and flower petals.

COMMON NAME: Golden Eye, for the yellow flower.

Vinca major **Bigleaf Periwinkle**

SCIENTIFIC NAME: *Vinca*, from Latin, *vinca pervinca*, in turn from, *vincio*, to bind. Reference is to the use of this plant in wreaths + *major*, Latin for large, for the leaf size.

COMMON NAME: Bigleaf, for the relatively large leaf. Periwinkle, from Middle English, *per wynke*, their name for this plant, it is derived from *vinca pervinca* also.

Vinca minor **Common Periwinkle**

SCIENTIFIC NAME: *Vinca* + *minor*, Latin for small, for the relatively small leaf size.

COMMON NAME: Common, most common type in its range. Periwinkle, see *Vinca major*.

Viola bicolor **Field Pansy**

SCIENTIFIC NAME: *Viola*, Latin for violet, any sweet-smelling flower + *bicolor*, Latin for having two colors, for the different colored flower petals.

COMMON NAME: Field, for the habitat. Pansy, for the resemblance to the garden pansy, from French, *pensee*, their name for this type of flower.

Viola lovelliana **Lovell's Violet**

SCIENTIFIC NAME: *Viola* + *lovelliana*, Latin for pertaining to Lovell, for Phoebe

Lovell, who discovered this flower in 1906, named by Ezra Brainerd (1844-1924).

COMMON NAME: Lovell's Violet, same as scientific name.

Viola missouriensis Missouri Violet

SCIENTIFIC NAME: *Viola + missouriensis,* Latin for belonging to Missouri, for the area of the type specimen.

COMMON NAME: Missouri Violet, same as scientific name.

Viola nephrophylla Northern Bug Violet

SCIENTIFIC NAME: *Viola + nephrophylla,* kidney leaf, from Greek, νεφρος, *nephos* kidney and φυλλον, *phullon,* leaf, for the shape.

COMMON NAME: Northern, for the range in the United States. Bug, for the habitat in damp places. Violet, same as genus name.

Viola palmata Wood Violet

SCIENTIFIC NAME: *Viola + palmata,* Latin for like a hand, for the lobed leaves.

COMMON NAME: Wood, for the habitat. Violet, same as genus name.

Viola pedata Bird's-Foot Violet

SCIENTIFIC NAME: *Viola + pedata,*

Latin for like a bird's foot. Reference is to the shape of the leaves.

COMMON NAME: Bird's-foot Violet, same as scientific name.

Viola pedatifida Prairie Violet

SCIENTIFIC NAME: *Viola + pedatifida,* Latin for cut like a bird's foot, for the shape of the leaves.

COMMON NAME: Prairie, for the habitat. Violet, same as genus name.

Viola primulifolia
Primroseleaf Violet

SCIENTIFIC NAME: *Viola + primulifolia,* Latin for having leaves like a primula (primrose).

COMMON NAME: Primroseleaf Violet, same as scientific name.

Viola pubescens Yellow Violet

SCIENTIFIC NAME: *Viola + pubescens,* Latin for downy hair, for the hairs on the leaves.

COMMON NAME: Yellow, for the flower color. Violet, same as genus name.

Viola sagittata Arrowleaf Violet

SCIENTIFIC NAME: *Viola + sagittata,* Latin for like an arrow, for the arrowhead-shaped leaves.

COMMON NAME: Arrowleaf, for the arrowhead-shaped leaf. Violet, same as genus name.

Viola sororia   **Common Blue Violet**

SCIENTIFIC NAME: *Viola* + *sororia,* Latin for sisterly, used here to mean very closely related to some other violets. It hybridizes with *Viola pedatifidia* and *Viola nephrophylla.*

COMMON NAME: Common in its range. Blue for flower color. Violet, same as genus name.

Viola villosa   **Carolina Violet**

SCIENTIFIC NAME: *Viola* + *villosa,* Latin for soft hairs, for the hairs on the leaves.

COMMON NAME: Carolina, for the area of the type specimen. Violet, same as genus name.

Warnockia scutellarioides
Prairie Brazoria

SCIENTIFIC NAME: *Warnockia,* for Barton Holland Warnock (1911-1998), an American botanist + *scutellarioides,* resembling *Scutellaria,* from the genus *Scutellaria* (skullcap) and Greek, ειδος, *eidos,* resembling.

COMMON NAME: Prairie, for the habitat. Brazoria, this plant was originally placed in the genus *Brazoria,* named for the range along the Brazos River.

Wedelia texana   **Hairy Wedelia**

SCIENTIFIC NAME: *Wedelia,* for Georg Wolfgang Wedel (1645-1721), a German physician and botanist + *texana,* Latin for pertaining to Texas, for the range.

COMMON NAME: Hairy, for the rough hairs on the leaves. Wedelia, same as genus name.

Xanthisma texanum   **Sleepy Daisy**

SCIENTIFIC NAME: *Xanthisma,* from Greek, ξανθισμα, *xanthisma,* dyed yellow, for the flower color + *texanum,* Latin for pertaining to Texas, for the range.

COMMON NAME: Sleepy Daisy, the flowers open at mid-morning and close in the late afternoon.

Xanthisma texanum   Sleepy Daisy

Xanthocephalum gymnospermoides
Gummy Broomweed

SCIENTIFIC NAME: *Xanthocephalum,*
yellow-headed, from Greek ξανθος,
xanthos, yellow and κεφαλǳ, *kephalē,* head
+ *gymnospermoides,* to look like a
Gymnosperma, from the genus
Gymnosperma and Greek, ειδος, *eidos,*
resembling.

COMMON NAME: Gummy, for the
resinous stems and leaves. Broomweed,
this plant was used as a broom in the past.

Yucca arkansana **Arkansas Yucca**

SCIENTIFIC NAME: *Yucca,* the Carib
word for cassava, inappropriately applied
to this plant + *arkansana,* Latin for of
Arkansas.

COMMON NAME: Arkansas, for the
area of the type specimen. Yucca, same as
genus name.

Yucca glauca **Small Soapweed**

SCIENTIFIC NAME: *Yucca + glauca,*
Latin for having a bloom, a white pow-
dery coating occuring on the leaves.

COMMON NAME: Small, for the
relative size. Soapweed, the root lathers in
water, may be used as soap or shampoo.

Yucca pallida **Pale Yucca**

SCIENTIFIC NAME: *Yucca + pallida,*
Latin for pale, for the glaucous leaves.

COMMON NAME: Pale Yucca, same as
scientific name.

Yucca rupicola **Texas Yucca**

SCIENTIFIC NAME: *Yucca + rupicola,*
Latin for living on cliffs, for the common
habitat.

COMMON NAME: Texas, for the
range. Yucca, same as genus name.

Yucca torreyi **Torrey Yucca**

SCIENTIFIC NAME: *Yucca + torreyi,* for
John Torrey (1796-1873), an American
physician and botanist who wrote *The
Flora of North America,* with Asa Gray
(1810-1888).

COMMON NAME: Torrey Yucca, same
as scientific name.

Zigadenus glaberrimus **Camas**

SCIENTIFIC NAME: *Zigadenus,* yoke
gland, from Greek, ζυγον, *zugon,* yoke
and αδεν, *aden,* gland. Reference is to the
flower glands, which sometimes are in
pairs (yoked) + *glaberrimus,* Latin for
completely hairless.

COMMON NAME: Camas, from
Chinook, *kamass,* a bulb.

Zigadenus nuttallii **Death Camas**

SCIENTIFIC NAME: *Zigadenus +
nuttallii,* for Thomas Nuttall (1786-1839),
an English botanist, explorer, printer,
ornithologist, and plant collector. He was
a fellow of the Linnaean Society.

COMMON NAME: Death, the bulb
and seeds contain toxic alkaloids. Camas,
from Chinook, *kamass,* a bulb.

Zinnia acerosa **Dwarf Zinnia**

SCIENTIFIC NAME: *Zinnia,* for
Johann Gottfried Zinn (1727-1759), a
German physcian and botanist + *acerosa,*
Latin for like a needle, for the sharp
pointed leaves.

COMMON NAME: Dwarf, for the
small size. Zinnia, same as genus name.

Zinnia grandiflora
Rocky Mountain Zinnia

SCIENTIFIC NAME: *Zinnia + grandiflora,* Latin for having large flowers.

COMMON NAME: Rocky Mountain,
for the area of the type specimen. Zinnia,
same as genus name.

Zizia aurea **Golden Alexander**

SCIENTIFIC NAME: *Zizia,* for Johann
Baptist Ziz (1779-1829), a German
botanist + *aurea,* Latin for golden, for the
flower color.

COMMON NAME: Golden, for the
flower color. Alexander, from Old French,
alissandre, their name for this type
of plant.

Zinnia grandiflora
Rocky Mountain Zinnia

BIBLIOGRAPHY

Ajilvsgi, Geyata. *Wildflowers of Texas.*
Fredericksburg, Tex.: Shearer, 1984.

Bell, Robert E. *Women of Classical Mythology: A
Biographical Dictionary.* Oxford: Oxford
University Press, 1991.

Brown, Roland W. *Composition of Scientific
Words.* Washington, D.C.: Smithsonian
Institution Press, 1956.

The Century Dictionary and Cyclopedia.
New York: Century Company, 1913.

Davidson, Gustav. *A Dictionary of Angels
Including the Fallen Angels.* New York:
Free Press, 1967.

Diggs, George M. Jr., Barney L. Lipscomb,
and Robert J. O'Kennon. *Shinners and
Mahler's Illustrated Flora of North Central
Texas.* Fort Worth: Botanical Research
Institute of Texas, 1999.

Freeman, Craig C., and Eileen K. Schofield.
*Roadside Wildflowers of the Southern Great
Plains.* Lawrence: University of Kansas Press,
1991.

Glare, P. G. W., ed. *Oxford Latin Dictionary.*
Oxford: Clarendon Press, 1982.

Gotch, A. F. *Latin Names Explained.*
New York: Facts on File, 1995.

Hopkins, Daniel J., ed. *Merriam-Webster's
Geographical Dictionary.* 3rd ed.
Springfield, Mass.: Merriam-Webster, 1997.

Hornblower, Simon, and Anthony Spawforth,
eds. *The Oxford Classical Dictionary.*
Oxford: Oxford University Press, 1996.

Jaeger, Edmund C. *A Source-Book of Biological
Names and Terms.* 3rd ed. Springfield, Ill.:
Charles C. Thomas, 1978.

Liddell, H. G., and R. Scott. *A Greek-English
Lexicon.* Oxford: Clarendon Press, 1996.

Loughmiller, Campbell and Lynn. *Texas
Wildflowers.* Austin: University of
Texas Press, 2002.

Morris, Richard B., ed. *Encyclopedia of
American History.* New York: Harper
and Row, 1961.

Nybakken, Oscar E. *Greek and Latin in
Scientific Terminology.*
Ames: Iowa State University Press, 1959.

Oxford English Dictionary. 2nd ed. Prepared by
I. A. Simpson and E. S. Weiner.
Oxford: Oxford University Press, 1989.

Quattrocchi, Umberto. *CRC World Dictionary
of Plant Names.* Boca Raton, Fla.:
CRC Press, 2000.

Rose, H. J. *A Handbook of Greek Mythology.*
New York: E. P. Dutton and Company,
1959.

Seyffert, Oskar. *A Dictionary of Classical
Antiquities, Mythology, Religion, Literature,
and Art.* Revised and edited from the
original German by Henry Nettleship and
J. E. Sandys. New York: Macmillian, 1904.

Skeat, Walter W., ed. *An Etymological
Dictionary of the English Language.* Oxford:
Oxford University Press, 1959.

Souter, Alexander. *A Glossary of Later Latin to
600 A.D.* Oxford: Clarendon Press, 1996.

Stearn, William T. *Botanical Latin.* 3rd ed.
London: David and Charles, 1983.

———. *Stearn's Dictionary of Plant Names for
Gardeners.* Portland, Ore.:
Timber Press, 1996.

Sweet, Henry. *The Student's Dictionary of
Anglo-Saxon.* Oxford: Oxford
University Press, 1911.

Torrey, John, and Asa Gray. *Flora of North
America.* New York: Hafner, 1969.
Reprint, Reprint Services Corp., 1994.

Warre Cornish, Francis, ed. *A Concise Dictionary
of Greek and Roman Antiquities.*
London: John Murray, 1898.

*Webster's New International Dictionary of the
English Language.* 2nd ed. Springfield, Mass.:
G & C Merriam, 1946.

Notes